FreeSWITCH 1.0.6

Build robust high performance telephony systems using FreeSWITCH

Anthony Minessale

Michael S. Collins

Darren Schreiber

[PACKT] open source *
PUBLISHING   community experience distilled

BIRMINGHAM - MUMBAI

FreeSWITCH 1.0.6

First published: July 2010

Production Reference: 1190710

Published by Packt Publishing Ltd.
32 Lincoln Road
Olton
Birmingham, B27 6PA, UK.

ISBN 978-1-847199-96-6

www.packtpub.com

Cover Image by Leisha Bryant (leishabryant@gmail.com)

Credits

Authors
Anthony Minessale
Michael S. Collins
Darren Schreiber

Reviewer
Justin Zimmer

Acquisition Editor
Usha Iyer

Development Editors
Neha Patwari
Tarun Singh

Technical Editors
Rupal J
Charumathi Sankaran

Copy Editors
Neha Shetty
Leonard D'Silva

Indexer
Tejal Daruwale

Editorial Team Leader
Aanchal Kumar

Project Team Leader
Priya Mukherji

Project Coordinator
Prasad Rai

Proofreader
Lynda Sliwoski

Graphics
Geetanjali Sawant

Production Coordinator
Shantanu Zagade

Cover Work
Shantanu Zagade

About the Authors

Anthony Minessale has been involved in telephony since 2003. Prior to that, he had spent over ten years as a CTO and platform designer for various companies during the height of the Internet revolution. He has spent over half a decade working as the creator and lead developer of the FreeSWITCH open source project and several years before that as a volunteer developer for the Asterisk open source PBX, and is a noted contributor of several features on that project as well.

Anthony is the creator and owner of FreeSWITCH Solutions LLC, responsible for the popular annual VoIP conference, ClueCon, held every summer in Chicago. Anthony also works for Barracuda Networks as the director of Engineering for the CudaTEL PBX appliance, a product he and his team handcrafted to work with FreeSWITCH as the telephony engine.

> I would like to thank the awesome FreeSWITCH community for their dedication to our project and the invaluable feedback they provide on a daily basis. A really big thank you to Michael Collins and Darren Schreiber for helping to put this book together. I would also like to thank Brian West and Michael Jerris for helping make FreeSWITCH even possible with all the time they devote to making it work. Finally I would like to thank the original Asterisk community who inspired us all to relentlessly push forward in open source telephony.

Michael S. Collins is a telephony and open source software enthusiast. He is a PBX veteran, having worked as a PBX technician for five years and as the head of IT for a call center for more than nine years. Michael is an active member of the FreeSWITCH community. He currently works for Barracuda Networks, Inc.

I would like to thank, first and foremost, my wife, Lisa, my daughter, Katherine, and my son, Sean, who keep me going each day. I would also like to thank the many FreeSWITCH experts around the world who are so willing to answer technical questions: Michael Jerris, Moises Silva, Raymond Chandler, Mathieu Réné and more. I would especially like to thank Brian K. West for taking me under his wing and educating me in the ways of VoIP. Finally, I would like to say thank you to Anthony Minessale for authoring an amazing piece of software and inviting me to work with the core FreeSWITCH development team.

Darren A. Schreiber is helping pioneer the way to distributed cloud telephony solutions. He is the founder of the 2600hz Project, the TCAI project, and is the author of the latest version of FreePBX, a popular open source telephony management system. He has worked in Enterprise IT for over 15 years and has lead teams in successful projects in telecom, marketing, and web-based SaaS spaces. He has been a serious telephony enthusiast from a young age and has been working extensively with VoIP technologies for the past seven years. Darren graduated from Rensselaer with a degree in Computer Science and Business Entrepreneurship.

About the Reviewer

Justin Zimmer has worked in the contact center technology field for over twelve years. During that time, he has performed extensive software and computer telephony integrations using both PSTN and IP telephony. His current projects include system designs utilizing open source softswitches over more traditional proprietary hardware-based telephony, and the integration of these technologies into market-specific CRM products.

As the Technical Partner of Unicore Technologies out of Phoenix, AZ, Justin is developing hosted contact center solutions for the low-end market. Unicore's solutions present contact centers with low startup costs in a turbulent economy, and allows those centers to scale their business while maintaining a consistent and familiar user interface.

I'd like to thank the countless community contributors that have provided enough online documentation to make this book as accurate and helpful as possible. And I'd like to thank my wife Nicole for putting up with the extra hours spent reviewing this book, as well as my boys Micah, Caden, and daughter Keira for giving up some of their daddy-time for this project.

Table of Contents

Preface

In 1999, the first shot of the telephony revolution was fired when the Asterisk PBX was released to the world. In the ensuing decade, open source telephony took the world by storm, lead by Asterisk and a host of other software packages such as OpenSER and YATE.

In 2006, an Asterisk developer named Anthony Minessale announced an ambitious project: a new telephony software engine, built from the ground up. Some thought this was crazy considering the wild success of the Asterisk platform. However, Anthony's vision was to create a telephony platform unlike any in existence—open source or proprietary. In May 2008, this new project reached a critical milestone with the release of FreeSWITCH 1.0.0.

Now that FreeSWITCH has been available for several years, some developers have migrated from Asterisk to FreeSWITCH. Others have added FreeSWITCH to an existing environment, having it work together with Asterisk, OpenSER, OpenSIPS, Kamailio, and other telephony applications.

Is FreeSWITCH right for you? The correct answer is, of course: It depends. When people ask the FreeSWITCH developers which telephony software they should use, the developers always reply with another correct answer: Use what works for your situation. To know the answer you will need to investigate further.

What FreeSWITCH is and what it is not

FreeSWITCH is a scalable softswitch. In practical terms this means that it can do anything a traditional PBX can do and much more. It can (and does) act as the core switching software for commercial carriers. It can scale up to handle thousands of simultaneous calls. It can also scale down to act as a simple softphone for your laptop or personal computer. It can also work in a cluster of servers.

FreeSWITCH is not a proxy server. If you need proxy server functionality, then consider OpenSIPS, Kamailio, or other similar software. FreeSWITCH is a **back-to-back user agent** or **B2BUA**. In this regard, it is similar to Asterisk and other IP PBX software.

Version and licensing

At the time of this writing this book, the FreeSWITCH developers were putting the finishing touches on FreeSWITCH version 1.2. While the examples presented in this book were specifically tested with version 1.0.6, they have also been confirmed to work with the latest FreeSWITCH development versions that form the basis of version 1.2. Do not be concerned about the fact that this material does not cover version 1.2 — it certainly does. The FreeSWITCH user interface is very stable between versions; therefore, this text will be applicable for years to come.

FreeSWITCH is released under the **Mozilla Public License** (**MPL**) version 1.1. Since FreeSWITCH is a library that can be implemented in other software applications and projects, the developers felt it important to strike a balance between the extremely liberal BSD license and the so-called "viral" GPL. The MPL fits this paradigm well and allows businesses to create commercial products based on FreeSWITCH without licensing concerns.

However, what about using FreeSWITCH with GPL-based software? It should suffice if we said that the developers wanted to make sure that anyone, including proprietary and GPL-based software users, could use FreeSWITCH. The powerful event socket gives us this functionality — a simple TCP socket-based interface that allows an external program to control FreeSWITCH. Regardless of the license you may be using for your own software, you can still connect to a FreeSWITCH server without any licensing issues.

What this book covers

Chapter 1, Architecture of FreeSWITCH gives a brief, but thorough introduction to the underlying architecture of FreeSWITCH.

Chapter 2, Building and Installation shows how to download and install FreeSWITCH on Windows and Unix-like operating systems.

Chapter 3, Test Driving the Default Configuration provides a hands-on look at the powerful and feature-rich default FreeSWITCH configuration.

Chapter 4, SIP and the User Directory offers an introduction to the concept of users and the directory as well as brief look at SIP user agents.

Chapter 5, Understanding the XML Dialplan explains the basics of creating and editing Dialplan extensions to add advanced functionality to a FreeSWITCH install.

Chapter 6, Using the Built-In XML IVR Engine discusses how to create menus and sound phrases for interacting with callers.

Chapter 7, Building IVR Applications with Lua introduces the concept of advanced call handling using the lightweight scripting language Lua.

Chapter 8, Advanced Dialplan Concepts builds upon the foundation laid in *Chapter 5* and shows how to handle more challenging routing scenarios.

Chapter 9, Controlling FreeSWITCH Externally introduces the incredibly powerful Event Socket and the Event Socket library that can be used to access and control a FreeSWITCH server.

Chapter 10, Advanced Features and Further Reading highlights some of the more powerful FreeSWITCH features like conferencing and offers some ideas on where to learn more about FreeSWITCH.

Appendix A, The FreeSWITCH Online Community gives a brief introduction to the worldwide online community and the tools used to stay in contact.

Appendix B, The History Of FreeSWITCH is a description of how FreeSWITCH came to be from one of the authors, Anthony Minessale.

Who this book is for

This book is for prospective FreeSWITCH administrators as well as enthusiasts who wish to learn more about how to set up, configure, and extend a FreeSWITCH installation. If you are already using FreeSWITCH, you will find that the information in this book compliments what you have already learned from your personal experience.

A solid understanding of basic networking concepts is very important. Previous experience with VoIP is not required, but will certainly make the learning process go faster.

Conventions

In this book, you will find a number of styles of text that distinguish between different kinds of information. Here are some examples of these styles, and an explanation of their meaning.

Code words in text are shown as follows: "If there is a match, (and there always will be), then this macro plays the vm-goodbye.wav file."

A block of code is set as follows:

```
<action application="playback"
  data="phrase:myphrase:arg1:arg2:arg3"/>
<action application="play_and_get_digits" data="2 5 3 7000 #
  phrase:myphrase:arg1 /invalid.wav my_var \d+"/>
```

When we wish to draw your attention to a particular part of a code block, the relevant lines or items are set in bold:

```
<input pattern="^(1):(.*)$" break_on_match="true">
  <match>
    <action function="play-file" data="voicemail/vm-you_have.wav"/>
    <action function="say" data="$1" method="pronounced"
      type="items"/>
    <action function="play-file" data="voicemail/vm-$2.wav"/>
    <action function="play-file" data="voicemail/vm-message.wav"/>
  </match>
</input>
```

Any command-line input or output is written as follows:

```
freeswitch@localhost>version
FreeSWITCH Version 1.0.6 (exported)
```

New terms and **important words** are shown in bold. Words that you see on the screen, in menus or dialog boxes for example, appear in the text like this: "New users should join only the **FreeSWITCH-users** list, until they are comfortable with the project."

> Warnings or important notes appear in a box like this.

> Tips and tricks appear like this.

Reader feedback

Feedback from our readers is always welcome. Let us know what you think about this book—what you liked or may have disliked. Reader feedback is important for us to develop titles that you really get the most out of.

To send us general feedback, simply send an e-mail to feedback@packtpub.com, and mention the book title via the subject of your message.

If there is a book that you need and would like to see us publish, please send us a note in the **SUGGEST A TITLE** form on www.packtpub.com or e-mail suggest@packtpub.com.

If there is a topic that you have expertise in and you are interested in either writing or contributing to a book, see our author guide on www.packtpub.com/authors.

Customer support

Now that you are the proud owner of a Packt book, we have a number of things to help you to get the most from your purchase.

> **Downloading the example code for the book**
>
> You can download the example code files for all Packt books you have purchased from your account at http://www.PacktPub.com. If you purchased this book elsewhere, you can visit http://www.PacktPub.com/support and register to have the files e-mailed directly to you.

Errata

Although we have taken every care to ensure the accuracy of our content, mistakes do happen. If you find a mistake in one of our books—maybe a mistake in the text or the code—we would be grateful if you would report this to us. By doing so, you can save other readers from frustration and help us improve subsequent versions of this book. If you find any errata, please report them by visiting http://www.packtpub.com/support, selecting your book, clicking on the **let us know** link, and entering the details of your errata. Once your errata are verified, your submission will be accepted and the errata will be uploaded on our website, or added to any list of existing errata, under the Errata section of that title. Any existing errata can be viewed by selecting your title from http://www.packtpub.com/support.

Piracy

Piracy of copyright material on the Internet is an ongoing problem across all media. At Packt, we take the protection of our copyright and licenses very seriously. If you come across any illegal copies of our works, in any form, on the Internet, please provide us with the location address or website name immediately so that we can pursue a remedy.

Please contact us at copyright@packtpub.com with a link to the suspected pirated material.

We appreciate your help in protecting our authors and our ability to bring you valuable content.

Questions

You can contact us at questions@packtpub.com if you are having a problem with any aspect of the book, and we will do our best to address it.

Architecture of FreeSWITCH

Welcome to FreeSWITCH! If you are reading this, then, undoubtedly, you are interested in things like telecommunications and Voice over Internet Protocol (VoIP). FreeSWITCH is revolutionary software created during a telephony revolution. Before looking at the architecture of this powerful software, let's take a look at the colorful world of telecommunications. This will help to put FreeSWITCH into perspective.

In this chapter, we cover:

- A telephony revolution
- Advantages of FreeSWITCH
- Endpoint and Dialplan modules
- How FreeSWITCH simplifies complex applications like Voicemail

A revolution has begun and secrets have been revealed

How and why the telephone works is a mystery to most people. It has been kept secret for years. We just plugged our phones into the wall and they worked, and most people do just that and expect it to work. The telephony revolution has begun, and we have begun to pry the secrets from the clutches of the legacy of the telephony industry. Now, everyday individuals like you and me are able to build phone systems that outperform traditional phone services and offer advanced features for relatively low cost. Some people even use FreeSWITCH to provide telephone services for making a profit. FreeSWITCH has been designed to make all of this easier, so we will go over the architecture to get a better understanding of how it works.

Do not be concerned if some of these concepts seem unnaturally abstract. Learning telephony takes time, especially VoIP. In fact, we recommend that you read this chapter more than once. Absorb as much as you can on the first pass, then come back after you complete *Chapter 5, Understanding the XML Dialplan*. You will be surprised at how much your understanding of VoIP and FreeSWITCH has improved. Then come back and skim it a third time after you have completed *Chapter 9, Controlling FreeSWITCH Externally*, at this point, you will have a firm grasp of VoIP and FreeSWITCH concepts. Give yourself plenty of time to digest all of these strange new concepts, and soon you will find that you are a skilled FreeSWITCH administrator. If you keep at it, you will be rewarded with a meaningful understanding of this strange and wonderful world we call telephony.

Telephones and the systems are very complicated and have evolved over the years into several varieties. The most popular type of phone in the U.K. and the U.S. is the traditional analog phone, which we affectionately refer to as **POTS** lines or **Plain Old Telephone Service**. From the traditional Ma Bell phone up to the long-range cordless phones that most of us have today, one thing has remained the same — the underlying technology. In the last 10-15 years, there has been a convergence of technology between computers and telephones that has produced a pair of affordable alternatives to POTS lines — Mobile phones and VoIP phones (also called Internet Phones).

FreeSWITCH fits into this big tangled mess of various telephone technologies by bridging them together, so that they can communicate despite being otherwise completely incompatible. FreeSWITCH also bridges telephone calls with computer programs that you can write yourself, and controls what happens in ways like never before. FreeSWITCH is software that runs on Windows and several UNIX varieties such as Mac OS X, Linux, Solaris, and BSD. This means you can install FreeSWITCH on your home PC or even a high-end server and use it to process phone calls. Installing FreeSWITCH is discussed in detail in *Chapter 2, Building and Installation*. We will be doing this as soon as we review the basic architecture.

The FreeSWITCH design: modular, scalable, and stable

The design goal of FreeSWITCH is to provide a modular, scalable system around a stable switching core, and provide a robust interface for developers to add to and control the system. Various elements in FreeSWITCH are independent of each other and do not have much knowledge about how the other parts are working, other than what is provided in what are called "exposed functions". The functionality of FreeSWITCH can also be extended with loadable modules, which tie a particular external technology into the core.

FreeSWITCH has many different module types that revolve around the central core, much like satellites orbiting a planet. The list includes:

Module Type:	Purpose:
Endpoint	Telephone protocols like SIP/H.323 and POTS lines.
Dialplan	Parse the call details and decide where to route the call.
Codec	Translate between audio formats.
Application	Perform a task such as play audio or set data.
Application Programming Interface (API)	Export a function that takes text input and returns text output, which could be used across modules or from an external connection.
File	Provide an interface to extract and play sound from various audio file formats.
Text-To-Speech (TTS)	Interface with text-to-speech engines.
Automated Speech Recognition ASR	Interface with speech recognition systems.
Directory	Connect directory information services, such as LDAP, to a common core lookup API.
Chat	Bridge and exchange various chat protocols.
Say	String together audio files in various languages to provide feedback to say things like phone numbers, time of day, spell words, and so on.

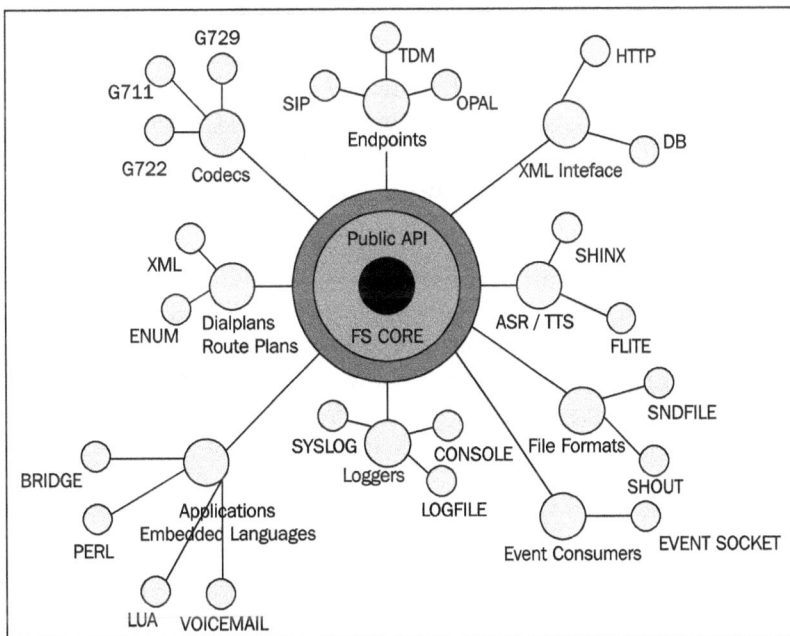

By combining the functionality of the various module interfaces, FreeSWITCH can be configured to connect IP phones, POTS lines, and IP-based telephone service. It can also translate audio formats and interfaces with a custom menu system, which you can create by yourself. You can even control a running FreeSWITCH server from another machine. Let's start by taking a closer look at one of the more widely used modules, namely, the Endpoint module.

Important modules: Endpoint and Dialplan

Endpoint modules are critically important and add some of the key features which make FreeSWITCH the powerful platform it is today. The primary role of these modules is to take certain common communication technologies and normalize them into a common abstract entity which we refer to as a **session**. A session represents a connection between FreeSWITCH and a particular protocol. There are several Endpoint modules that come with FreeSWITCH, which implement several protocols such as SIP, H.323, Jingle (Google Talk), and some others. We will spend some time examining one of the more popular modules named `mod_sofia`.

Sofia-SIP (`http://sofia-sip.sourceforge.net`) is an open source project sponsored by Nokia, which is determined to make a programming interface to the **Session Initiation Protocol** or **SIP**. We use this library in FreeSWITCH in a module we call `mod_sofia`. This module registers to all the hooks in FreeSWITCH necessary to make an Endpoint module, and translates the native FreeSWITCH constructs into SIP constructs and back again. Configuration information is taken from the central FreeSWITCH configuration files, which allows `mod_sofia` to load user-defined preferences and connection details. This allows FreeSWITCH to accept registration from SIP phones and devices, register to other SIP Endpoints such as service providers, send notifications, and provide services to the phones such as voicemail.

When a SIP call is established between FreeSWITCH and another SIP device, it will show up in FreeSWITCH as an active session. If the call is inbound, it can be transferred or bridged to interactive voice response (IVR) menus, hold music, or one or more extensions, though numerous other options are available. Let's examine a typical scenario where a SIP phone registered as extension 2000 calls extension 2001, with the hope of establishing a call.

First, the SIP phone sends a call setup message to mod_sofia over the network (mod_sofia is "listening" for such messages). After receiving the message, mod_sofia in turn parses the relevant details and passes the call into the core *state machine* in FreeSWITCH. The state machine (in the FreeSWITCH core) then sends the call into the ROUTING state. The next step is to locate the **Dialplan** module, based on the configuration data for the calling Endpoint. The default and most widely used Dialplan module is the **XML Dialplan** module. This module is designed to look up a list of instructions from the central XML registry within FreeSWITCH. The XML Dialplan module will parse a series of XML extension objects using regular expression pattern-matching. As we are trying to call 2001, we hope to find an XML extension testing the destination_number field for something that matches "2001" and routes accordingly. The Dialplan is not limited to matching only a single extension. In fact, in *Chapter 5, Understanding the XML Dialplan*, you will get an expanded definition of the term "extension". The XML Dialplan module builds a sort of "task list" for the call. Each extension that matches it will have its actions added to the call's task list.

Assuming FreeSWITCH finds at least one extension, the XML Dialplan will insert instructions into the session object with the information it needs to try and connect the call to 2001. Once these instructions are in place, the state of the calling session changes from ROUTING to EXECUTE where the next handler drills down the list and executes the instructions obtained by the ROUTING state. This is where the application interface comes into the picture.

Each instruction is added to the session in the form of an application name and a data argument that will be passed to that application. The one we will use in this example is the bridge application. The purpose of this application is to create another session with an outbound connection, then connect the two sessions for direct audio exchange. The argument we will supply to bridge will be user/2001, which is the easiest way to generate a call to extension 2001. A Dialplan entry for "2001" might look like this:

```
<extension name="example">
  <condition field="destination_number" expression="^2001$">
    <action application="bridge" data="user/2001"/>
  </condition>
</extension>
```

The extension is named "example", and it has a single condition to match. If the condition is matched, it has a single application to execute. In plain language, the mentioned extension could be expressed like this: If the caller dialed "2001", then this establishes a connection between the calling party and the endpoint (that is, telephone) at 2001. Consider how this happens.

Once we have inserted the instructions into the session, the session's state will change to EXECUTE, and the FreeSWITCH core will use the data collected to perform the desired action. First, the default execute state handler will parse the command to execute bridge on user/2001, then it will look up the bridge application and pass the user/2001 data in. This will cause the FreeSWITCH core to create a new outbound session of the desired type. User 2001 is also a SIP phone, so the user/2001 will resolve into a SIP dial string, which will be passed to mod_sofia to ask it to create a new outbound session.

If the setup for that new session is successful, there will now be two sessions in the FreeSWITCH core. The bridge application will take the new session and the original session (the caller's phone) and call the bridge function on it. This allows the audio to flow in both directions, once the person at extension 2001 actually answers the phone. If that user was unable to answer or was busy, a timeout (that is, a failure) would occur and send the corresponding message back to the caller's phone. If a call is unanswered or an extension is busy, many routing options are possible, including call forwarding or voicemail.

All of this happens from the simple action of picking up the phone handset and dialing 2 0 0 1. FreeSWITCH takes all of the complexity of SIP and reduces it to a common denominator. From there, it reduces the complexity further by allowing us to configure a single instruction in the Dialplan to connect the phone at 2000 to the phone at 2001. If we want to allow the phone at 2001 to be able to call the phone at 2000, we can add another entry in the Dialplan going the other way.

```
<extension name="example 2">
  <condition field="destination_number" expression="^2000$">
    <action application="bridge" data="user/2000"/>
  </condition>
</extension>
```

In this scenario, the Endpoint module turned SIP into a FreeSWITCH session and the Dialplan module turned XML into an extension. The bridge application turned the complex code of creating an outbound call, and connecting the audio into a simple application/data pair. Both the Dialplan module and the application module interface are designed around regular FreeSWITCH sessions. Therefore, not only does the abstraction make life easier for us at the user level, it also simplifies the design of the application and the Dialplan because they can be made agnostic of the actual endpoint technology involved in the call. It is because of this abstraction, when we make up a new Endpoint module tomorrow for something like Skype (there is actually such a thing present, by the way), that we can reuse all the same application and Dialplan modules. The same principle applies to the Say, ASR, TTS, and other such modules.

It is possible that you may want to work with some specific data provided by the Endpoint's native protocol. In SIP, for instance, there are several arbitrary headers as well as several other bits of interesting data from the SIP packets. We solve this problem by adding variables to the channel. Using *channel variables*, mod_sofia can set these arbitrary values as they are encountered in the SIP data where you can retrieve them by name from the channel in your Dialplan or application. This way we share our knowledge of these special variables with the SIP Endpoint. However, the FreeSWITCH core just sees them as arbitrary channel variables, which the core can ignore. There are also several special reserved channel variables that can influence the behavior of FreeSWITCH in many interesting ways. If you have ever used a scripting language or configuration engine that uses variables, then you are at an advantage because channel variables are pretty much the same concept. There is simply a variable name and a value that is passed to the channel and the data is set.

There is even an application interface for this: the set application that lets you set your own variables from the Dialplan.

```
<extension name="example 3">
  <condition field="destination_number" expression="^2000$">
    <action application="set" data="foo=bar"/>data="foo=bar"/>
    <action application="bridge" data="user/2000"/>
  </condition>
</extension>
```

The recent example is almost identical to the previous example, but instead of just placing the call, we first set the variable "foo" equal to the value "bar". This variable will remain set throughout the call and can even be referenced at the end of the call in the detail logs.

The more we build things in small pieces, the more the same underlying resources can be reused, making the system simpler to use. For example, the codec interface knows nothing else about the core, other than its own isolated world of encoding and decoding audio packets. Once a proper codec module has been written, it becomes usable by any Endpoint interface capable of carrying that codec in its audio stream. This means that if we get a Text-To-Speech module working, we can generate synthesized speech on any and all Endpoints that FreeSWITCH supports. It does not matter which one comes first as they have nothing to do with each other. However, the addition of either one instantly adds functionality to the other. The TTS module becomes more useful because it can use more codecs; the codecs have become more useful because we added a new function that can take advantage of them. The same idea applies to applications. If we write a new application module, the existing endpoints will immediately be able to run and use that application.

Complex applications made simple

FreeSWITCH removes much of the complexity of more advanced applications. Let's look at two examples of a more complex application.

Voicemail

The first application we will discuss is the voicemail application. The general purpose of this application is probably pretty easy to deduce. It provides voicemail service. This application is useful to add right after the bridge application as a second option, in case the call was not completed. We can do this with a careful combination of application choices, and one of those fancy "special" variables that we were discussing earlier. Let's look at a new version of our last extension that also allows us to leave a voicemail:

```
<extension name="example 4">
  <condition field="destination_number" expression="^2000$">
    <action application="set" data="hangup_after_bridge=true"/>
    <action application="bridge" data="user/2000"/>
    <action application="voicemail" data="default ${domain} 2000"/>
  </condition>
</extension>
```

Here we see two uses of channel variables. First we set `hangup_after_bridge=true` telling the system to just hang up once we have had at least one successfully bridged call to another phone and to disregard the rest of the instructions. We are also using the `domain` variable as seen in brackets prefixed with a dollar sign, `${domain}`. This is a special variable that defaults to the auto-configured domain name, which all the phones are using from the configuration.

In the example, we check if someone is dialing "2000". We then try to bridge the call to the phone registered to extension 2000. If the call fails or there is no answer, we will continue to the next instruction, which is to execute the `voicemail` application. We provide the information the application needs to know, and which extension the voicemail is for so it knows how to handle the situation. Next, the `voicemail` application plays the pre-recorded greeting or generates one for you using the `Say` module's interface we briefly discussed earlier. It strings together sound files to make a voice say "The person at extension 2 0 0 0 is not available, please leave a message". Next, `mod_voicemail` prompts you to record a message, and now is your chance to leave your mark in that person's inbox by leaving a voice message. As an additional feature, if you are not satisfied with your recording, you can repeat it as many times as you wish. Once you finally commit, a FreeSWITCH `MESSAGE_WAITING` *event* is fired into the core *event system*, which is picked up by `mod_sofia` by way of an *event consumer*, where the event information is translated into SIP. If everything goes as planned, the phone registered on extension 2000 will illuminate its message-waiting indicator light!

Again in this example, not only have we seen how to play a greeting, record a message, and send it to a user, we have also uncovered another unsung hero of the FreeSWITCH core—the event system. The FreeSWITCH event system is not a module interface like the other examples, it is a core engine that you can use to bind to named events and react accordingly when an event is received. In other words, throughout the FreeSWITCH core, there are events that are sent and received. Modules can bind to (that is "listen" for) various events. They can also "fire" events into the event engine; other modules can listen for those events. As we discussed, the Sofia SIP module binds or subscribes to the event designated for MESSAGE_WAITING information. This allows our mod_voicemail module to interact with mod_sofia, without either system having any knowledge about the other's existence. The event is fired by mod_voicemail, received by mod_sofia, and translated into the proper SIP message—all seemingly magical, courtesy of the event system.

There are several challenges with such a complex interactive system when considering all of the possible languages it may need to support as well as what files to play for the automated messages and how they are strung together. The Say module supplies a nice way to string files together, but it is somewhat limited to something specific like spelling a word, counting something, or saying a certain date. The way we overcome this is by defining a more complex layer on top of the Say module called Phrase Macros. **Phrase Macros** are a collection of XML expressions that pull out a list of arguments by matching a regular expression and executing a string of commands. This is very similar to how the XML Dialplan works, only custom-tailored for interactive voice response scenarios (IVR). For example, when mod_voicemail asks you to record your message, rather than coding in the string of files to make it say that, the code just calls a Phrase Macro called voicemail_record_message. This arbitrary string is shared between mod_voicemail and the Phrase Macro section in the configuration allowing us, the users, to edit the file without doing any fancy programming.

```
<macro name="voicemail_record_message">
  <input pattern="^(.*)$">
    <match>
      <action function="play-file" data="voicemail/vm
      record_message.wav"/>
    </match>
  </input>
</macro>
```

When `mod_voicemail` executes the `voicemail_record_message` macro, it first matches the pattern, which, in this case, is just to match everything, as this particular macro has no input. If the macro did have input, the pattern matching could be used to perform different actions based on different input. Once a match is found, the `match` tag is parsed in the XML for `action` tags just like in our Dialplan example. This macro just plays the file `vm_record_message.wav`, but more complicated macros, like the ones for verifying your recording or telling you how many messages you have in your inbox, may use combinations of various `say` modules and playing of audio files. Phrase Macros are discussed in detail in *Chapter 6, Using the Built-in XML IVR Engine* and used extensively in *Chapter 7, Building IVR Applications With Lua*.

Once again, we have cooperation among the phrase system, the audio file, and the `say` modules loaded by the core being joined together to enable powerful functionality. The `say` modules are written specifically for a particular language or "voice" within a language. We can programmatically request to say a particular time and have it translated into the proper `say` module based on input variables. The Phrase Macro system is a great way to put bigger variable concepts into your code, which can be easily tweaked later by everyday users. For example, if we wanted to make a small IVR that asks us to dial a four-digit number and then just read it back and hang up, we could make one macro called "mypp_ask_for_digits" and the other called "myapp_read_digits". In our code, we would execute these macros by name—the first one when it is time to ask for the digits and the other one to read back the

digits by passing in the value we entered. Once this is in place, a less-experienced individual could implement the XML files to play the proper sounds. He/she can use the `say` modules to read back the number, and it could all be working in multiple languages with no further coding necessary. Voicemail is just one example of FreeSWITCH in use as an application server. There are endless possibilities when we use FreeSWITCH to connect phone calls with computers.

Multi-party conferencing

Another popular feature of FreeSWITCH is delivered by the `mod_conference` conferencing module. The `mod_conference` module provides dynamic conference rooms that can bridge together the audio from several audio channels. This can be used to hold meetings where there are several callers who want to interact on the same call. Each new session that connects to the same conference room will join the others, and instantly be able to talk to all of the other participants at the same time. By using a Dialplan example, similar to the one we used for bridging to another phone, we can make an extension to join a conference room:

```
<extension name="example 4">
  <condition field="destination_number" expression="^3000$">
    <action application="conference" data="3000@default"/>
  </condition>
</extension>
```

This is just as simple as bridging a call, but what is special about this extension is that many callers can call extension 3000 and join the same conference. If three people joined this conference and one of them decides to leave, the other two would still be able to continue their conversation. The conference module also has other special features, such as the ability to play sound files or text to speech to the whole conference or even just to a single member of the conference. As you may have guessed, we are able to do this by using the TTS and sound file interfaces provided by their respective modules. Once again, the smaller pieces come together to extend the functionality without needing explicit knowledge of the other components in the system.

The conference module also uses the event system in a special way called **custom events**. A module such as mod_conference can reserve a special event **namespace** called a **subclass** when it first loads. When something interesting happens, such as when a caller joins or leaves a conference, it fires those events on the CUSTOM event channel in the core. When we are interested in receiving such events, all we have to do is subscribe to the CUSTOM event supplying an extra subclass string, which specifies the specific CUSTOM events we are interested in. In this case, it is conference::maintenance. This makes it possible to look out for important things such as when someone joins or leaves the conference or even when they start and stop talking. Conferencing is discussed in detail in *Chapter 10, Advanced Features and Further Reading*.

The FreeSWITCH API (FSAPI)

Another very powerful module interface in FreeSWITCH is the **FSAPI** module. The principle of this type of interface is very simple — it takes a single string of text as input, which may or may not be parsed, especially by the following code. The return value is also a string that can be of any size, from a single character up to several pages of text, depending on the function that was called. One major benefit of FSAPI functions is that a module can use them to call routines in another module, without directly linking into the actual code. The command-line interface of FreeSWITCH or CLI uses FSAPI functions to pass commands from your prompt.

Here is a small example of how we can execute the `status` FSAPI command from the FreeSWITCH CLI:

```
freeswitch> status

API CALL [status()] output:

UP 0 years, 3 days, 23 hours, 31 minutes, 31 seconds, 524 milliseconds,
576 microseconds

438 session(s) since startup

6 session(s) 0/30

1000 session(s) max
```

What's really happening here is that when we type `status` and press the **Enter** key, the word "status" is used to look up the `status` FSAPI function from the module in which it was implemented. The underlying function is then called, and the core is queried for its status message. Once the status data is obtained, the output is written to a stream that comes back and prints as the result of the command.

We have already learned that a module can create and export FSAPI functions, which can be executed from anywhere such as the CLI. But wait, there's more! Modules can also be written to push commands into the FSAPI interface, and send the result over a specific protocol. There are two modules included in FreeSWITCH that do just that—`mod_event_socket` and `mod_xml_rpc` (`mod_event_socket` discussed in detail in *Chapter 9, Controlling FreeSWITCH Externally*.) Consider the example of `mod_xml_rpc`. This module implements the standardized XML-RPC protocol as a FreeSWITCH module. Clients using an XML-RPC interface can connect to FreeSWITCH and execute any FSAPI command they choose. So a remote client could execute an RPC call to `status`, and get a similar status message to the one we saw in the previous example. This same module also provides FreeSWITCH with a general web server, which allows FSAPI commands to be accessed with a direct URL hit. For example, one could point a browser to `http://example.freeswitch.box:8080/api/status` to access the status command directly over the World Wide Web. By using this technique, it's possible to create FSAPI commands that work similar to a CGI, providing a dynamic web application that has direct access to FreeSWITCH internals.

As we can see, the FSAPI interface is very versatile. Now we know it can be used to provide a CLI interface, a way for modules to call functions from each other and a way to export WWW or XML-RPC functions. There is still one more use for FSAPI functions that we have not covered. We touched slightly on the concept of channel variables earlier, noting that we can use the expression `${myvariable}` to get the value of a certain variable. FSAPI functions can also be accessed this way in the format `${myfunction()}`. This notation indicates that the FSAPI command "myfunction" should be called, and that the expression should be replaced with the output of that function call. Therefore, we can use `${status()}` anywhere when variables are expanded to gain access to the status command. For example:

```
<action application="set" data="my_status=${status}"/>
```

The value placed in the `my_status` variable will be the output from the `status` command.

The drawback to all the versatility provided by a single module interface is that in order to achieve all of this, we have to "loosely type" the functionality. This means that there are several cases where a single FSAPI command could easily be accessed, using all of the ways we have discussed. In addition, there are also some other specific functions that are specifically designed for a particular access method. For instance, if we made an FSAPI command that produced HTML intended to be accessed with a web browser, we would not want to access it from the CLI or by referencing it as a variable. Similarly, if we made an FSAPI function that computed some kind of value based on call details, which was designed to be used from the Dialplan, it would not be very useful at the CLI or from the Web. So, with great power comes great responsibility, and this is one case where we need to use common sense to decide when and where to use the proper FSAPI functions to get the most out of them.

The XML registry

We have now discussed many of the fundamental components of the FreeSWITCH core and how they interact with each other. We have seen how the event system can carry information across the core, and how the XML Dialplan can query the XML registry for data. This would be a good time to explain the XML registry a bit more. The **XML registry** is a centrally managed XML document that holds all of the critical data, which FreeSWITCH needs to operate properly. The initial document is loaded from your hard drive and passed into a special *pre-processor*. This pre-processor can include other XML documents and other special operations, such as setting global variables, which can be resolved by the pre-processor further down in the document.

Once the entire document and all of the included files are parsed, replaced, and generated into a static XML document, this document is loaded into memory. The XML registry is divided into several sections—`configuration`, `dialplan`, `directory`, and `phrases`. The core and the modules draw their configuration from the `configuration` section. The XML Dialplan module draws its Dialplan data from the `dialplan` section. The SIP authentication, user lookup, and the voicemail module read their account information from the `directory` section. The Phrase Macros pull their configuration from the `phrases` section. If we make a change to any of the documents on the disk, we can reload the changes into memory by issuing the `reloadxml` command from the CLI. (This is an example of using the FSAPI interface to communicate with the FreeSWITCH core.)

Language modules

One distinct type of module that does not have a direct interface to FreeSWITCH-like files and Endpoints, but still offers an immensely powerful connection to existing technology, is the **Language** module. Language modules embed a programming language like Lua, JavaScript, or Perl into FreeSWITCH, and transfer functionality between the core and the language's runtime. This allows things like IVR applications to be written in the embedded language, with a simple interface back to FreeSWITCH for all the heavy lifting. Language modules usually register into the core with the application interface and the FSAPI interface and are executed from the Dialplan. Language modules offer lots of opportunities and are very powerful. Using language modules, you can build powerful voice applications in a standard programming language. In some respects, you can actually control a telephone with a programming language.

The default configuration

Understanding all of these concepts right off the bat is far from easy, and as the maintainers of the software, we do not expect most people to have everything "just click". This is the main reason that every new layer we put on top of the core, makes things simpler and easier to learn. The default configuration of FreeSWITCH is the last line of defense between new users of the software and all of the crazy, complicated, and sometimes downright evil stuff, better known as telephony. We try very hard to save the users from such things.

The main purpose of the default configuration in FreeSWITCH is to showcase all of the hundreds of parameters there are to work with. We present them to you in a working configuration that you could actually leave untouched and play with a bit before venturing into the unknown and trying your own hand at changing some of the options. Think of FreeSWITCH as a Lego set. FreeSWITCH and all of its little parts are like a brand new bucket Lego bricks, with plenty of parts to build anything we can imagine. The default configuration is like the sample spaceship that you find in the instruction booklet. It contains step-by-step instructions on exactly how to build something you know will work. After you pick up some experience, you might start modifying your Lego ship to have extra features, or maybe even rebuild the parts into a car or some other creation. The good news about FreeSWITCH is that it comes out of the box already assembled. Therefore, unlike the bucket of Lego bricks, if you get frustrated and smash it to bits, you can just re-install the defaults and you won't have to build it again from scratch. The default configuration is discussed in *Chapter 3, Test Driving the Default Configuration.*

Once FreeSWITCH has been successfully built on your system, you simply have to launch the program without changing one line in the configuration file. You will be able to point a SIP telephone or software-based SIP *soft phone* to the address of your computer and make a test call. If you are brave and have ambition of connecting a traditional analog phone, you may want to get the SIP thing under your belt first. This is because it involves a little more work (including purchasing a hardware card for your computer or a magic device called an ATA — analog telephone adapter).

If you have more than one phone, you should be able to configure them to each having an individual extension in the range 1000-1019, which is the default extension number range that is pre-defined in the default configuration. Once you get both phones registered, you will be able to make calls across them or have them to meet in a conference room in the 3000-3399 range. If you call an extension that is not registered or let the phone ring at another extension for too long, the voicemail application will use the phrase system to indicate that the party is not available, and ask you to record a message. If you dial 5000, you can see an example of the IVR system at work, presenting several menu choices demonstrating various other neat things FreeSWITCH can do out of the box. There are a lot of small changes and additions that can be made to the default configuration while still leaving it intact.

For example, using the pre-processor directives we went over earlier, the default configuration loads a list of files into the XML registry from certain places, meaning that every file in a particular folder will be combined into the final XML configuration document. The two most important points where this takes place are where the user accounts and the extensions in the Dialplan are kept. Each of the 20 extensions that are preconfigured with the defaults are stored into their own file. We could easily create a new file with a single user definition and drop it into place to add another user, and simply issue the `reloadxml` at the `FreeSWITCH CLI`. The same idea applies to the example dialplan. We can put a single extension into its own file, and load it into place whenever we want.

Summary

FreeSWITCH is a complex system of moving parts that is intertwined to produce a solid, stable core with flexible and easy-to-extend add-ons. The core extends its interfaces to modules. These modules simplify the functionality further and extend it up to the user. The modules also can bring outside functionality into FreeSWITCH by translating various communication protocols into a common, well-known format. We looked at the various module types, and demonstrated how they revolve around the core and interact with each other to turn simple abstract concepts into higher-level functionalities. We touched base on a few of the more popular applications in FreeSWITCH — the conferencing and voicemail modules and how they, in turn, make use of other modules in the system without ever knowing it. This agnosticism is accomplished by means of the event system. We also saw how the default configuration provides several working examples, to help take the edge off of an otherwise frightening feat of staring down the business end of a full-featured soft-switch.

Now that we have a general idea of what makes FreeSWITCH tick, we will take a closer look at some of these concepts with some real-world examples for you to try. First we obtain a copy of the source code from the Internet, so we can build the software package and install it. From there, we will test out the configuration, so be sure to get yourself a SIP phone or at least a soft-phone. Once we try a few things, we will dive a litter deeper into how things work and create a few things of our own like an extension or two and an IVR menu. So take a deep breath and get ready to dive into the world of telephony with FreeSWITCH!

2
Building and Installation

FreeSWITCH is open source software. Basically this means that anyone can obtain, read, compile, mangle, fix, or anything that comes to mind, the raw source code of the application. Many users, especially beginners, will find that dealing with source code is somewhat a daunting task, but rest assured, we are doing our best to make this experience as painless as possible. In the future, we will be adding binary packages into various popular Linux distributions, but for the time being, we will explain how to manually obtain and install FreeSWITCH for Unix and Windows. (For the purpose of this chapter, the terms "Unix-like" and "Linux/Unix" refer not only to Unix and Linux but also to FreeBSD and Max OSX.) Try not to fret if it seems overwhelming. With a little patience and luck, the whole process will go smoothly. It's not entirely unlike a root canal. It's been said that many root canals are pulled off without a hitch and when they go wrong, they go horribly wrong; and that is where the horror stories, which we all hear, come from.

In this chapter, we will discuss how to download and install FreeSWITCH from the source code for Unix-like environments as well as for Windows. We will cover the necessary prerequisites for each operating system. Finally, we will explain how to launch FreeSWITCH and how to run it in the background.

In this chapter, we will cover the following:

- Setting up the FreeSWITCH environment
- Downloading and installing FreeSWITCH
- Launching FreeSWITCH and running it in the background
- The first order of business is to lay the groundwork for our FreeSWITCH installation

Setting up the FreeSWITCH environment

FreeSWITCH, like many other software applications, requires a suitable environment. Primarily that means choosing appropriate operating system for your hardware and having the proper LAN/WAN connectivity and physical environment.

Operating system

The first question to consider here is: which operating system should be used? Generally speaking, it is good to use an operating system with which you are comfortable and familiar. One caveat to consider is 32-bit versus 64-bit. Some users have reported problems when running a 32-bit OS on a 64-bit hardware platform. We strongly recommend that you use a 64-bit OS if you have 64-bit hardware.

For those who prefer a Windows environment you can use XP, Vista, Windows 7, Server 2003, or Server 2008. Several users have reported good success with production systems running on modern hardware, and using Windows Server 2008.

On the other hand, there is a wide variety of Unix-like operating systems available, many of which are freely downloadable. Most of us have an operating system (Linux, BSD, Solaris, and so on), and distribution (CentOS, Debian, Ubuntu, and so on.) that we prefer to use. The FreeSWITCH developers do not advocate any particular operating system or distribution.

Some have asked which platform is "the best" for FreeSWITCH. There are many factors to consider when choosing a platform on which to run a telephony application. FreeSWITCH is cross-platform, and therefore, it compiles and runs on numerous systems. However, through hard-earned experience we know which operating systems and distributions lend themselves to real-time telephony applications. The bottom line is that you want your system to be stable and reliable. Our experience is that installation on Red Hat Enterprise Linux (RHEL), or its free cousin, CentOS, yields the best performance and fewest problems.

Some have characterized RHEL and CentOS as "boring and predictable". These qualities are perfect for running real-time telephony applications like FreeSWITCH.

Operating system prerequisites

Each operating system has its own set of prerequisites. Make sure that you have met the prerequisites for your platform.

Linux/Unix

The following items frequently are already installed on your system. Note that an SVN or Git client is not required:

- SVN: **A Subversion (SVN)** client gives you access to the current code repository (recommended for those who simply want the latest code)
- Git: A Git client also gives you access to the current code repository (recommended especially for developers)
- GNUMAKE: The GNU version of make
- AUTOCONF: Version 2.60 or higher
- AUTOMAKE: Version 1.9 or higher
- LIBTOOL: Version 1.5.14 or higher
- GCC: Version 3.3 or higher
- WGET: Any recent version
- LIBNCURSES: Any recent version

Mac OS X

It is strongly recommended that Mac users have, at the very least, OS X Version 10.4. Compiling FreeSWITCH on OS X requires the installation of the Apple XCode Developer Tools. You may download them from `http://connect.apple.com`. Free registration is required.

Windows

FreeSWITCH in a Windows environment has two primary requirements. They are as follows:

1. Microsoft Visual C++ 2008 (or 2008 Express Edition)
2. A file decompression utility

FreeSWITCH in Windows is compiled and built using Microsoft Visual C++ 2008 (MSVC) or Visual C++ 2008 Express Edition (MSVCEE). The Express Edition is free to download though registration is required. It can be obtained at `http://www.microsoft.com/Express/VC`. The other requirement for Windows is a file decompression utility like WinZip (`www.winzip.com`) or WinRAR (`www.rarlab.com`). A free alternative is 7-Zip (`www.7-zip.org`). Each of these utilities will add a right-click menu option to Windows Explorer.

Text editors and XML

Working with FreeSWITCH requires you to have a text editor with which you are comfortable. Regardless of your editor choice, we strongly recommend that you use a text editor that supports XML syntax highlighting. You will find that editing XML configuration files is much easier on the eyes with highlighting turned on.

If you do not already have a preferred editor, then we suggest trying one or two for your platform. Be aware that if you are in a Linux/Unix environment that does not have GUI (Graphical User Interface), then your choices will be fewer. However, there are several excellent text-only editors available:

- Emacs—This is a text-only editor available for just about any Unix-like environment, including Mac OS X. It can highlight source code, XML, HTML, and more. This is the editor of choice for the FreeSWITCH development team. (A GUI version of Emacs is also available.)

- Vi/Vim—This is a text-only editor available for just about and Unix-like environment. Like Emacs it can highlight source code and markup languages. (A GUI version of Vim is also available.)

- Notepad++—This is a graphical text editor for Windows environment. It supports highlighting of many programming and markup languages. It is a very useful and free text editor for Windows.

Downloading the source

Most open source projects have their source code divided into two general categories: *stable* and *latest*. While the latest FreeSWITCH code is usually quite stable, we recommend that you begin with the latest stable release. You can update to the latest trunk at a later point. (See the *Building From the latest Code* section in this chapter.) One other point to keep in mind: binary distributions of FreeSWITCH might be available for your platform. While they are certainly convenient, in our experience it is easier to troubleshoot, update, and customize your FreeSWITCH installation when compiling from the source.

Be sure that your system has Internet access because the build process will occasionally need to download additional files.

The source code can be obtained from the following FreeSWITCH download site: `http://files.freeswitch.org`. Locate a file named `freeswitch-1.0.6.tar.gz`, and download it into a local directory on your computer, then decompress it. A typical session in Linux might look like the following:

```
#>cd /usr/src
#>wget http://files.freeswitch.org/freeswitch-1.0.6.tar.gz
#>tar zxvf freeswitch-1.0.6.tar.gz
```

This will create a new directory that contains the FreeSWITCH source code, ready for you to compile on your system. (From now on, this will be referred to as the FreeSWITCH source directory.)

Windows users should create a new directory and download the source file. See the *Compiling FreeSWITCH For Windows* section, later in this chapter.

Building from the latest code

If you prefer to be on the latest version of FreeSWITCH, then you will need a Subversion (SVN) client or a Git client. The FreeSWITCH developers recently migrated from Subversion to Git for the development tree. However, they are maintaining a read-only SVN mirror, so you can still get the latest code via SVN. You can also get the latest code with a Git client; however, developers who wish to have commit-access will need a Git client. Most Linux/Unix environments already have, or can easily have, a Subversion client installed. In Windows, a popular (and free) Subversion client is TortoiseSVN (`tortoisesvn.tigris.org`). There is also TortoiseGit (`code.google.com/p/tortoisegit`). In Windows, the build procedure is essentially the same: open the appropriate solution file and then build it.

In Linux/Unix environments it is necessary to "bootstrap" prior to compiling. However, there is a shortcut available. The following commands will download and build a fresh SVN checkout of FreeSWITCH, with the default configuration and all the sound files:

```
#>cd /usr/src ; wget http://www.freeswitch.org/eg/Makefile ; make
#>make all
#>cd freeswitch.trunk
#>make install
#>make cd-sounds-install
#>make cd-moh-install
```

The preceding commands will take some time to complete. You can automate the process a bit by chaining the commands together with the && operator.

Compiling FreeSWITCH for Linux/Unix/ Mac OS X

The install procedure is essentially the same for Linux, Unix, or Mac OS X. However, make sure that your system has met the prerequisites listed in the previous section.

Compiling FreeSWITCH

Compiling FreeSWITCH requires just a few steps, although it will take some time depending upon the speed of your system. The basic procedure for compiling FreeSWITCH is as follows:

- Edit modules.conf file to customize which modules are compiled by default
- Run configure script
- Run make and make install to compile and install
- Edit modules.conf.xml to customize which modules are loaded by default
- Install the sound and music files

Following are detailed step-by-step instructions for compiling FreeSWITCH.

Step 1: Edit modules.conf

The modules.conf file contains a list of the various FreeSWITCH modules that will be configured and compiled. The default modules.conf file has a sensible set of modules, pre-selected to be compiled. However, there is one optional module that we will enable now. You should have a new subdirectory named freeswitch-x.y.z, where x.y.z is the version number. For example, if the latest stable version is 1.0.6 then your source directory will be /usr/src/freeswitch-1.0.6. Follow the steps below:

1. Change directory into the new FreeSWITCH source directory:

   ```
   #>cd /usr/src/freeswitch-1.0.6
   ```

2. Open modules.conf in a text editor. Scroll down to the following line:

   ```
   #asr_tts/mod_flite
   ```

3. Remove the # character from the beginning of the line, then save and exit. The `mod_flite` module enables FreeSWITCH to use the open source Festival Lite text-to-speech (TTS) engine. (The Flite TTS engine does not produce particularly high quality speech synthesis. However, it is very handy for doing TTS testing.)

After editing `modules.conf` we are ready to start the build process.

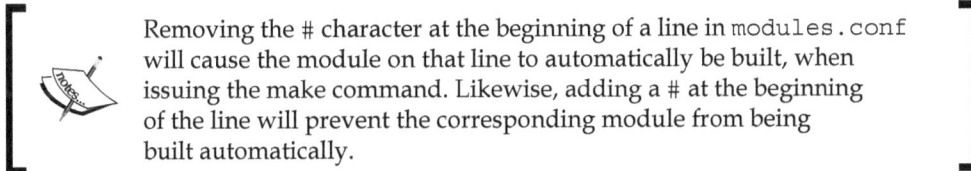

> Removing the # character at the beginning of a line in `modules.conf` will cause the module on that line to automatically be built, when issuing the make command. Likewise, adding a # at the beginning of the line will prevent the corresponding module from being built automatically.

Step 2: Run configure script

Like many open source projects, FreeSWITCH in UNIX-like environments makes use of the now famous `configure` script. From within the FreeSWITCH source directory, launch the configure script, as follows:

```
#>./configure
```

The `configure` script performs many tasks, including making sure that the prerequisites have been met. If a prerequisite has not been met then the `configure` script will exit, and tell you which dependency has not been met. If this occurs then you must resolve the issue and rerun the `configure` script. You will need to make sure that all of the prerequisites have been met before the `configure` script will run to completion.

During the configuration process you will see the configure script run multiple times. FreeSWITCH makes use of many libraries like Apache Portable Runtime (APR) and Perl Compatible Regular Expressions (PCRE). Each of these elements has its own specific `configure` script that is customized to its own needs.

After some time the `configure` script finishes, and returns you to the system prompt. You will undoubtedly see a lot of output on the screen from the configuration process, but if you do not see any errors then you may proceed to the compilation process.

Step 3: Run make and make install

The configuration process in the previous step actually creates what is called a **Makefile** for FreeSWITCH, its libraries, and its various modules. The compilation and installation of FreeSWITCH are both handled by the make utility. First run *make*, and then run *make install*. Many users will run them both with one command line, which is as follows:

```
#>make && make install
```

Like the configure script, the make process takes a while, and will stop if there are any errors. Usually things go well, and at the end of the compilation and installation you are greeted with the following message:

```
+-------- FreeSWITCH install Complete ----------+
+ FreeSWITCH has been successfully installed.   +
+                                               +
+       Install sounds:                         +
+       (uhd-sounds includes hd-sounds, sounds) +
+       (hd-sounds includes sounds)             +
+       ------------------------------------    +
+               make cd-sounds-install          +
+               make cd-moh-install             +
+                                               +
+               make uhd-sounds-install         +
+               make uhd-moh-install            +
+                                               +
+               make hd-sounds-install          +
+               make hd-moh-install             +
+                                               +
+               make sounds-install             +
+               make moh-install                +
+                                               +
+       Install non english sounds:             +
+       replace XX with language                +
+       (ru : Russian)                          +
+       ------------------------------------    +
+               make cd-sounds-XX-install       +
+               make uhd-sounds-XX-install      +
+               make hd-sounds-XX-install       +
+               make sounds-XX-install          +
+                                               +
+       Upgrade to latest:                      +
+       ------------------------------------    +
```

```
+                 make current               +
+                                            +
+       Rebuild all:                         +
+       ----------------------------------   +
+                 make sure                  +
+                                            +
+       Install/Re-install default config:   +
+       ----------------------------------   +
+                 make samples               +
+                                            +
+                                            +
+       Additional resources:                +
+       ----------------------------------   +
+       http://www.freeswitch.org            +
+       http://wiki.freeswitch.org           +
+       http://jira.freeswitch.org           +
+       http://lists.freeswitch.org          +
+                                            +
+       irc.freenode.net / #freeswitch       +
+                                            +
+--------------------------------------------+
```

If you see a message like the last one then you have successfully compiled FreeSWITCH, and can proceed to the next step. If an error occurs then the compilation process will stop and report it. You will need to correct the problem before you can continue. If the error message is unfamiliar to you then you should contact the FreeSWITCH community using the resources listed in Appendix A (The FreeSWITCH Online Community).

Step 4: Edit modules.conf.xml

The modules.conf.xml file contains a list of modules that FreeSWITCH will load when it is launched. The default modules.conf.xml file corresponds with the default modules.conf file. The modules that are built by default in modules.conf are also enabled by default in modules.conf.xml. As we enabled mod_flite to be built in modules.conf, we need to enable mod_flite in modules.conf.xml, so that it will be loaded automatically when FreeSWITCH starts. As a rule of thumb, any module that you wish to load automatically when FreeSWITCH starts must be enabled in modules.conf.xml.

The `modules.conf.xml` file is located in the `conf/autoload_configs` subdirectory. The default location is `/usr/local/freeswitch/conf/autoload_configs/ modules.conf.xml`. Open the file in a text editor and locate the following line near the end of the file:

```
<!-- <load module="mod_flite"/> -->
```

Remove the `<!--` and `-->` tags so that it looks like the following:

```
<load module="mod_flite"/>
```

Save the file and exit. You are almost ready to start the FreeSWITCH application.

> What's the difference between `modules.conf` and `modules.conf. xml` files? The `modules.conf` file is found in the source directory, and is used to control FreeSWITCH modules which are compiled when running `make`. The `modules.conf.xml` file is part of the default XML configuration, and is found in the FreeSWITCH `autoload_configs` subdirectory. It controls which modules are loaded when FreeSWITCH is launched.

Step 5: Install sound and music files

Sound and music files are not absolutely required. However, they are highly recommended. Without them you will not have music on hold, nor will features like voicemail and the sample IVR be functional. FreeSWITCH has sample sound and music files available in four different sampling rates. We recommend installing all of them so that you can take advantage of high quality audio connections wherever possible.

To install the sound files just issue the following command in the FreeSWITCH source directory:

```
#>make cd-sounds-install
```

To install the music files issue the following command:

```
#>make cd-moh-install
```

These commands will download and install the sound and music files in 8 kHz, 16 kHz, 32 kHz, and 48 kHz. FreeSWITCH will use the appropriate sampling rate when playing a sound or music file to a caller.

You are now ready to start FreeSWITCH. The next section covers compiling FreeSWITCH in the Windows environment, so skip down to the section named *Starting FreeSWITCH*.

Compiling FreeSWITCH for Windows

As mentioned in the *Operating system prerequisites* section, FreeSWITCH is built with MSVC or MSVCEE. The steps presented here are specifically for the Express Edition; however, the steps for using the standard edition are essentially the same.

Building the solution with MSVC/MSVCEE

There are several small steps to take prior to building with MSVC. They are as follows:

1. Create a new folder and copy the `tar.gz` file into it. In our example, we'll use `C:\FreeSWITCH\freeswitch-1.0.6.tar.gz`.

2. Right-click `freeswitch-1.0.6.tar.gz` and extract the files with your decompression utility. You will now have a new file named, `freeswitch-1.0.6.tar`.

3. Right-click `freeswitch-1.0.6.tar` and extract files. This process will take a few moments. You will then see a window similar to the following screenshot:

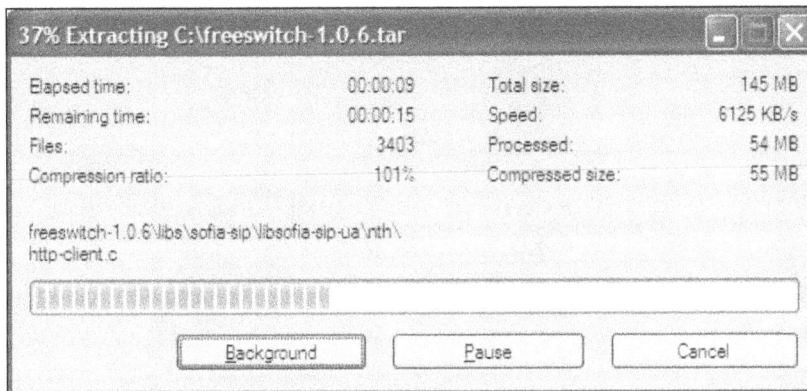

Note: WinRAR decompresses both the `.gz` and `.tar` files in a single step.

4. After extraction you will have a new sub-folder named after the latest version of FreeSWITCH. In our example, we now have a sub-folder named `freeswitch-1.0.6`. Double-click on the folder to see the complete FreeSWITCH source tree. It will be similar to the screen in the following screenshot:

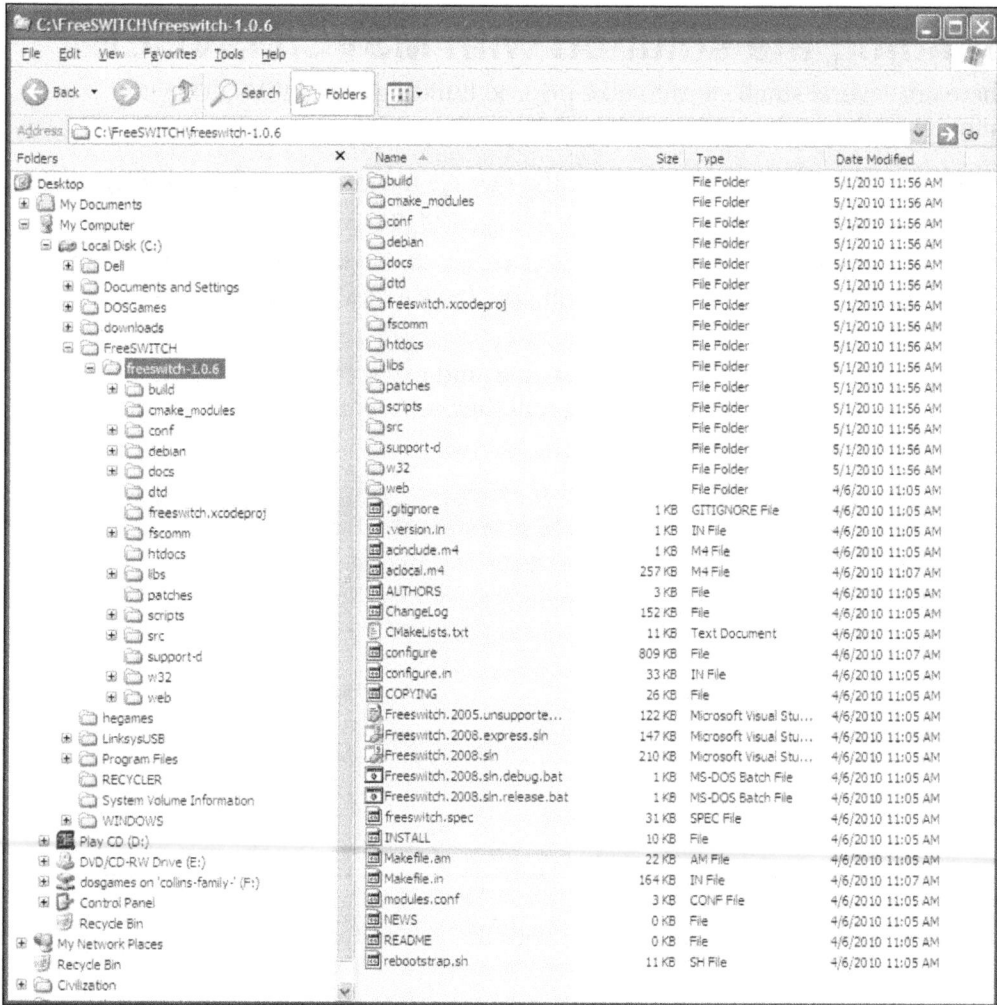

5. While there are many files, the only ones we care about right now are the two solution files. For MSVC, the file is named `Freeswitch.2008.sln` and for MSVCEE, it is named `Freeswitch.2008.express.sln`. Double-click the appropriate solution file for your edition of MSVC. The screenshots in this example will show MSVC 2008 Express Edition. However, the Standard and Professional editions will be very similar.

6. After the solution file loads, click `Build > Build Solution` or press *F7*. The solution will start building. Numerous messages will appear in the Output window. When the solution has finished building, you will see a message at the bottom of the Output window as in the following screenshot:

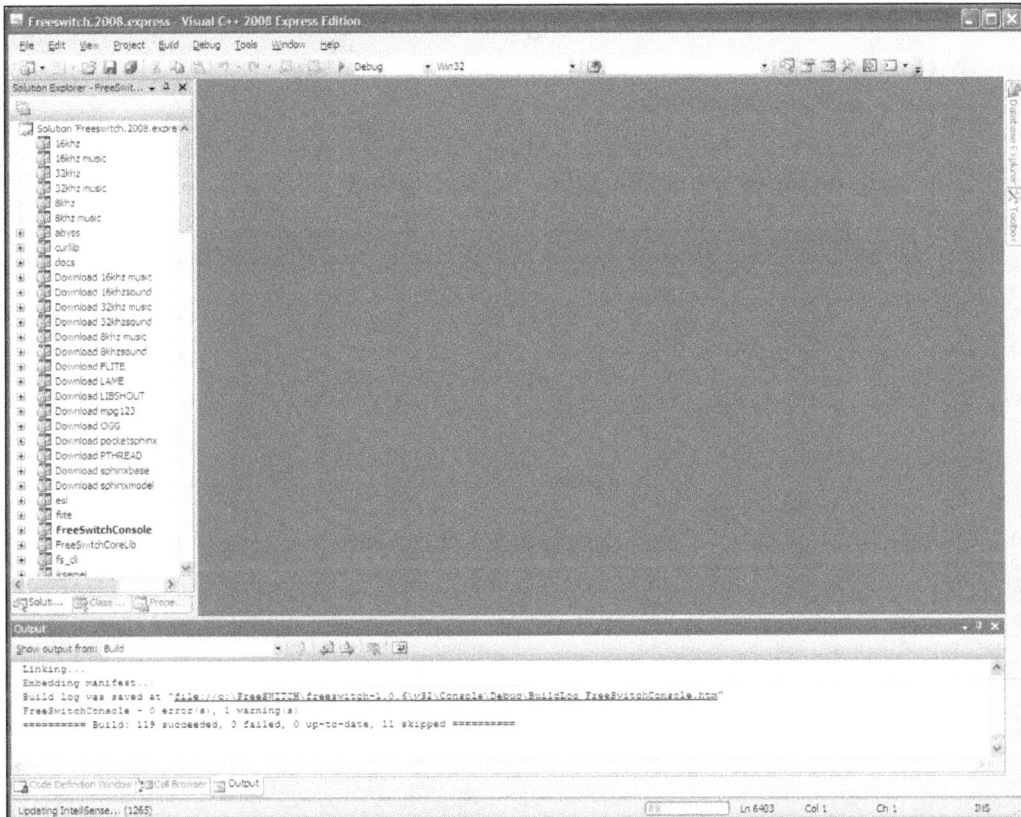

7. Note: The MSVC/EE solution files will automatically perform several steps that are usually done manually in a Linux/Unix installation. These include downloading of all the sound and music files, and building optional modules like Flite (text-to-speech) and PocketSphinx (speech recognition). However, these optional modules still need to be enabled in `modules.conf.xml` if you wish to have them automatically loaded when FreeSWITCH starts. (See the next screenshot.)

8. Once the solution is built you can close MSVC. All remaining steps are performed from the Windows Explorer or the Windows command line.

9. Go back to the Windows Explorer. You will see that the build process has created a new folder named Debug. This is the FreeSWITCH installation directory. The last step before launching FreeSWITCH is to edit the modules. conf.xml file in order to enable mod_flite to be loaded by default when FreeSWITCH is started. We will be using the mod_flite text-to-speech (TTS) engine in several examples throughout this book.

10. Double-click the conf folder, then double-click on the autoload_configs folder.

11. Open modules.conf.xml in an editor. In our example, we'll use Notepad++ to edit the file as seen in the following screenshot:

12. Locate the following line near the end of the file:

```
<!-- <load module="mod_flite"/> -->
```

Remove the `<!--` and `-->` tags so that it looks like the following:

```
<load module="mod_flite"/>
```

Save the file and exit the editor. You are now ready to launch FreeSWITCH for the first time.

Starting FreeSWITCH

Once you have compiled FreeSWITCH, it is time to launch the application.

Linux/Unix/OS X: run `/usr/local/freeswitch/bin/freeswitch`.

Windows: run `freeswitch.exe` from the `Debug` directory.

The system will start loading, and numerous messages will display on the screen. Console messages are color-coded for readability. Do not worry about all of the messages right now, just make sure that your system starts up and you get to the FreeSWITCH console, which we call the command-line interface (CLI). The CLI prompt looks like the following:

```
freeswitch@localhost>
```

Let's issue a few commands to verify that the system is operational. First, issue the `version` command to verify the version of FreeSWITCH that we have installed, as follows:

```
freeswitch@localhost>version

FreeSWITCH Version 1.0.6 (exported)
```

Next, issue the `status` command which displays a few statistics about your system, as follows:

```
freeswitch@localhost>status

UP 0 years, 0 days, 0 hours, 0 minutes, 36 seconds, 839 milliseconds, 449
microseconds

0 session(s) since startup

0 session(s) 0/30

1000 session(s) max
```

These are just a few of the many commands you will learn about in FreeSWITCH. Type `help` to see a complete list of commands that are available. Lastly, shut down FreeSWITCH with this command: `fsctl shutdown`. The system will display numerous messages as it shuts down, and will return you to the system command prompt. (If you launched `FreeSWITCH.exe` from the Windows explorer then the FreeSWITCH window will simply close.)

Running FreeSWITCH in the background

In most cases, you will want FreeSWITCH to run in the background. In a Unix/Linux environment this is frequently called running as a *daemon*. In Windows this is called running as a service.

To launch FreeSWITCH as a daemon in Unix/Linux:

```
#>/usr/local/freeswitch/bin/freeswitch -nc
```

The various Linux and Unix distributions take different approaches to automatically running a daemon at system start up. Several `init` script examples are available on the FreeSWITCH wiki: `wiki.freeswitch.org/wiki/Freeswitch_init`. Consult the system administration documentation for your specific distribution for instructions, on how to configure the init script to launch FreeSWITCH at system startup.

Windows requires just a few steps to have FreeSWITCH run as a service. They are as follows:

1. Open a Windows command-line session (Click on `Start | Run`, type `cmd`, and then click the OK button).

2. Change the directory into your FreeSWITCH installation directory, as follows:

    ```
    cd FreeSWITCH\freeswitch-1.0.6\Debug
    ```

3. Run `freeswitch.exe` (or just `freeswitch`) with the `-install` argument, as follows:

    ```
    freeswitch -install FreeSWITCH
    ```

4. The last step is to configure the service itself. Open the services tool, click on **Start | Control Panel | Administrative Tools | Services**.

   FreeSWITCH should now appear in the list of services:

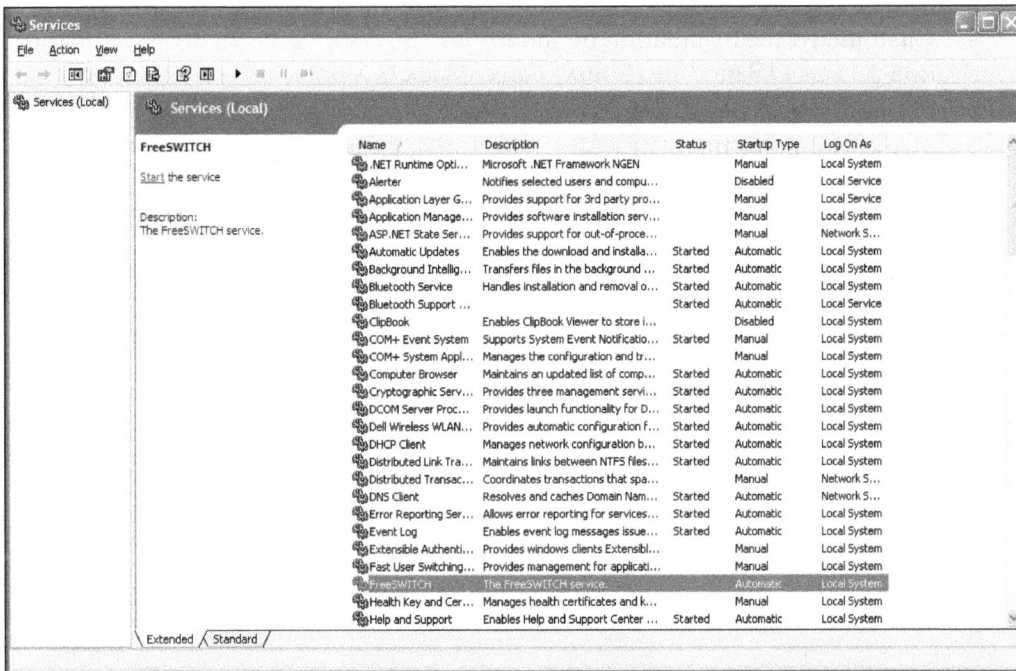

5. Right-click **FreeSWITCH** and click start. The service will take a moment to start up.

6. Confirm that the service is running by using the `fs_cli.exe` utility found in the `Debug` folder:

   fs_cli.exe

7. You will see a welcome screen and a command prompt. Issue the status command, to confirm that the system is running.

8. Type `/exit` to close the `fs_cli.exe` program.

You now have FreeSWITCH running as a service in Windows.

The `fs_cli` utility is discussed in greater detail in *Chapter 9, Controlling FreeSWITCH Externally*.

Summary

In this chapter, we accomplished a number of objectives. They are as follows:

- Downloaded and installed FreeSWITCH
- Customized the installation by modifying the `modules.conf` to compile the `mod_flite` TTS module (Linux/Unix/Mac OS X only)
- Customized the FreeSWITCH configuration by modifying `modules.conf.xml` to automatically load `mod_flite`, when FreeSWITCH is launched
- Launched FreeSWITCH and issued several commands to confirm its operational status
- Launched FreeSWITCH as a daemon (Linux/Unix) or as a service (Windows)

In the following chapter, we will put our new installation into action as we explore the default configuration of FreeSWITCH.

3
Test Driving the Default Configuration

Now that you have FreeSWITCH installed, it is time to explore the default configuration. The standard FreeSWITCH installation comes preconfigured with users, a Dialplan, security settings, and more. The default configuration is designed to make your first experience with FreeSWITCH as simple as possible. Let's start by considering some important concepts.

Important concepts to understand

FreeSWITCH is a very versatile software. One of the biggest reasons that it's so versatile is because the world of telephony is very dynamic. As the developers of the software, we often faced difficult choices when making decisions about how FreeSWITCH should behave in various situations. Quite often, we faced conundrums where a large number of potential users required the software to work in a specific way, and the others expected the exact opposite behavior. We easily support devices that behave properly, but at the same time we must adapt to tolerate many devices that blatantly violate specifications. FreeSWITCH was designed to scale, so we also had to design things so you can start out with a self-contained static configuration, and be able to scale into using live dynamic configurations without missing a beat. This is a lot to swallow for a new user but don't fret. When you installed FreeSWITCH in the last chapter, you also installed a fully functional default configuration that will get you through most of this book, with only a few minor modifications.

As we discussed in *Chapter 1, Architecture of FreeSWITCH*, FreeSWITCH is based on a central core fuelled by a central XML registry, and orbited by several modules that communicate with each other via the core. We are going to use the default settings in the XML registry, to register some phones and make a few test calls. When you make the call, the SIP module will push a request to the XML Dialplan where the digits you dialed are matched against a series of pattern matches called **regular expressions**. Once a match has been found, the data from the XML extension that matched is copied into the channel locally, so it has a list of instructions that it will execute in the next stage of the call. It's possible to match more than one extension on the same pass of the dialplan, depending on the choice of configuration keywords. For these first few tests, just a single extension will be put to use, and you will have a chance to see all of the call data that is available whenever a channel is in the ROUTING state.

In Telephony jargon, we call a connection between two devices a **call leg**. Consider the following illustration:

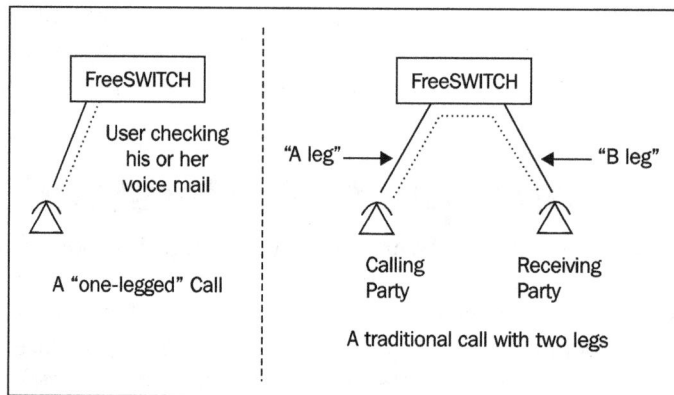

If you are using a softphone to call and listen to a demo extension then there is one call leg in use, that is, the connection between your phone and FreeSWITCH. If you dial digits that end up calling another phone currently registered to FreeSWITCH or push the call to a service provider to call your cellular phone, you then have two call legs—the first one we explained, and another connects FreeSWITCH and the other phone or service provider. Each leg of the call has its own unique properties, and a special relationship with the opposite leg in that particular call. When one or more legs of call are exchanging media with each other, we call that a **bridge**. In a bridged call, either leg of the call can perform certain operations on the other leg in the same bridge such as put it on *hold*, *transfer* it to another extension, or join it with a third party to form a **three-way call**.

Some calls only have one leg—there is a connection between one phone and FreeSWITCH, and FreeSWITCH interacts with the caller directly. This type of interface is referred to as an **IVR** or **Interactive Voice Response** menu. IVRs are very powerful and you certainly have used them before, if you have ever called a system that provides a list of choices, and asks you to dial a digit indicating the choice you want to make. If you have ever used a calling card, this is also a form of IVR that asks you to dial your destination digits before completing your call. Some IVRs can even detect speech and react purely on special words that you may say at the appropriate time. With FreeSWITCH it is simple to make an IVR, and we will learn a few ways to do this in *Chapter 6, Using the Built-In XML IVR Engine* and *Chapter 7, Building IVR Applications with Lua*.

The XML Dialplan separates the extensions into special groups called **contexts**. A context is an XML tag containing several extension elements. An **extension** is a collection of patterns to match against the dialed digits and a relative set of instructions to execute based on a positive or negative match against the patterns. Consider the following figure:

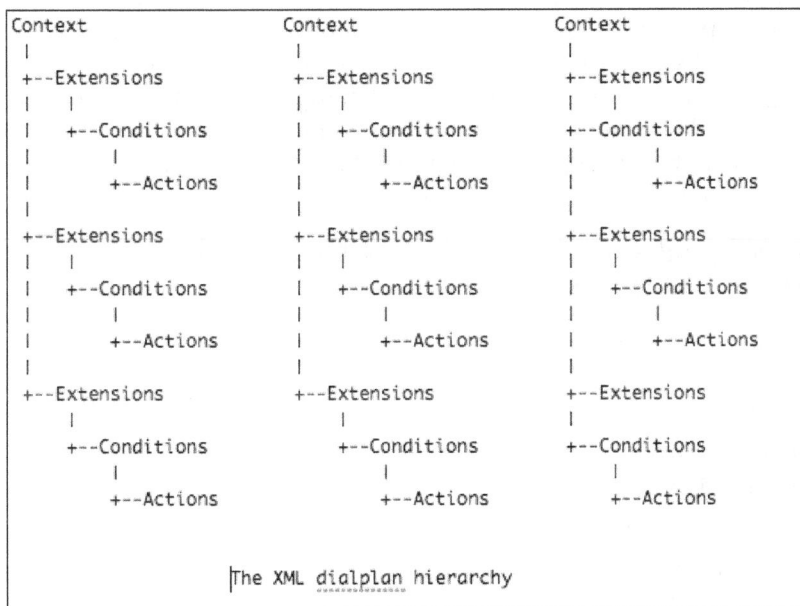

```
Context              Context              Context
|                    |                    |
+--Extensions        +--Extensions        +--Extensions
|   |                |   |                |   |
|   +--Conditions    |   +--Conditions    +--Conditions
|       |            |       |            |       |
|       +--Actions   |       +--Actions   |       +--Actions
|                    |                    |
+--Extensions        +--Extensions        +--Extensions
|   |                |   |                |   |
|   +--Conditions    |   +--Conditions    |   +--Conditions
|       |            |       |            |       |
|       +--Actions   |       +--Actions   |       +--Actions
|                    |                    |
+--Extensions        +--Extensions        +--Extensions
|                    |                    |
    +--Conditions        +--Conditions        +--Conditions
        |                    |                    |
        +--Actions           +--Actions           +--Actions


            The XML dialplan hierarchy
```

Every new call that enters the FreeSWITCH core must have a pre-ordained set of context, Dialplan, and extension digits to indicate where the call should be routed. In our examples, we will be using the XML Dialplan, the default context. The extension digits will depend on what you dialed when you placed the call. Once you dial an extension, the SIP endpoint module will insert all of the call data it has decoded from your SIP phone, set the Dialplan to XML, the context to default, and push the call's state to ROUTING. The default ROUTING logic in the core will lookup the XML Dialplan module and push the call into its call hunt handler routine. This routine connects to the XML registry and searches the list of contexts for the default context. Once the context has been located, it parses each extension in the context, testing the patterns held in the *condition* tag, until it finds one that matches. Each *action* tag within that condition tag contains an *application* and an optional data argument. These applications provided by the application modules we discussed in *Chapter 1, Architecture of FreeSWITCH*, will be executed in order until the last one is reached or the call ends.

The arguments to the applications can contain **channel variables**, a special group of name/value pairs that are designed to influence the channel behavior, and provide a way to store important call data. They look similar to the special pre-processor variables we recently discussed, but only a single dollar sign is used, rather than two. *${destination_number}* for instance, tells you what digits the caller dialed, and is the primary value used to route calls. The condition tags use the *field* attribute to denote which value to run the pattern match against. If this value is one of the special variables held in the caller profile, you can omit the ${} for simplicity's sake.

The special *caller profile* variables are as follows. Some may seem unusual at first but as you use FreeSWITCH more, you will see where these all come into play:

* username
* Dialplan
* caller_id_name
* caller_id_number
* callee_id_name
* callee_id_number
* network_addr
* ani
* aniii
* rdnis
* destination_number
* source
* uuid
* context

The caller profile is just a collection of special information that every call has in common, which is passed along from one leg to another. This information can be accessed the same way as other variables, and should be considered "read-only", as the data is provided by the initial call setup. Following is a real example from the default configuration, which uses the tone generator in the core to play a rendition of the popular song from the 1980's video game, Tetris:

```
<extension name="tone_stream">
    <condition field="destination_number" expression="^9198$">
        <action application="answer"/>
        <action application="playback"
        data="tone_stream://path=${base_dir}
        /conf/tetris.ttml;loops=10"/>
    </condition>
</extension>
```

As you can see, it uses `field="destination_number"` to check if you dialed 9198 and if you do, it answers the call and plays the tone stream. It uses `${base_dir}` to denote the location where the configuration is stored, so it can deduce the path to the correct file containing the tone data. We will be discussing this all once more. You have had a chance to see FreeSWITCH in action, by making a few test calls to the various demonstration extensions we provide in the defaults. Channel variables can be very useful when integrating outside information about a call, which you may want to set and retrieve later in your own applications. These variables might contain information such as the caller's account number, which is useful if she calls in to manage her account. There is an interface to set variables in the application interface provided by the set application, which is as follows:

```
<action application="set" data="customer_id=1234"/>
```

As the XML registry can be rather large and scary, we have designed it to be loaded from several smaller files spread out into the configuration directory in logical order. This means that rather than digging into one giant file, you can locate smaller, simpler files, each of which can be used to configure a specific type of functionality in FreeSWITCH.

> The FreeSWITCH wiki contains a large diagram showing how the default Dialplan is laid out: http://wiki.freeswitch.org/wiki/Default_config#Overview_Diagram_of_the_Default_Configuration.

Once FreeSWITCH loads the main registry or `freeswitch.xml`, the file is run through a special pre-processor that scans the file for special directives, which are replaced on the file with the contents of other files. In some cases, the pre-processor also sets global variables. This means that you can set important variables once in the top-level configuration file, and reference them later in the deeper sections of the registry. Take an IP address or domain name for instance. Pretend that you have some significant IP address, say, 74.112.132.98. If you use this value multiple times in your configuration, you can put the following line somewhere at the top of the first file that is loaded.

```
<X-PRE-PROCESS cmd="set" data="my_ip=74.112.132.98"/>
```

Now anywhere else in your configuration you can place $${my_ip} where you want your IP address to appear. This expansion is done by the pre-processor, so in the final XML generated and loaded by FreeSWITCH, the IP will appear as if it was hardcoded into the file everywhere the $${my_ip} appeared.

Another great feature of the XML pre-processor is the ability to include other files into place with a single line. Following is an example line used in the default configuration, to load all the files from a particular directory in place inside the default Dialplan context:

```
<X-PRE-PROCESS cmd="include" data="default/*.xml"/>
```

This means that every single file in the "default" folder that ends with `.xml` will be included in place of the preceding line. This makes it possible to make up new extensions in their own dedicated files, and include them into your Dialplan without disturbing the `default.xml` (the file containing the default context).

Putting FreeSWITCH to work

Now that we have covered the basics, it is time to roll up our sleeves and really put FreeSWITCH to work. We will first learn a bit more about the main tool for controlling FreeSWITCH, the Command Line Interface, after which we will configure one or two telephones and make some test calls.

Controlling FreeSWITCH with the CLI

In *Chapter 2, Building and Installation*, we briefly discussed a utility called `fs_cli`. As we generally will run FreeSWITCH as a daemon (Linux/Unix) or a service (Windows), it is important to become familiar with using `fs_cli`. For convenience, you can add `fs_cli.exe` to your path in Windows. In Linux/Unix you can create a symbolic link, as follows:

```
#>ln -s /usr/local/freeswitch/bin/fs_cli /usr/local/bin/fs_cli
```

Now, if you simply type `fs_cli` at the system command prompt, it will launch the `fs_cli` program for you.

> **Executable Files: Linux/Unix versus Windows**
>
> Generally speaking, Windows executable files will have `.exe` at the end of the filename. On Windows systems the `fs_cli` program is named `fs_cli.exe`. Windows users can type `fs_cli.exe` or just `fs_cli` whereas Linux/Unix users should type `fs_cli`, to launch the FreeSWITCH command-line utility.

Launch the command-line utility:

#>fs_cli

You will be greeted with the following FS CLI welcome message:

```
#>:fs_cli
     _____ _____    _____ _      _____
    |  ___/  ___|  / ___|| |    |_   _|
    | |_  \ `--.  / /   | |      | |
    |  _|  `--. \ | |   | |      | |
    | |   /\__/ / | \___| |____ _| |_
    \_|   \____/   _____/ \___/

    ********************************************************
    * Anthony Minessale II, Ken Rice, Michael Jerris       *
    * FreeSWITCH (http://www.freeswitch.org)               *
    * Brought to you by ClueCon http://www.cluecon.com/    *
    ********************************************************


    Type /help <enter> to see a list of commands


    +OK log level   [7]
    freeswitch@internal>
```

Once connected, everything you type will be sent to the FreeSWITCH server, except for commands that begin with a / (slash) character. These *slash commands* control the behavior of the `fs_cli` program itself. Issue the `/help` command to see the list of available `fs_cli` slash commands:

```
freeswitch@internal>/help
Command                            Description
-------------------------------------------------
/help                              Help
/exit, /quit, /bye, ...            Exit the program.
/event, /noevent, /nixevent       Event commands.
/log, /nolog                       Log commands.
/filter                            Filter commands.
/debug [0-7]                       Set debug level.

freeswitch@internal>
```

Note that there are several different slash commands for exiting the system: `/exit`, `/quit`, and `/bye`. Also, there is the ellipsis (...) shortcut. All four of these commands will exit the `fs_cli` utility and return you to the system prompt. They are all equivalent, so use whichever suits you. Keep in mind that when running FreeSWITCH from the console, that is, not as a daemon or service, the ellipsis shortcut will perform a FreeSWITCH system shutdown!

The other slash command to keep in mind is `/log`. By default, `fs_cli` starts up with full debug logging enabled. (The welcome screen mentions this fact with **+OK log level [7]** displayed at startup.) The `/log` command will let you control what level of debug logging will be displayed during your `fs_cli` session. You can change the log level at any point during your session. When you exit and restart `fs_cli`, the log level will reset to 7. (This behavior can be controlled with the `-d` or `--debug` command line parameters.) Unless you wish to see a lot of debug information, it is best to set the log level to 6, as follows:

```
freeswitch@internal>/log 6

+OK log level 6 [6]
```

Each number from 0 to 7 represents a different debug level as noted in the following table:

Debug Level:	Name:	Text Display Color:
0	Console	White
1	Alert	Red
2	Critical (CRIT)	Red
3	Error (ERR)	Red
4	Warning	Violet

Debug Level:	Name:	Text Display Color:
5	Notify	Orange
6	Information (INFO)	Green
7	Debug	Yellow

You may use the name (case-insensitive) as well as the number when specifying the log level:

```
freeswitch@internal>/log info
+OK log level info [6]
```

All the other commands you type will be sent to the FreeSWITCH server. There are a few basic commands to become familiar with. They are as follows:

- `help` — It displays a list of available CLI commands; these commands are called FSAPI commands or just APIs for short
- `version` — It displays the FreeSWITCH version you are running
- `status` — It displays some statistics about the currently running instance of FreeSWITCH
- `show channels` — It displays a list of individual channels that are active
- `show calls` — It displays a list of bridged calls

A channel is a single *call leg*. A call is defined as two calls *bridged* together. An example of a "one-legged" call is a user checking his or her voicemail. On the other hand, a "call" is two individual call legs bridged (that is, connected) together. Be sure to understand the difference between show channels and show calls.

In the next section, we will learn a few more commands that will help us configure phones to work with FreeSWITCH.

Configuring a SIP phone to work with FreeSWITCH

Most of the devices that we connect to FreeSWITCH will be SIP-based. SIP, Session Initiation Protocol, is a very common *signaling* protocol for telephone calls. (SIP is not limited to voice; it can handle chat, video, and other "session" types.) SIP phones come in two varieties: hard phones and soft phones. A **hard phone** is a standalone device with headset, keypad, and usually a digital display. A **soft phone** is a software application that runs on a computer, and utilizes the speakerphone or an external headset. We will examine the setup process for a free soft phone called **X-Lite**, as well as the basic SIP configuration options for hard phones from Aastra, Polycom, and Snom.

SIP settings

All SIP devices have a minimum set of configuration parameters that must be set. Like all complex protocols, SIP has its share of obscure and sometimes arcane configuration options. However, they are well beyond the scope of this book. We will be limiting our discussion to the basics that are necessary to make a SIP device connect to FreeSWITCH, and perform standard PBX functions: make and receive calls, transfer calls, put calls on hold, and so on.

In our SIP configuration, we will have our SIP devices register with our FreeSWITCH server. When a SIP device is registered with a *SIP registrar,* then that registrar knows how to route calls to the SIP device. FreeSWITCH acts as a SIP registrar. SIP allows for *digest authentication* for SIP endpoints that wish to register. It is possible to allow unauthorized SIP endpoints to register, but it is not recommended. (A good analogy might be that of an open relay SMTP server. If you just let anyone into your system to send an email, or make phone calls, then bad things are bound to happen. Please do not do it!)

SIP users bear other semblances to e-mail. A SIP URI contains *user@domain* just like an e-mail address. There is also a "real" name or "display" name in addition to the username, as well as a domain. There is also an authorization username and password. The authorization username does not need to be the same as the username but in many cases it is.

FreeSWITCH comes preconfigured with 20 SIP user accounts. (In *Chapter 4, SIP and the User Directory,* we will discuss these in more detail, including how to configure additional users.) The user names are 1000, 1001 through 1019. You can use any of these users for testing.

The following are the SIP settings for user 1000:

- User Name: 1000
- Authorization Username: 1000
- Password: 1234
- Domain: [IP address of your FreeSWITCH server]

Keep these settings handy for setting up your SIP device. Let's look at the configuration process for several different SIP phones. Even if your device is not specifically mentioned here, you can still use the basic principles of configuring the SIP device and you should be able to get your phone connected without much hassle. In each of the following examples, we will connect a different telephone to a FreeSWITCH server running on a local LAN with an IP address of 10.15.0.210.

X-Lite softphone

X-Lite (`http://www.counterpath.com`) is a free soft phone. (X-Lite is, however, not open source.) Download and install X-Lite on a computer that is on the same LAN as your FreeSWITCH server. Note: While it is technically possible to run a soft phone on the same machine as your FreeSWITCH server, this is neither recommended nor supported. Launch the X-Lite application. You will see a "phone" like the following:

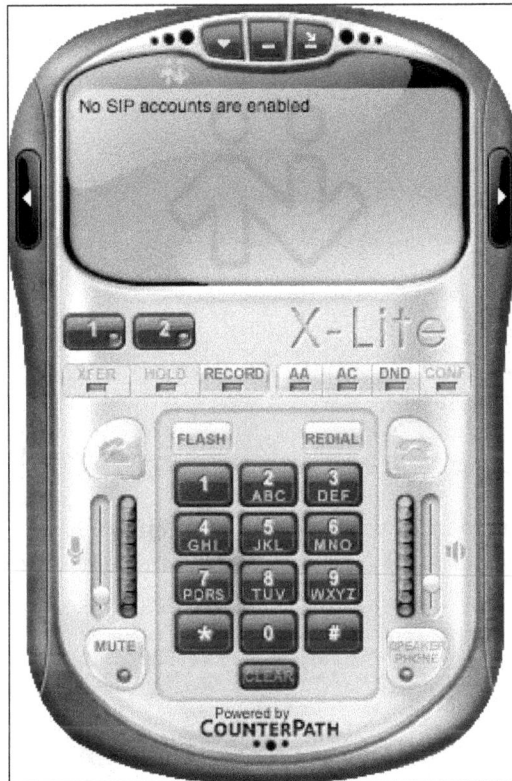

Click the small down arrow icon near the top of the phone, and then click **SIP Account Settings...** to open the SIP account menu. X-Lite supports just a single SIP account. Click **Add** to open up the Account properties screen. Fill in the form fields. Setting up extension 1005 would look like the following screenshot:

Click **OK** to close the properties window and then click **Close**. The phone will now attempt to register to FreeSWITCH. A successful registration will look like the following:

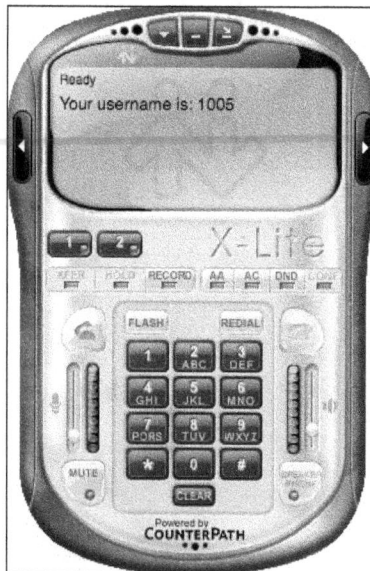

This phone is now registered. If you receive a different message in the display, then there was most likely a configuration error. Two common errors are 403 and 408:

- 403 — Forbidden: This means that the authorization username or password is incorrect.
- 408 — Timeout: Usually this means that the domain is not correct, or there is a network problem. Linux users can check IPTables and Windows users can check their firewalls to make sure that port 5060 is getting through.

Now that your phone is registered you can begin making test calls. Skip to the *Testing the default Dialplan* section.

Hard phones

We will take a brief look at setting up a few different kinds of hard phones. After reviewing the sample set up for Aastra, Polycom, and Snom phones you will know the basic principles, and should be able to set up any SIP-compliant telephone.

Before you start, be sure that you have at least the following basic information for your phone:

- IP Address — You will need to know the IP address of the phone if you wish to use the web interface. Most phones also have a small menu system for configuring the phone itself.
- Admin Name — Most phones will have an admin user.
- Admin Password — Most phones also require an admin password.

If you are unsure of the telephone's default username and password, consult the manufacturer's website for more information.

Hard phone tip: firmware

Most hard phones are field upgradable, that is, the manufacturer supplies updated firmware that can be downloaded and installed on each phone. Visit the manufacturer's website to find out what is the latest firmware for your phone, and what features it includes.

Aastra phones

Aastra phones have a standard web-based interface. Point a browser to the phone's IP address and then log in. Click the **Global SIP** link on the navigation pane. The interface for the Aastra 9112i will look as follows:

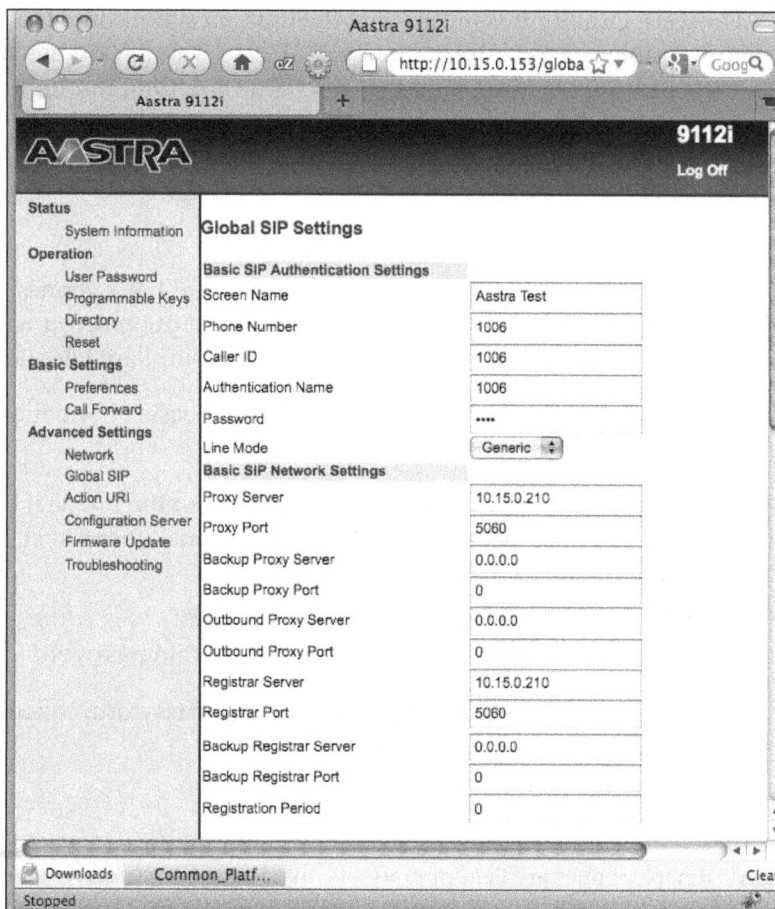

Fill in all the fields under **Basic SIP Authentication Settings**. Under **Basic SIP Network Settings** fill in the **Proxy Server**, **Proxy Port**, **Registrar Server**, and **Registrar Port** fields. Scroll down and click on **Save Settings**, then restart the phone by clicking the **Reset** link on the navigation pane. The phone will restart and connect to FreeSWITCH.

If the registration is successful then the display name ("Aastra Test"), and the phone number ("**1006**") will show in the telephone display. Now that your phone is registered, you can begin making test calls. Skip to the *Testing the default Dialplan* section.

Polycom phones

Polycom phones have a web interface as well as a menu on the phone. You can use either; however, it is easier to use the web interface. Point a browser at the phone's IP address and log in. Click the **Lines** link. Like many SIP phones, the SoundPoint IP 330 can register to more than one server. In this example, we'll use **Line 1** to connect to FreeSWITCH. The web interface for a Polycom SoundPoint IP 330 looks like the following:

For **Line 1**, fill in the following fields: **Display Name**, **Address**, **Auth User ID**, **Auth Password**, and **Label**. Under **Server 1**, fill in the **Address** and **Port** fields. Scroll down and click the **Submit** button. The phone will reboot and then connect to FreeSWITCH.

Now that your phone is registered you can begin making test calls. Skip to the *Testing the default Dialplan* section.

Snom phones

Snom phones have a full-featured web interface for configuration. Point a browser at your phone's IP address to open up the web interface. Notice that Snom phones have the concept of **identities**, which allow you to connect to more than one server. Click the **Identity 1** link on the navigation pane and fill in the SIP configuration fields. The web interface for a Snom 300 looks like the following screenshot:

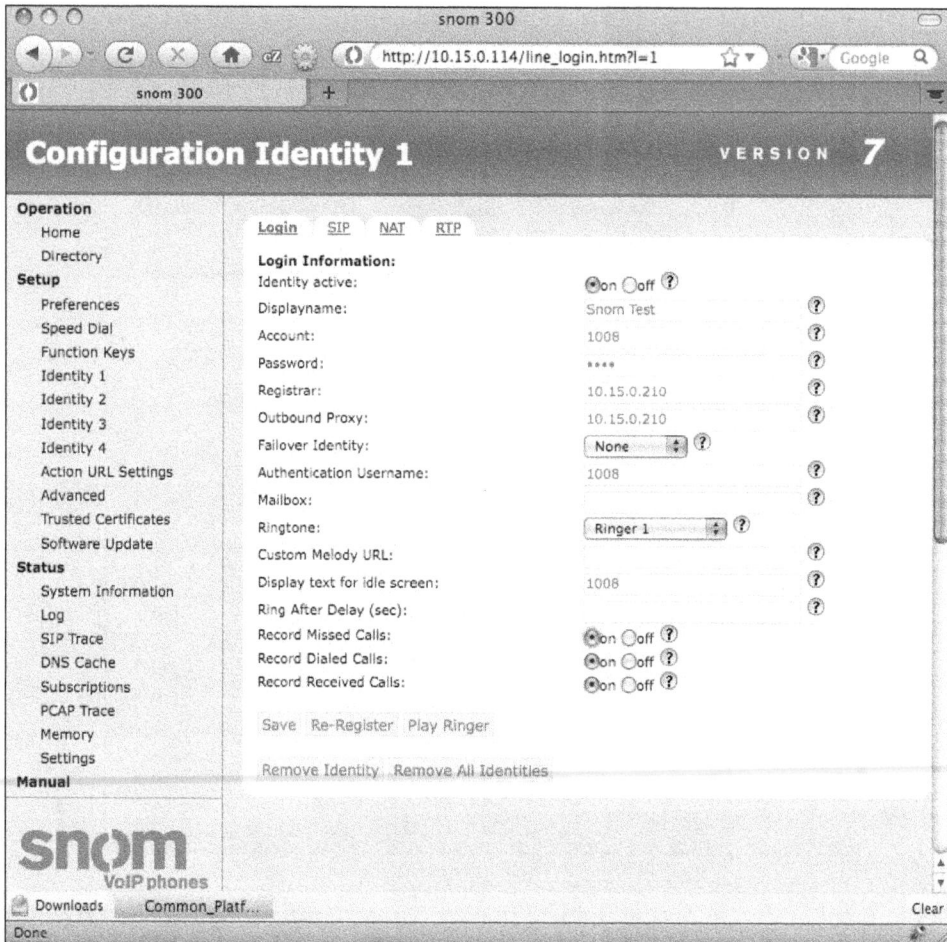

Configure **Identity 1** by filling in the fields under **Login Information: Display Name, Account, Password, Registrar, Outbound Proxy, Authentication Username**, and **Display test for idle screen**. Click **Save** then click **Re-Register**. The phone will immediately connect to FreeSWITCH.

Now that your phone is registered you can begin making test calls. Skip to the *Testing the default Dialplan* section.

PortAudio: The alternative telephone

FreeSWITCH supports the use of the local sound card or an external headset that is connected to the FreeSWITCH server. The optional PortAudio module (mod_portaudio) can be compiled and enabled in the same manner as the mod_flite example discussed in *Chapter 2, Building and Installation*. See http://wiki.freeswitch.org/wiki/ Mod_portaudio for details on how to configure and use the PortAudio module with FreeSWITCH.

Testing the default Dialplan

Now that you have a phone configured you can perform several kinds of test calls. If you can get two different phones configured, then you can make a few additional types of test calls. Before you begin dialing, be sure that you have installed the default sounds and music files. (Windows users will have them installed by default. Linux/Unix users please refer to *Step 5:5: Install sound and music files* section in Chapter 2 for more information.)

Test calls for a single phone

The following tests are simple ways to confirm that FreeSWITCH is operating properly, as well as learning more about what it can do. In each case, you simply need to dial the four-digit number and click your phone's **Send** button.

The "Tetris" extension

Dial *9198*. You will hear what hopefully sounds like the Tetris theme song. The sound is generated solely using tone generation. (See http://wiki.freeswitch. org/wiki/TGML for more information on TGML, the tone generation markup language used in FreeSWITCH.)

Echo test

Dial *9196*. Speak into the phone and the audio will be echoed back to you. This test confirms that audio is flowing in both directions.

Music on hold

Dial *9664*. The system will play the default music on hold. If you hear the music, then your *music on hold* files are properly installed, and FreeSWITCH is correctly playing those sound files.

Demonstration IVR

Dial *5000*. The demonstration IVR menu will play. You will be given the options that are described below:

- 1: Call FreeSWITCH public conference
- 2: Echo Test
- 3: Music on Hold
- 4: Register for ClueCon
- 5: Listen to screaming monkeys (yes, really)
- 6: Sample IVR sub-menu

The FreeSWITCH public conference is quite literally a public conference room, which anyone may call into. Note that your FreeSWITCH system will need to have Internet access, and that your firewall and NAT must be configured to allow SIP and RTP traffic.

The *echo* test and *music on hold* test are identical to dialing 9196 and 9664, respectively.

ClueCon is an annual developer conference. Dialing 4 will transfer you to an operator who will be glad to get you registered for the conference.

The *screaming monkeys* option is an example of an enum lookup. (See `http://en.wikipedia.org/wiki/E.164` for more information.)

The sample sub-menu is very simple: press * to return to the main menu.

The demonstration IVR menu is found in `conf/autoload_configs/ivr.conf.xml`.

The "Information" application

Dial *9192*. This extension is very simple. Before dialing, be sure to open up the `fs_cli` utility. The `info` application will dump a lot of debug data about the current phone call, and then hang up immediately. Change the debug level to 6 (INFO) before you dial. Following is a sample of the output:

```
freeswitch@internal> /log 6
+OK log level 6 [6]
freeswitch@internal> 2009-11-03 17:55:25.145056 [NOTICE] switch_
channel.c:613 New Channel sofia/internal/1007@10.15.0.210 [1e708e72-
c8e5-11de-83a4-41a0a2e37086]
2009-11-03 17:55:25.150076 [INFO] mod_dialplan_xml.c:397 Processing
Polycom Test->9192 in context default
2009-11-03 17:55:25.161531 [NOTICE] mod_dptools.c:653 Channel [sofia/
internal/1007@10.15.0.210] has been answered
```

```
2009-11-03 17:55:25.164043 [INFO] mod_dptools.c:911 CHANNEL_DATA:
Channel-State: [CS_EXECUTE]
Channel-State-Number: [4]
Channel-Name: [sofia/internal/1007@10.15.0.210]
Unique-ID: [1e708e72-c8e5-11de-83a4-41a0a2e37086]
Call-Direction: [inbound]
Presence-Call-Direction: [inbound]
Answer-State: [answered]
Channel-Read-Codec-Name: [PCMU]
Channel-Read-Codec-Rate: [8000]
Channel-Write-Codec-Name: [PCMU]
Channel-Write-Codec-Rate: [8000]
Caller-Username: [1007]
Caller-Dialplan: [XML]
Caller-Caller-ID-Name: [Polycom Test]
Caller-Caller-ID-Number: [1007]
Caller-Network-Addr: [10.15.0.110]
Caller-Destination-Number: [9192]
Caller-Unique-ID: [1e708e72-c8e5-11de-83a4-41a0a2e37086]
Caller-Source: [mod_sofia]
Caller-Context: [default]
Caller-Channel-Name: [sofia/internal/1007@10.15.0.210]
Caller-Profile-Index: [1]
Caller-Profile-Created-Time: [1257299725145056]
Caller-Channel-Created-Time: [1257299725145056]
Caller-Channel-Answered-Time: [1257299725161531]
Caller-Channel-Progress-Time: [0]
Caller-Channel-Progress-Media-Time: [0]
Caller-Channel-Hangup-Time: [0]
Caller-Channel-Transfer-Time: [0]
Caller-Screen-Bit: [true]
Caller-Privacy-Hide-Name: [false]
Caller-Privacy-Hide-Number: [false]
variable_sip_received_ip: [10.15.0.110]
variable_sip_received_port: [5060]
variable_sip_via_protocol: [udp]
variable_sip_authorized: [true]
variable_sip_number_alias: [1007]
variable_sip_auth_username: [1007]
variable_sip_auth_realm: [10.15.0.210]
variable_number_alias: [1007]
```

```
variable_user_name: [1007]
variable_domain_name: [10.15.0.210]
variable_toll_allow: [domestic,international,local]
variable_accountcode: [1007]
variable_user_context: [default]
variable_effective_caller_id_name: [Extension 1007]
variable_effective_caller_id_number: [1007]
variable_outbound_caller_id_name: [FreeSWITCH]
variable_outbound_caller_id_number: [0000000000]
variable_callgroup: [techsupport]
variable_record_stereo: [true]
variable_default_gateway: [example.com]
variable_default_areacode: [918]
variable_transfer_fallback_extension: [operator]
variable_sip_from_user: [1007]
variable_sip_from_uri: [1007@10.15.0.210]
variable_sip_from_host: [10.15.0.210]
...
variable_local_media_ip: [10.15.0.210]
variable_local_media_port: [18102]
variable_sip_nat_detected: [true]
variable_endpoint_disposition: [ANSWER]
variable_current_application: [info]

2009-11-03 17:55:25.423972 [NOTICE] mod_dptools.c:637 Hangup sofia/
internal/1007@10.15.0.210 [CS_EXECUTE] [NORMAL_CLEARING]
2009-11-03 17:55:25.423972 [NOTICE] switch_core_session.c:1159 Session
7 (sofia/internal/1007@10.15.0.210) Ended
2009-11-03 17:55:25.423972 [NOTICE] switch_core_session.c:1161 Close
Channel sofia/internal/1007@10.15.0.210 [CS_DESTROY]
```

Don't worry about what all of that means right now. Just remember that FreeSWITCH stores a lot of information for each call leg that is active. The `info` Dialplan application is useful for debugging your custom Dialplan entries.

Test calls for two or more phones

The true power of FreeSWITCH is seen in how it can handle calls from multiple endpoints. The following tests will give you an idea of some of the features that FreeSWITCH supplies. The tests in this section require at least two different telephones to be configured.

Calling another telephone

Dial *1000*, *1001*, and so on. Simply dial the other phone's extension number and it should ring. Most SIP phones are like regular telephones, so just pick up the handset to answer.

Parking a call

Call another telephone and wait for an answer. Click the **Transfer** button and dial *6001*. Hang up. The other party is now parked and will hear music on hold. Retrieve the call in one of the following ways:

Dial *6001*. The parked call is automatically unparked and bridged to you.

Dial *6000*, wait for the system to answer. The system will prompt you for the extension number.

Dial *6001*. The parked call is automatically unparked and bridged to you.

Calling a conference

Dial *3000*. Default Dialplan Quick Reference.

Consult the following table for a list of extension numbers and their functions:

Extension:	Function:
1000 – 1019	Local Extensions
** + Extension Number	Intercept a ringing phone (that is, "call pickup")
2000	Sample call group: Sales
2001	Sample call group: Support
2002	Sample call group: Billing
3000-3399	Sample conference rooms
4000 or *98	Retrieve voicemail
5000	Demo IVR
5900	FIFO queue park
5901	FIFO queue retrieve
6000	Valet park retrieval, manual
6001-6099	Valet park/retrieval, automatic
9178	Example fax receive
9179	Example fax transmit
9180	Ring test, far end generates ring tone
9181	Ring test, send U.K. ring tone

Extension:	Function:
9182	Ring test, send music as ring tone
9183	Answer, then send U.K. ring tone
9184	Answer, then send music as ring tone
9191	ClueCon registration
9192	Information dump
9195	Delayed echo test
9196	Echo test
9197	Milliwatt tone (test signal quality)
9198	Tetris
9664	Music on hold

The bulk of the default Dialplan is defined in `conf/dialplan/default.xml`.

Summary

In this chapter, we were introduced to the default configuration of FreeSWITCH. Among the topics we discussed, were the following:

- The important concepts behind how and why FreeSWITCH behaves when you make calls
- Basic use of `fs_cli`, the FreeSWITCH command-line interface utility.
- How to configure SIP devices to connect to FreeSWITCH using the predefined user accounts
- Testing the default Dialplan by dialling a number of different extensions

We now turn our attention to another important aspect of FreeSWITCH: the user directory.

In the next chapter, we will take a closer look at the FreeSWITCH user directory.

4
SIP and the User Directory

In the previous chapter, we briefly introduced SIP, the Session Initiation Protocol, where we discussed how to register a telephone with FreeSWITCH. In this chapter, we will build upon that foundation and learn more about how we use SIP to connect users, both locally and around the world. SIP is a ubiquitous protocol in the VoIP landscape. In this chapter, we will:

- Learn the principle behind the FreeSWITCH user Directory
- Explore and configure the FreeSWITCH user Directory for the first time
- Learn how to connect FreeSWITCH to service providers
- Make modifications to the Dialplan and directory XML configuration
- Briefly discuss SIP profiles and User Agents

Understanding the FreeSWITCH user directory

The FreeSWITCH user directory is based on a centralized XML document, comprised of one or more `<domain>` elements. Each `<domain>` can contain either `<user>` elements or `<groups>` elements. A `<groups>` element contains one or more `<group>` elements, each of which contains one or more `<user>` elements. A small, simple example would look like the following:

```
<section name="directory">
  <domain name="example.com">
    <groups>
      <group name="default">
        <user id="1001">
          <params>
            <param name="password" value="1234"/>
```

```
            </params>
          </user>
        </group>
      </groups>
    </domain>
  </section>
```

Some more basic configurations may not have a need to organize the users in groups so it is possible to omit the `<groups>` element completely, and just insert several `<user>` elements into the top `<domain>` element.

The important thing is that each `user@domain` derived from this directory is available to all components in the system — it's a single centralized directory for storing all of your user information. If you register as a user with a SIP phone or if you try to leave a *voicemail* message for a user, FreeSWITCH looks in the same place for user data. This is important because it limits duplication of data, and makes it more efficient than it would be if each component kept track of its users separately.

This system should work well for a small system with a few users in it, but what about a large system with thousands of users? What if a user wants to connect his existing database to FreeSWITCH to provide the user directory? Well, using `mod_xml_curl` that we discussed in the first chapter, we can create a web service that gets the request for the entries in the user directory, in the same way a web page sends the results of a form submission. In turn, that web service can query an existing database of users formatted any way possible, and construct the XML records in the format that FreeSWITCH registry expects. `mod_xml_curl` returns the data to the module requesting the lookup. This means that instant, seamless integration with your existing setup is possible; your data is still kept in its original, central location.

The user directory can be accessed by any subsystem within FreeSWITCH. This includes modules, scripts, and the FSAPI interface among others. In this chapter, we are going to learn how the Sofia SIP module employs the user directory to authenticate your softphone or hardware SIP phone. If you are a developer you may appreciate some nifty things you can do with your user directory, such as adding a `<variables>` element to either the `<domain>`, the `<group>`, or the `<user>` element. In this element you can set many `<variable>` elements, allowing you to set channel variables that will apply to every call made by a particular authenticated user. This can come in very handy in the Dialplan because it allows you to make user-specific routing decisions. It is also possible to define IP address ranges using CIDR notation, which can be used to authenticate particular users based on what remote network address they connect from. This removes the need for a login and password, if your user always logs in from the same remote IP address.

Authentication versus authorization

Authentication is the process of identifying a user. **Authorization** is the process of determining the level of access of a user. Authentication answers the question, "Is this person really who he says he is?" Authorization answers the question, "What is this person allowed to do here?" When you see expressions such as "IP Auth" and "Digest Auth", remember that they are referring to the two primary ways of identifying (that is, authenticating) a user. IP authorization is based upon the user's IP address. Digest authentication is based upon the user supplying a username and password. SIP (and FreeSWITCH) can use either method. Visit `http://en.wikipedia.org/wiki/Digest_access_authentication` for a discussion of how digest authentication works.

The directory is implemented in pure XML. This is advantageous for several reasons, not the least of which is the "X" in XML: Extensible. Since XML is, by definition, extensible, the directory structure is also extensible. If we need to add a new element into the directory, we can do so simply by adding to the existing XML structure.

Working with the FreeSWITCH user directory

The default configuration has one domain with a directory of 20 users. Users can be added or removed very easily. There is no set limit to how many users can be defined on the system. The list of users is collectively referred to as the **directory**. Users can belong to one or more **groups**. Finally, all the users belong to a single *domain*. By default, the **domain** is the IP address of the FreeSWITCH server.

In the following sections we will discuss these topics:

- User features
- Adding a user
- Testing voicemail
- Groups of users

User features

Let's begin by looking at the XML file that defines a user. Locate the file
conf/directory/default/1000.xml and open it in an editor. You should
see a file like the following:

```
<include>
  <user id="1000">
    <params>
      <param name="password" value="$${default_password}"/>
      <param name="vm-password" value="1000"/>
    </params>
    <variables>
      <variable name="toll_allow"
      value="domestic,international,local"/>
      <variable name="accountcode" value="1000"/>
      <variable name="user_context" value="default"/>
      <variable name="effective_caller_id_name" value="Extension
      1000"/>
      <variable name="effective_caller_id_number" value="1000"/>
      <variable name="outbound_caller_id_name"
      value="$${outbound_caller_name}"/>
      <variable name="outbound_caller_id_number"
      value="$${outbound_caller_id}"/>
      <variable name="callgroup" value="techsupport"/>
    </variables>
  </user>
</include>
```

The XML structure of a user is simple. Within the <include> tags the user has
the following:

- The user element with the id attribute

- The params element, wherein parameters are specified

- The variables element, wherein channel variables are defined

Even before we know what much of the specifics mean, we can glean from this file
that the user id is 1000 and that there is both a password and a vm-password. In
this case, the password parameter refers to the SIP authorization password. (We
discussed this under the *Configuring a SIP phone to work with FreeSWITCH* section in
Chapter 3.) The expression $${default_password} refers to the value contained in
the global variable default_password which is defined in the conf/vars.xml file.
If you surmised that vm-password means "voicemail password" then you are correct.
This value refers to the digits that the user needs to dial when logging in to check
his or her voicemail messages. The value of id is used both as the authorization
username and the SIP username.

Additionally, there are a number of channel variables that are defined for this user. Most of these are directly related to the default Dialplan. The following table lists each variable and what it is used for:

Variable	Purpose
toll_allow	Specifies which types of calls this user can make
accountcode	Arbitrary value that shows up in CDR data
user_context	The Dialplan context that is used when this person makes a phone call
effective_caller_id_name	Caller ID name displayed on called party's phone when calling another registered user
effective_caller_id_number	Caller ID number displayed on called party's phone when calling another registered user
outbound_caller_id_name	Caller ID name sent to provider on outbound calls
outbound_caller_id_number	Caller ID number sent to provider on outbound calls
callgroup	Arbitrary value that can be used in Dialplan or CDR

In summary, a user in the default configuration has the following:

- A username for SIP and for authorization
- A voicemail password
- A means of allowing/restricting dialling
- A means of handling caller ID being sent out
- Several arbitrary variables that can be used or ignored as needed

Let's now add a new user to our directory.

Adding a user

Adding one or more users is a simple two-step process, which is as follows:

- Create a new XML file for the user, usually by copying an existing file
- Modify the Local_Extension Dialplan entry

In this example, we will create a new user for a person named "Gwen" and a username of "1100". Follow these steps:

- Open a terminal window, change directory to conf/directory/default
- Make a copy of 1000.xml and name it 1100.xml. A Linux/Unix session looks like the following:

```
#>cd /usr/local/freeswitch/conf/directory/default
#>cp 1000.xml 1100.xml
```

- Open `1100.xml` in an editor and make the following changes:
    ○ Replace all occurrences of "1000" with "1100"
    ○ Change the value of `effective_caller_id_name` to "Gwen"

The new file should look like the following:

```
<include>
  <user id="1100">
    <params>
      <param name="password" value="$${default_password}"/>
      <param name="vm-password" value="1100"/>
    </params>
    <variables>
      <variable name="toll_allow"
      value="domestic,international,local"/>
      <variable name="accountcode" value="1100"/>
      <variable name="user_context" value="default"/>
      <variable name="effective_caller_id_name" value="Gwen"/>
      <variable name="effective_caller_id_number" value="1100"/>
      <variable name="outbound_caller_id_name"
      value="$${outbound_caller_name}"/>
      <variable name="outbound_caller_id_number"
      value="$${outbound_caller_id}"/>
      <variable name="callgroup" value="techsupport"/>
    </variables>
  </user>
</include>
```

Save the file. Next, we need to edit the Dialplan entry for `Local_Extension`. Open `conf/dialplan/default.xml` in an editor and locate the following lines:

```
<extension name="Local_Extension">
  <condition field="destination_number" expression="^(10[01][0-9])$">
```

This Dialplan extension, as its name implies, routes calls to local extensions. In our case, a local extension is a phone registered to a user in our directory. Recall that FreeSWITCH comes with 20 directory users predefined, numbered 1000 through 1019. This extension corresponds to those 20 users. By default, any call made to 1000, 1001, ... 1019 will be handled by the `Local_Extension` Dialplan entry. We need to add "1100" to the regular expression. Edit the `expression` value so that it looks like the following:

```
^(10[01][0-9]|1100)$
```

Save the file. (Regular expressions are discussed in greater detail in *Chapter 5, Understanding the XML Dialplan.*)

The last thing we need to do is reload the XML configuration. Launch `fs_cli` and issue the `reloadxml` command as follows:

```
freeswitch@internal> reloadxml
+OK [Success]

freeswitch@internal> 2009-11-20 16:47:36.986620 [INFO] mod_enum.c:808
ENUM Reloaded
2009-11-20 16:47:36.986620 [INFO] switch_time.c:661 Timezone reloaded 530
definitions
```

> Linux/Unix users can save time by opening two terminal windows.
> Run `fs_cli` in one window and your editor in the other. For advanced
> handling of multiple windows check out the GNU Screen utility. For
> more information check: `http://www.gnu.org/software/screen`.

Our new extension has been defined, and we should now be able to register a SIP phone to user 1100. Using the methods described in *Chapter 3, Test Driving the Default Configuration*, register a SIP phone to user 1100. An X-Lite configuration looks like this:

The registered phone can now make outbound calls, and can receive inbound calls from those who dial 1100.

[💡 To see which SIP phones are registered issue this command at the FreeSWITCH command line: `sofia status profile internal`.]

Now that we have successfully added a user, let's test a common feature: voicemail.

Testing voicemail

Each user in the directory has a voice "mailbox" where others can leave voice messages. By default, unanswered calls to a user will go to the user's voicemail after 30 seconds. Make a test call to confirm that everything is working. Dial the destination extension and let it ring. After about 30 seconds the voicemail system will answer; record a message of at least three seconds (the minimum message length), and then hang up. (If you have only one phone for testing, then try dialing your own extension.) The user's phone will now have a message-waiting indicator. An X-Lite softphone with a message waiting looks like the following image:

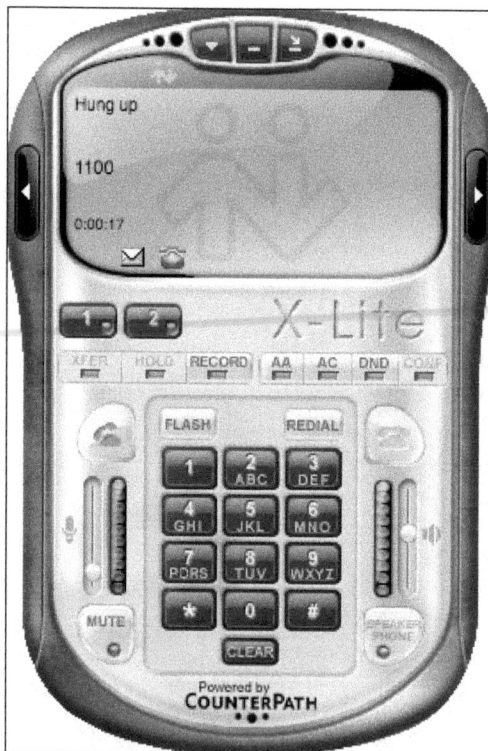

Notice the envelope icon and the red telephone icon. These indicate a new message waiting and a missed call, respectively.

> Save time when leaving a voice message by pressing #, to skip past the user's outbound greeting.

Retrieving the message is also simple: Dial *98 or *4000*. The voicemail system will guide you through logging in and listening to new or saved messages. A typical session would look like the following:

4000

"Welcome to your voicemail. Please enter your ID, followed by the pound sign."

1100#

"Please enter your password, followed by the pound sign."

1100#

"You have one new message."

When a user has a new message, the system will automatically play it along with the date and time that the message was left. The default voicemail menus are configured as follows:

Main Menu

> 1 — Listen to new messages
>
> 2 — Listen to saved messages
>
> 5 — Options menu (recorded name, greeting, and so on)
>
> # — Exit voicemail

While Listening to a Message

> 1 — Replay message from the beginning
>
> 2 — Save message
>
> 4 — Rewind
>
> 6 — Fast-forward
>
> 0 — Pause playback

After Listening to a Message

> 1 – Replay message from the beginning
>
> 2 – Save message
>
> 4 – Send to e-mail (requires configuration)
>
> 7 – Delete message
>
> 8 – Undelete message

Feel free to try out some of these options. Log in to your voicemail and record an outbound greeting. By default you can record up to ten different greetings; however, most users only record a single greeting. Typically we will use greeting number one.

> All of the voicemail options are customizable. Look in the file `conf/autoload_configs/voicemail.conf.xml`. You can edit the default voicemail profile or even create your own custom voicemail profiles.

Now that we have voicemail working, we can concentrate on one other useful feature: groups of users.

Groups of users

Larger installations frequently need the ability to dial multiple telephones. For example, a department in a company might have several users, all of whom are responsible for answering calls to that department. At the same time, they each have their own extension number, so they may individually receive calls. FreeSWITCH has a directory feature that allows users to be grouped together. A user can belong to multiple groups.

> Some PBX systems employ an advanced form of inbound call routing called **ACD** or **Automatic Call Distribution**. Call groups are not used for this kind of application. Although it is beyond the scope of this publication, FreeSWITCH users wanting advanced functionality are encouraged to investigate FIFO queues. See `http://wiki.freeswitch.org/wiki/Mod_fifo` for more information.

Groups are defined in the file `conf/directory/default.xml`. Open the file and locate the `groups` node. Notice that there are four groups already defined. They are as follows:

* Default – All users in the directory
* Sales – 1000 to 1004
* Billing – 1005 to 1009
* Support – 1010 to 1014

The latter three groups are merely arbitrarily defined groups that can be modified or removed as needed. The `default` group, though, is a bit more interesting. It contains every user in the directory. (Use with caution!) Let's add a new group and then examine how groups work:

1. Add the following lines inside the groups node:

```
<group name="custom">
  <users>
    <user id="1000" type="pointer"/>
    <user id="1100" type="pointer"/>
  </users>
</group>
```

2. If you have two or more telephones registered then use their extension numbers instead of 1000 and 1100. Save the file.

3. Launch `fs_cli` and issue the `reloadxml` command.

Confirm that the new custom group has been added by using the `group_call` command. Your output should be similar to the following:

```
freeswitch@internal> group_call custom
[presence_id=1000@10.15.0.91] error/user_not_registered, [presence_
id=1100@10.15.0.91] sofia/internal/sip:1100@10.15.0.136:31354;rinstance=5e
39ede358ffc0c8
```

What significance does this chunk of apparently random gibberish hold? The `group_call` command is used to create a *dialstring* for calling multiple telephones. In our example, user 1000 is not registered and therefore would not receive a call. (Hence the "error" of `user_not_registered`.) However, user 1100 is indeed registered. If a user in a group is not registered, then when the group is called, that user is effectively ignored. Before we can call our new group we need to add it to the Dialplan, as follows:

1. Open `conf/dialplan/default.xml` and locate the `group_dial_billing` extension shown as follows:

```
<extension name="group_dial_billing">
  <condition field="destination_number" expression="^2002$">
    <action application="bridge"
      data="group/billing@${domain_name}"/>
  </condition>
</extension>
```

2. Insert the following new lines after the `</extension>` tag of the `group_dial_billing` extension:

```
<extension name="group_dial_custom">
  <condition field="destination_number" expression="^2003$">
    <action application="bridge"
      data="group/custom@${domain_name}"/>
  </condition>
</extension>
```

3. Save the file.

4. Launch `fs_cli` and issue the `reloadxml` command.

5. Test your group by dialing *2003*. All the extensions in your group should ring.

When all of the phones in a group are ringing, the first one to answer will "win" and receive the call. All the other phones will stop ringing.

We have seen how we can connect telephones to FreeSWITCH, as well as the many features they have. Now let's discuss how to make phone calls outside the local FreeSWITCH server.

Connecting to the world with gateways

The counterpart to having a user register to your FreeSWITCH server is to have your server register as a user on a remote server. This is accomplished using **gateways**. A gateway is quite simply an outbound registration to another SIP server. Telephone service providers use very large servers to provide SIP *trunks* to their subscribers. In FreeSWITCH, we can use a gateway to connect to a SIP provider. We can also use a gateway to connect to another SIP server, such as another FreeSWITCH server or any SIP-compliant IP-PBX.

Setting up a new gateway

A gateway simply connects to a SIP server just like a SIP phone connects to FreeSWITCH. As such, a gateway configuration bears some resemblance to a SIP phone configuration. Like a SIP phone registering to FreeSWITCH, a gateway has some minimum requirements. They are as follows:

- Username and password
- Server address or IP, and port

These values are supplied by the service provider. Occasionally there are other parameters, like a proxy server and port. If you already have an account with a SIP provider then you can use it for your gateway. In this example, we will use an account from `iptel.org`.

> Visit `http://www.iptel.org` to sign up for a free SIP account.

To add a new gateway, follow these steps:

1. Create a new XML file in `conf/sip_profiles/external`. This example will use `iptel.org.xml`. Add the following lines, inserting the proper values for your provider:

    ```
    <include>
      <gateway name="iptel">
      <param name="username" value="MY_USER_NAME"/>
      <param name="password" value="MY_PASSWORD"/>
      <param name="realm" value="iptel.org"/>
      <!-- iptel.org requires a 'proxy' parameter -->
      <param name="proxy" value="sip.iptel.org"/>
      </gateway>-->
    </include>
    ```

2. Save the file and then launch `fs_cli`.

3. Issue the command `/log 6` to decrease the verbosity of debug messages.

4. Simply reloading the XML configuration will not add the new gateway. Issue the following command: `sofia profile external restart reloadxml`. The output will look as follows:

    ```
    freeswitch@internal> sofia profile external restart reloadxml

    Reload XML [Success]

    restarting: external

    freeswitch@internal> 2009-11-21 16:29:23.509986 [INFO] mod_enum.
    c:808 ENUM Reloaded

    2009-11-21 16:29:23.511578 [INFO] switch_time.c:661 Timezone
    reloaded 530 definitions

    2009-11-21 16:29:24.118566 [NOTICE] sofia_reg.c:85 UN-Registering
    iptel

    2009-11-21 16:29:24.713768 [NOTICE] sofia.c:1218 Waiting for
    worker thread
    ```

```
2009-11-21 16:29:24.713768 [NOTICE] sofia_glue.c:3690 deleted
gateway example.com
2009-11-21 16:29:24.713768 [NOTICE] sofia_glue.c:3690 deleted
gateway iptel
2009-11-21 16:29:24.713768 [NOTICE] sofia_reg.c:2237 Added gateway
'iptel' to profile 'external'
2009-11-21 16:29:24.713768 [NOTICE] sofia_reg.c:2237 Added gateway
'example.com' to profile 'external'
2009-11-21 16:29:24.713768 [NOTICE] sofia.c:3149 Started Profile
external [sofia_reg_external]
2009-11-21 16:29:25.736445 [NOTICE] sofia_reg.c:333 Registering
iptel
```

5. Confirm that the gateway is registered properly. Issue the command `sofia status`. The output should look similar to the following:

```
freeswitch@internal> sofia status
                    Name       Type             Data                      State
=================================================================================
        external   profile    sip:mod_sofia@10.15.0.91:5080    RUNNING   (0)
     example.com   gateway          sip:joeuser@example.com    NOREG
           iptel   gateway       sip:MY_USER@sip.iptel.org     REGED
        internal   profile    sip:mod_sofia@10.15.0.91:5060    RUNNING   (0)
   internal-ipv6   profile      sip:mod_sofia@[::1]:5060       RUNNING   (0)
     10.15.0.91    alias                       internal        ALIASED
=================================================================================
3 profiles 1 alias
```

The gateway's state should be REGED. If it says something else, like FAIL_WAIT, then most likely there is a configuration problem. Confirm your settings and try again.

> Restarting a profile will disconnect all active calls that are currently routed through that profile. An alternate command to add a newly created gateway without restarting the entire profile is:
> `sofia profile external rescan reloadxml`

Now that our gateway is added, we need to modify the Dialplan so that we can make and receive calls.

Making calls

We will make a simple Dialplan entry that sends calls out our new gateway. Our new extension will accept the digit 9 and then the digit 1, followed by exactly ten more digits representing the telephone number to be dialed. (In a production environment there are many other possible strings, which can even be alphanumeric. Some of these will be considered in *Chapter 5, Understanding the XML Dialplan*.)

To get started with making outbound calls, add your new extension to the Dialplan, following these steps:

1. Create a new file in `conf/dialplan/default` named `01_custom.xml`.

2. Add the following text to the file:

```
<include>
  <extension name="Dial Out Custom Gateway">
    <condition field="destination_number"
      expression="^9(1\d{10})$">
      <action application="bridge"
        data="sofia/gateway/custom/$1"/>
    </condition>
  </extension>
</include>
```

3. Save the file. Launch `fs_cli` and issue the `reloadxml` command.

The new extension is now ready to be tested. From a phone that is registered to FreeSWITCH, dial 9 plus a ten-digit phone number. For example, dial *9, 1-800-555-1212*. It may take a moment for the call to be established. Confirm that audio is flowing in both directions and that each party can hear the other. If audio is flowing in only one direction, then most likely there is a problem with the NAT device on your local network.

Receiving calls

Generally, when you register your gateway with a SIP provider, the provider allows you to receive calls. (Telephones that register with FreeSWITCH are an example of this.) By default, FreeSWITCH treats incoming calls as inherently untrusted, even if they come from the opposite end of a registered gateway. These calls come into the "public" Dialplan context. From there they can be discarded or routed as needed. Let's set up a simple Dialplan entry to handling inbound calls to our `iptel.org` account.

1. Create a new file in `conf/dialplan/public` named `01_iptel.xml`.

2. Add these lines to the file, using your account name as follows:

```
<include>
  <extension name="iptel-inbound">
    <condition field="destination_number"
    expression="^(MY_IPTEL_USERNAME)$">
      <action application="set" data="domain_name==$${domain}"/>
      <action application="bridge" data="1000 XML default"/>
    </condition>
  </extension>
</include>
```

3. Save the file. Launch `fs_cli` and execute the `reloadxml` command.

Inbound calls will now be routed to extension 1000. You can route calls to any valid extension, including all the extensions we tested in *Chapter 3, Test Driving the Default Configuration*.

Making calls without a gateway

Sometimes it is not necessary to use a gateway. For example, not all services require digest authorization. An example of this is the FreeSWITCH public conference server. In fact, the default Dialplan contains an extension for dialling the conference: *9888*. (Actually, there are several different conference "rooms" on the public FreeSWITCH conference server.) Let's look at this extension. Open `conf/dialplan/default.xml` in an editor and locate the `freeswitch_public_conf_via_sip` extension. Note the `bridge` line:

```
<action application="bridge" data="sofia/${use_profile}/$1@conference.
freeswitch.org"/>
```

The value in `${use_profile}` defaults to "internal" (as defined in `conf/vars.xml`). When a user dials *9888* the dialstring that is sent out is actually as follows:

```
sofia/internal/888@conference.freeswitch.org
```

Notice that there is no mention of a gateway. Instead, FreeSWITCH simply sends the call out to the `internal` SIP profile. In other words, the local FreeSWITCH server sends a call to `conference.freeswitch.org` without actually authorizing it. This is possible because the server at `conference.freeswitch.org` does not require authorization for incoming calls. (This is where the gateway comes in—if the target server issues a challenge then the gateway will respond to that challenge with authorization credentials, namely the username and password.)

Not all SIP providers explicitly require digest authorization of calls; some perform IP authorization instead. In those cases you do not need to create a gateway. Instead, simply send the call out a SIP profile. Usually the internal SIP profile is sufficient for these kinds of calls.

SIP profiles and user agents

Before we finish our discussion of SIP and the user directory, it would be good to touch upon a subject that some users initially find a bit daunting: SIP profiles. In the strictest sense of the word, a SIP profile in FreeSWITCH is a *User Agent*. In practical terms, this means that each SIP profile "listens" on a particular IP address and port number. The `internal` profile listens on port 5060, and the `external` profile listens on port 5080. Not only does the profile listen but it can respond as well. For example, when a phone sends a SIP REGISTER packet to FreeSWITCH (at port 5060), the `internal` profile "hears" the registration request and acts accordingly. The files in `conf/sip_profiles/` are ones which determine how the profiles behave. Many of the parameters in these profiles are to customize how FreeSWITCH handles various SIP traffic scenarios. In most cases the defaults are reasonable and should work. In other cases, though, you may find that because of the peculiarities in various VoIP phones and vendors, you will need to make adjustments.

Lastly, do not let the profile names `internal` and `external` be a source of confusion. Each profile is simply a user agent that is streamlined for a specific purpose. The `internal` profile is optimized to handle telephone registrations and calls between registered phones. The `external` profile is optimized for outbound gateway connections and several NAT traversal scenarios.

For a deeper discussion of user agents and the concept of a back-to-back user agent (B2BUA) see `http://en.wikipedia.org/wiki/Back-to-back_user_agent`.

Summary

In this chapter, we discussed the following:

- How FreeSWITCH collects users into a directory
- How FreeSWITCH uses a VoIP protocol, SIP, to connect users to each other, and to the world
- SIP is similar to e-mail in that it has users and domains
- Employing various user features like voicemail
- Adding a new user and modifying the Dialplan accordingly
- Connecting to the outside world with gateways
- SIP profiles and user agents

In this chapter, we made some minor modifications to the default XML Dialplan, and we learned how to set up users and domains within the XML user directory. Now that we have a general understanding of how these modifications work, we will continue to build upon this foundation. We will now begin to form a much more detailed understanding of FreeSWITCH as we further explore the XML Dialplan module, the default and most commonly used call routing engine available in FreeSWITCH.

5
Understanding the XML Dialplan

The Dialplan is a crucial part of any FreeSWITCH installation. Indeed, any PBX must have a Dialplan, sometimes called a numbering plan, in order to handle the routing of calls. In simple terms, a Dialplan is a list of instructions on where to route a call. For example, when a user picks up a phone and dials 1000, how does the system know what to do with that call? The default Dialplan knows to connect the calling party to the telephone registered as with user id 1000. However, the Dialplan can do much more than merely connect the calling and called parties. In many cases, the Dialplan will contain instructions on what the call should do and how it should behave.

In the previous chapter, we made small modifications to the Dialplan. In this chapter, we will build upon that foundation and introduce the basics of routing and controlling calls as we discuss the following topics:

- Overview of the XML Dialplan
- Contexts, extensions, and actions
- Conditions, patterns, and regular expressions
- Channel variables
- Creating and testing a new extension
- Important Dialplan applications
- Writing dialstrings

FreeSWITCH XML Dialplan elements

The default FreeSWITCH XML Dialplan is contained in three main files and two directories, located in `conf/dialplan/`:

- `default.xml` — The primary FreeSWITCH Dialplan configuration
- `public.xml` — Handles calls coming in to FreeSWITCH from another location
- `features.xml` — A special context for handling specific dialing features
- `default/` — Files in this directory get included in the default context
- `public/` — Files in this directory get included in the public context

The default XML configuration has many instructions for routing calls, all of which make use of the basic building blocks of a Dialplan: contexts, extensions, conditions, and actions. A context is a logical grouping of one or more extensions. An extension contains one or more conditions that must be met. Conditions contain actions that will be performed on the call, depending on the whether the condition is met or not. Before discussing these building blocks further, though, let's revisit some of the concepts we first considered in *Chapter 3, Test Driving the Default Configuration*.

Call legs and channel variables

Phone calls to and from FreeSWITCH consist of one or more call legs.
A "one-legged" connection might be something like a user dialing into his or her voicemail. A traditional call between two parties is a connection with two call legs. Recall the following illustration from *Chapter 3, Test Driving the Default Configuration*:

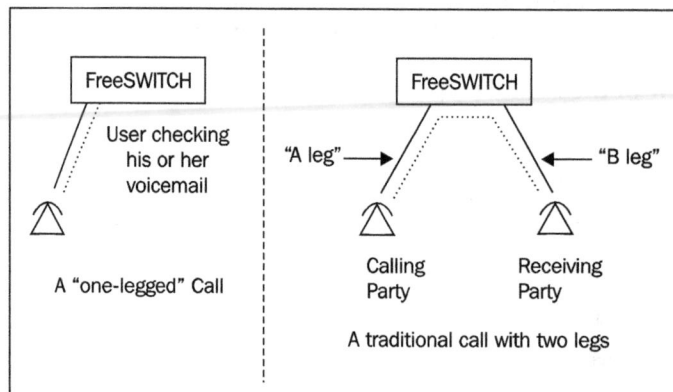

A call between two different telephones consists of an **A-leg** (calling or originating party) and a **B-leg** (receiving party). Each call leg is also known as a **channel**, as in an audio channel. Each channel has a set of logical attributes, what you might call a list of facts about that particular call leg. Each of these attributes is stored in a corresponding channel variable. In the previous chapter, we learned that a registered user has several channel variables defined, and these variables are included in call legs involving that user. To get an idea of just how much information is available for a call, you can call the `information` extension at *9192* following the steps below:

1. Launch `fs_cli` and issue the command `/log 6`

2. From a registered phone dial *9192*

You will see dozens of lines of information. Following is an excerpt from an `info` dump:

```
2009-12-09 13:50:40.685247 [INFO] mod_dptools.c:916 CHANNEL_DATA:
Channel-State: [CS_EXECUTE]
Channel-State-Number: [4]
Channel-Name: [sofia/internal/1001@10.15.0.94]
Unique-ID: [dd9fbb65-971e-4b65-9f2e-586bde83a6bf]
Call-Direction: [inbound]
Presence-Call-Direction: [inbound]
Channel-Presence-ID: [1001@10.15.0.94]
Answer-State: [answered]
Channel-Read-Codec-Name: [PCMU]
Channel-Read-Codec-Rate: [8000]
Channel-Write-Codec-Name: [PCMU]
Channel-Write-Codec-Rate: [8000]
Caller-Username: [1001]
Caller-Dialplan: [XML]
Caller-Caller-ID-Name: [Michael Collins]
Caller-Caller-ID-Number: [1001]
Caller-Network-Addr: [10.15.0.124]
Caller-ANI: [1001]
Caller-Destination-Number: [9192]
...
variable_sip_received_ip: [10.15.0.124]
variable_sip_received_port: [29935]
variable_sip_via_protocol: [udp]
variable_sip_authorized: [true]
variable_sip_number_alias: [1001]
```

```
variable_sip_auth_username: [1001]
variable_sip_auth_realm: [10.15.0.94]
variable_number_alias: [1001]
variable_toll_allow: [domestic,international,local]
variable_accountcode: [1001]
variable_user_context: [default]
variable_effective_caller_id_name: [Michael Collins]
variable_effective_caller_id_number: [Michael Collins]
...
```

The lines beginning with "variable_" show the values in the respective channel variables. For example, the line `variable_sip_authorized: [true]` is showing that the value of `sip_authorized` channel variable is "true". You will also notice that there are numerous other data elements such as `Unique-ID` and `Call-Direction`. These are **info application variables**. Most (but not all) of these are available as read-only values, which can be accessed just like channel variables.

Accessing channel variables

Within the Dialplan, variables are accessed with a special notation: `${variable_name}`. Consider the following example:

```
<action application="log" data="INFO The value in sip_authorized is
  '${sip_authorized}' "/>
```

This action would print out a log message to the FreeSWITCH command such as the following:

```
2009-12-09 14:32:48.904383 [INFO] mod_dptools.c:897 The value in sip_
authorized is 'true'
```

Accessing the read-only values is much the same. Each of these values has a corresponding channel variable name. For example:

```
<action application="log" data="INFO The value of Unique-ID is
  '${uuid}' "/>
```

This will print a log line on the FreeSWITCH command line such as the following:

```
2009-12-09 14:46:31.695458 [INFO] mod_dptools.c:897 The value of Unique-
ID is '169ae42e-29f5-4e1c-9505-8ee6ef643081'
```

> A complete list of `info` application variables and their corresponding channel variable names can be found at the following address: http://wiki.freeswitch.org/wiki/Channel_Variables#variable_xxxx.

Channel variables are discussed further in *Chapter 8, Advanced Dialplan Concepts*.

Regular expressions

The FreeSWITCH XML Dialplan makes extensive use of Perl-compatible regular expressions (PCRE). A regular expression is a means of executing a true/false test on a string of characters. This is commonly called **pattern matching**. When a regular expression is applied to a string of characters we answer a simple question: does it match the pattern? If the answer is yes, then usually it means that a particular condition is met, and therefore, the extension in question can be executed. In some cases, we want to do something if a pattern is not met. (See the *Actions and anti-actions* section of this chapter.)

Perl-compatible regular expressions follow a very specific syntax. It can be overwhelming at first. However, once you learn the basics you will appreciate just how powerful they are. Following are some sample regular expressions and their meanings:

Pattern:	Meaning:
123	Match any string containing the sequence "123"
^123	Match any string beginning with the sequence "123"
123$	Match any string ending with the sequence "123"
^123$	Match any string that is exactly the sequence "123"
\d	Match any single digit (0-9)
\d\d	Match two consecutive digits
^\d\d\d$	Match any string that is exactly three digits long
^\d{7}$	Match any string that is exactly seven digits long
^(\d{7})$	Match any string that is exactly seven digits long, and store the matched value in a special variable named $1
^1?(\d{10})$	Matching any string that optionally begins with the digit "1" and contains an additional ten digits; store the matched value in $1
^(3\d\d\d)$	Match any four-digit string that begins with the digit "3", and store the matched value in $1

You can no doubt see that regular expressions can be used to match virtually any conceivable pattern of dialed digits. They also can match letters and punctuation marks. Look through `conf/dialplan/default.xml` and you will see many different expressions used.

If you would like to know if a particular string matches a specific pattern, then use the `regex` command at the FreeSWITCH command line. (The term "regex" is short for "regular expression" and is generally pronounced REJ-ex.) The `regex` command needs at least two arguments: the data to test and the pattern to match against. The arguments are separated by a | (pipe) character. The `regex` command will return "true" if the data and the pattern match, otherwise it will return "false". Following are some examples that you can try at the `fs_cli`:

```
freeswitch@internal> regex 1234|\d
true
freeswitch@internal> regex 1234|\d\d\d\d
true
freeswitch@internal> regex 1234|\d{4}
true
freeswitch@internal> regex 1234|\d{5}
false
freeswitch@internal> regex 1234|^1234$
true
freeswitch@internal> regex 1234|234
true
freeswitch@internal> regex 1234|^234
false
```

Use the `regex` command to quickly test data strings and patterns.

> Regular expressions are useful in numerous other computer-related endeavors. You may find it handy to know more than just the basic pattern matching syntax. The FreeSWITCH wiki contains links to many online resources for learning more: http://wiki.freeswitch.org/wiki/Regular_Expression.

Contexts

Contexts are logical groups of extensions. Think of contexts as sections of the Dialplan. Each section has a specific purpose and contains only extensions that are related to that purpose. One such purpose is to isolate extensions from one another. A typical example of this is **multi-tenancy**. A FreeSWITCH server can service more than one business entity (tenant), and providing each tenant with its own context prevents numbering conflicts. Each tenant could, for example, have a "dial zero for the operator" extension. Users in one tenant can dial 0 to reach their front desk extension, while users in another tenant can also dial 0 to reach a completely different extension. Another consideration for contexts is security. Phone calls that are being routed through a context have access only to the resources specifically allotted, perhaps long-distance or international dialing, or the use of other resources like multi-party audio conference rooms.

There is no limit to the number of extensions that may be defined. The default XML Dialplan defines three different contexts. They are as follows:

Default

The `default` context contains all of the extension definitions that are available to registered users of the system. When we added extension 1100 to `conf/dialplan/default.xml`, we were actually modifying an extension in the default context. Most of the features of the default XML Dialplan are defined in this file.

Public

The `public` context is a good example of using contexts for the sake of security. All unauthorized calls coming in to the FreeSWITCH server will be handled by the public context. The name "public" means "inherently untrusted". By default, FreeSWITCH is paranoid about what unauthorized callers can do in the system. Generally speaking, the public context is used to route incoming DID (Direct Inward Dial) phone numbers to a specific internal extension. (See `conf/dialplan/public/00_inbound_did.xml` for an example.) You can use the `public` context to let in only the calls that you deem appropriate for your system.

Features

The `features` context is a good example of grouping together extensions by function. These extensions could just as easily be added to the `default` context; however, putting them in their own context helps keep things organized. The extensions defined in the features context mostly are not endpoints in themselves but rather "helper" extensions, which perform a function and then transfer the caller elsewhere. An example of this is the `please_hold` extension which sets the music on hold for the caller, tells the caller, "Please hold while I connect your call", and then transfers the caller to the destination extension.

Extensions

The term "extension" can sometimes be misleading. In the traditional PBX environment an extension is simply a phone connected to the phone system, typically with a three-digit or four-digit extension number. In FreeSWITCH an extension is actually a set of instructions on what to do with a call. It can be as simple as dialing a three-digit or four-digit number, and having someone's desk phone ring. In fact, this is precisely what we did in *Chapter 4, The User Directory*, when we added a new user and a corresponding "extension" to allow her phone to be dialed.

An extension definition begins with an `<extension>` tag and ends with a closing `</extension>` tag. All of the conditions, actions, and anti-actions in between are part of the extension definition. Extensions have two optional attributes: `name` and `continue`. The `name` attribute is used primarily to keep your Dialplan readable. You can imagine how difficult it would be to look at a Dialplan file with dozens of `<extension>` tags without any names. The `continue` attribute determines the Dialplan parser's behavior when it finds a matching extension. An extension is said to "match" if all of the conditions for that extension evaluate to true. By default extensions do not continue after the first Dialplan match. Setting `continue=true` will cause the parser to keep looking for more extensions to match. (See the *How Dialplan Processing Works* section in this chapter.)

Conditions

Conditions are the logical pieces of the Dialplan that determine which extensions get executed when a particular phone number is dialed. Keep in mind that conditions are not limited just to which phone number was dialed. Conditions can also be based on date and time, caller ID, the IP address of the sending server, and even channel variables. Looking through the default Dialplan you will mostly see conditions like the following:

```
<condition field="destination_number" expression="^(1234)$">
```

The `destination_number` is by far the most common field tested, as most of the time we need to route a call based upon the digits dialed by a user.

Many extensions have just a single condition:

```
<extension name="Simple example">
  <condition field="destination_number" expression="^(1234)$">
    <!-- actions performed here -->
  </condition>
</extension>
```

However, you can also "stack" conditions to create a logical AND such as the following:

```
<extension name="Two condition tags example">
  <condition field="ani" expression="^(1111)$"></condition>
  <condition field="destination_number" expression="^(1234)$">
    <!-- actions performed here but only if both of the above
      conditions are true -->
  </condition>
</extension>
```

In the preceding example, both conditions must be true for the actions inside the second `<condition>` tag. The `ani` field (which is the calling party's phone number) must be "1111", and the `dialed_number` must be "1234" for the actions to be executed. The plain-language description of this extension would be, "If the caller is '1111' and the destination is '1234' then execute these actions". Putting multiple `<condition>` tags inside of a single extension is sometimes called "stacking the conditions". Note that the first condition is still a valid XML node and requires a closing tag. XML allows a syntactic shortcut for this which is as follows:

```
<condition field="ani" expression="^(1111)$"/>
```

The trailing / (forward slash) character closes the `<condition>` tag.

An additional feature of `<condition>` tags is the `break` attribute. When stacking multiple conditions, the `break` attribute can control how the parser behaves after each condition is evaluated. The `break` attribute can have the following four values:

1. *on-true* — Stop searching further conditions in this extension if the current condition is true
2. *on-false* — Stop searching further conditions in this extension if the current condition is false (this is the default)
3. *never* — Keep searching further conditions regardless of whether the current condition true or false
4. *always* — Stop searching further conditions regardless of whether the current condition is true or false (very rarely used)

The default behavior is to break out of searching for more conditions as soon as the first failed match occurs. Let's try the same extension with a `break` attribute:

```
<extension name="Two condition tags example">
  <condition field="ani" expression="^(1111)$" break="never">
    <!-- actions performed here if caller is 1111 -->
  </condition>
  <condition field="destination_number" expression="^(1234)$">
    <!-- actions performed here if caller dialed 1234 even if caller
      was not 1111 -->
  </condition>
</extension>
```

We added `break="never"` to the first condition. The parser will now behave differently when it gets to this condition. If the condition fails, then the parser moves on to the next condition within the same extension. Without the `break="never"` attribute the parser would have stopped all further parsing of this extension, and moved on in the Dialplan. But what happens if this condition is true? The actions inside the first condition will be added to the task list, and then the parser moves on to the next condition in this extension. The net result is that we get a set of actions performed if the caller dialed 1234, but we have other actions that get performed if the caller happens to be 1111.

A note of caution is warranted here. Some users attempt to "nest" conditions in their Dialplans, that is, they try to put a `<condition>` inside another `<condition>` tag:

```
<extension name="WRONG! Do not nest conditions">
  <condition field="ani" expression="^(1111)$">
    <condition field="destination_number" expression="^(1234)$">

    </condition>
  </condition>
</extension>
```

The inner condition will never be executed. Instead, the console will display an error which is as follows:

```
2009-12-10 13:04:49.330959 [ERR] mod_dialplan_xml.c:122 Nested conditions
are not allowed!
```

There is never a reason to nest conditions in the XML Dialplan.

More advanced conditions are considered in *Chapter 8, Advanced Dialplan Concepts*.

Actions and anti-actions

Actions represent what actually happens to the call when it is traversing the Dialplan. Actions and anti-actions both tell FreeSWITCH to act upon a call. The difference between the two is simple: actions are executed if the condition is met and anti-actions are executed if the condition is *not* met. Consider the following example:

```
<extension name="Action vs. anti-action example">
  <condition field="destination_number" expression="^(9101)$">
    <action application="log" data="INFO You dialed 9101"/>
    <anti-action application="log" data="INFO You did NOT dial
      9101"/>
  </condition>
</extension>
```

In the preceding example, the extension will log some information to the FreeSWITCH command line depending upon what the user dialed. If the user dials *9101*, the action is executed and the log displays, "You dialed 9101". If the user dials anything other than 9101, then the anti-action is executed and the log displays, "You did NOT dial 9101".

Most extensions you create (and indeed, in the default Dialplan) will have many actions but few anti-actions. In most cases, actions execute Dialplan *applications* which in turn may accept *arguments*. In the preceding example, the `log` application is executed and the `data` attribute contains the argument passed to it.

How Dialplan processing works

Understanding the Dialplan is easier if you can visualize what happens when a call comes in. Often, we hear expressions like "the call traverses the Dialplan" or "the call hits the Dialplan". What exactly does that mean? Let's walk through the processing of a call, so that we can really understand what XML Dialplan is doing.

The Dialplan has two phases: parsing and executing. The Dialplan parser looks for extensions to execute. When it finds a matching extension, it then adds the actions (or anti-actions) to a list of tasks. When the parser finishes looking for extensions, the execution phase begins, and the actions in the task list are performed.

A good way to see all of this in action is to watch the FreeSWITCH console in debug mode while making a test phone call. Launch `fs_cli`, make a test call to 9196 (music on hold), and then hang up the phone. Scroll back in your terminal and look for a line that looks something like the following:

```
2009-12-09 22:23:16.727746 [INFO] mod_dialplan_xml.c:408 Processing Test
User->9196 in context default
```

This is the start of the Dialplan processing. A telephone whose user is named "Test User" has dialed 9196. (Your console will display the name of the user associated with the phone from which you dialed.) The lines following begin with "Dialplan:" and are debug messages, showing which extensions matched and which ones did not. The first extension parsed is called "unloop". It is an important extension, but is not very interesting for our Dialplan discussion. Look down to the next extension that gets parsed. In our example, *call the debug* output is as follows:

```
Dialplan: sofia/internal/1001@10.15.0.91 parsing [default->tod_example]
continue=true
Dialplan: day of week[4] =~ 2-6 (PASS)
Dialplan: hour[22] =~ 9-18 (FAIL)
Dialplan: sofia/internal/1001@10.15.0.91 Date/Time Match (FAIL) [tod_
example] break=on-false
```

The extension `tod_example` (time of day example) is shown being parsed. These debug lines correspond to the `tod_example` extension found in `conf/dialplan/default.xml`:

```
<extension name="tod_example" continue="true">
  <condition wday="2-6" hour="9-18">
    <action application="set" data="open=true"/>
  </condition>
</extension>
```

This extension simply checks the time of the day and the day of the week. If the call is made on a weekday (Monday through Friday) during business hours, (9 AM to 6 PM) then it sets the channel variable `open` to "true". This call was made on a Wednesday at 10:23 PM. Therefore, it passed the `wday` (day of week) test but not the `hour` (hour of day) test. Had the call been made between 9 AM and 6 PM then both conditions would have been met, and the set application would have been added to the task list. Notice that the `tod_example` extension has `continue="true"`. This means that the Dialplan will continue parsing extensions even if `tod_example` matches.

The parser continues trying to match extensions, most of which fail:

```
Dialplan: sofia/internal/1001@10.15.0.91 parsing [default->global-
intercept] continue=false
Dialplan: sofia/internal/1001@10.15.0.91 Regex (FAIL) [global-intercept]
destination_number(9196) =~ /^886$/ break=on-false
Dialplan: sofia/internal/1001@10.15.0.91 parsing [default->group-
intercept] continue=false
Dialplan: sofia/internal/1001@10.15.0.91 Regex (FAIL) [group-intercept]
destination_number(9196) =~ /^\*8$/ break=on-false
Dialplan: sofia/internal/1001@10.15.0.91 parsing [default->intercept-ext]
continue=false
Dialplan: sofia/internal/1001@10.15.0.91 Regex (FAIL) [intercept-ext]
destination_number(9196) =~ /^\*\*(\d+)$/ break=on-false
Dialplan: sofia/internal/1001@10.15.0.91 parsing [default->redial]
continue=false
Dialplan: sofia/internal/1001@10.15.0.91 Regex (FAIL) [redial]
destination_number(9196) =~ /^870$/ break=on-false
Dialplan: sofia/internal/1001@10.15.0.91 parsing [default->global]
continue=true
Dialplan: sofia/internal/1001@10.15.0.91 Regex (FAIL) [global] ${call_
debug}(false) =~ /^true$/ break=never
Dialplan: sofia/internal/1001@10.15.0.91 Regex (FAIL) [global] ${sip_
has_crypto}() =~ /^(AES_CM_128_HMAC_SHA1_32|AES_CM_128_HMAC_SHA1_80)$/
break=never
```

The preceding debug lines are all failed matches, which is completely normal. Next, we see some interesting output as follows:

```
Dialplan: sofia/internal/1001@10.15.0.91 parsing [default->global]
continue=true

Dialplan: sofia/internal/1001@10.15.0.91 Regex (FAIL) [global] ${call_
debug}(false) =~ /^true$/ break=never

Dialplan: sofia/internal/1001@10.15.0.91 Regex (FAIL) [global] ${sip_
has_crypto}() =~ /^(AES_CM_128_HMAC_SHA1_32|AES_CM_128_HMAC_SHA1_80)$/
break=never

Dialplan: sofia/internal/1001@10.15.0.91 Absolute Condition [global]

Dialplan: sofia/internal/1001@10.15.0.91 Action hash(insert/${domain_
name}-spymap/${caller_id_number}/${uuid})

Dialplan: sofia/internal/1001@10.15.0.91 Action hash(insert/${domain_
name}-last_dial/${caller_id_number}/${destination_number})

Dialplan: sofia/internal/1001@10.15.0.91 Action hash(insert/${domain_
name}-last_dial/global/${uuid})
```

Notice the debug line that mentions "**Absolute Condition**". An absolute condition simply means that the condition is always evaluated as *true*, and the actions within are always executed. This `condition` tag is located in the `global` extension further down in `default.xml`. It is listed, as follows, with XML comments removed:

```xml
<extension name="global" continue="true">
  <condition field="${call_debug}" expression="^true$" break="never">
    <action application="info"/>
  </condition>
  <condition field="${sip_has_crypto}"
    expression="^(AES_CM_128_HMAC_SHA1_32|AES_CM_128_HMAC_SHA1_80)$"
    break="never">
    <action application="set" data="sip_secure_media=true"/>
  </condition>
  <condition>
    <action application="hash" data="insert/${domain_name}-
      spymap/${caller_id_number}/${uuid}"/>
    <action application="hash" data="insert/${domain_name}-
      last_dial/${caller_id_number}/${destination_number}"/>
    <action application="hash" data="insert/${domain_name}-
      last_dial/global/${uuid}"/>
  </condition>
</extension>
```

The third <condition> tag (highlighted) in the global extension has no field or expression and thus always evaluates to true, and therefore, the actions within are added to the task list. This does raise a good question: Normally the parser stops parsing the current extension as soon as a condition fails, so why did the parser not skip past the global extension after its first condition failed? The answer lies in the break attribute. Notice that we have break="never" specified in the first two <condition> tags in this extension. This tells the parser to keep parsing the current extension for further conditions regardless of whether this condition is true or false. (See the *Conditions* section earlier in this chapter.)

Most of the following conditions fail to match until the parser reaches the echo extension:

```
Dialplan: sofia/internal/1001@10.15.0.91 parsing [default->echo]
continue=false
Dialplan: sofia/internal/1001@10.15.0.91 Regex (PASS) [echo] destination_
number(9196) =~ /^9196$/ break=on-false
Dialplan: sofia/internal/1001@10.15.0.91 Action answer()
Dialplan: sofia/internal/1001@10.15.0.91 Action echo()
```

The parser adds the answer and echo Dialplan applications to the task list.

At this point, the parsing is done and now the execution phase begins. You will see some debug lines that begin with "EXECUTE" and show what exactly is being executed, as in the following:

```
EXECUTE sofia/internal/1001@10.15.0.91 hash(insert/10.15.0.91-spymap/
1001/19b7689d-5d05-409f-aaef-a7477742a0cd)
EXECUTE sofia/internal/1001@10.15.0.91 hash(insert/10.15.0.91-last_
dial/1001/9196)
EXECUTE sofia/internal/1001@10.15.0.91 hash(insert/10.15.0.91-last_dial/
global/19b7689d-5d05-409f-aaef-a7477742a0cd)
EXECUTE sofia/internal/1001@10.15.0.91 answer()
...
EXECUTE sofia/internal/1001@10.15.0.91 echo()
```

Preceding is a complete example of a call "hitting the Dialplan" and being processed. Though it takes us several minutes to discuss this process, it happens very quickly on the server. This "parse first, execute second" processing strategy makes the XML Dialplan relatively efficient. As an exercise, try watching the debug output while calling *9664* (music on hold) and dialing from one registered telephone to another.

Now that you have seen the Dialplan parser in action, let's create a new extension.

Creating a new extension

Let's create a brand new extension. Start by opening the following XML file we created in *Chapter 4, The User Directory*: `conf/dialplan/default/01_Custom.xml`. This file will contain the custom extensions that we create from now on.

> Always begin your custom Dialplan filenames with a digit sequence. The reason for this is that the XML parser reads the XML files in ASCII order. The last file in `conf/dialplan/default/` that we want parsed is `99999_enum.xml`. This file contains the ENUM extension which is used as a "last resort" if the dialed number does not match any other extensions. See `http://wiki.freeswitch.org/wiki/Mod_enum` for more information.

A Dialplan XML file can contain one or more extension definitions. The only restriction is that the file should begin and end with the XML tags `<include>` and `</include>` respectively.

Our new extension will be simple, but it will also demonstrate the power and flexibility of the FreeSWITCH Dialplan. The extension will have the following characteristics:

- Answer the call
- Read back the calling user's extension number in two different formats
- Sleep for two seconds
- Say goodbye to the caller
- Hang up
- The extension will be executed when the caller dials 9101

To create the new extension follow these steps:

1. Add the following content to your `01_Custom.xml` file:

   ```xml
   <include>
     <extension name="simple test">
       <condition field="destination_number" expression="^(9101)$">
         <action application="answer"/>
         <action application="say" data="en number iterated ${ani}"/>
         <action application="sleep" data="1000"/>
         <action application="say" data="en number pronounced
           ${ani}"/>
         <action application="sleep" data="1000"/>
         <action application="playback" data="voicemail/vm-
           goodbye.wav"/>
   ```

```
            <action application="sleep" data="2000"/>
            <action application="hangup"/>
        </condition>
      </extension>
    </include>
```

2. Save the file. Launch `fs_cli` and issue `reload_xml`, or press *F6*.

The new extension is now added. To test your new extension, simply dial *9101*. (You can also watch the FreeSWITCH command line to get a sense of what the system is doing as it processes your extension.) The system should answer, play a few sound prompts, and then hang up. Let's step through each line of the extension and discuss what it does:

```
<extension name="simple test">
```

This tag simply marks the beginning of the extension definition. The `name` attribute is actually optional. However, it helps with making the Dialplan more readable. The extension definition ends with the `</extension>` tag.

```
<condition field="destination_number" expression="^(9101)$">
```

The `condition` tag defines the matching parameters for this extension. Here we match the value in `destination_number` against the pattern `^(9101)$`. In plain language, this condition says, "If the user dialed the exact digits 9101, then execute the actions in this extension." All of the actions between this tag and the closing `</condition>` tag are executed.

```
<action application="answer"/>
```

The `answer` application does just what it says: it answers the call.

```
<action application="say" data="en number iterated ${ani}"/>
```

This executes the `say` application, which uses the pre-recorded sound prompts to voice numbers, letters, currency amounts, and so on. The first three arguments to say are the say engine (usually a language), pronunciation type, and pronunciation method. In this example, we are asking the `say` application to use the en engine (that is, use the English sound files) and to pronounce a number in iterated fashion. The number "1234" will be voiced as, "One-two-three-four". The say application is further described in the *Important Dialplan Applications* section of this chapter.

```
<action application="sleep" data="1000"/>
```

The preceding action simply sleeps, that is, pauses the execution for 1000 milliseconds (1 second).

```
<action application="say" data="en number pronounced ${ani}"/>
```

This executes the say application again, this time using the pronounced method. With the pronounced method, the say application will pronounce the number instead of merely listing the digits. The number "1234" will be voiced as, "One thousand, two hundred thirty-four".

```
<action application="sleep" data="1000"/>
```

This pauses the execution for another 1000 milliseconds.

```
<action application="playback" data="voicemail/vm-goodbye.wav"/>
```

The preceding action executes the playback application. The playback application plays an audio file to the caller. The filename is specified as the argument. In this case, we specify a file normally used with the FreeSWITCH voicemail application. The playback application is further described in the *Important Dialplan Applications* section of this chapter.

FreeSWITCH contains a number of pre-recorded audio files. The English filenames and contents are list in docs/phrase/en.xml under the FreeSWITCH source directory.

```
<action application="sleep" data="2000"/>
```

This pauses execution for 2000 milliseconds (2 seconds).

```
<action application="hangup"/>
```

The last action of our extension hangs up, disconnecting the caller.

That's it! You have now gone through the basic steps necessary to add custom extensions to your system. Most of the extensions that we create will go into the default context, because they are designed for the users of our system. In a few cases we may add extensions to another context, for example, to handle incoming DID calls. We may also define a custom context to handle a specific need, such as when using a single FreeSWITCH server to handle multiple departments or multiple companies.

Important Dialplan applications

FreeSWITCH has about one hundred different Dialplan applications. However, a few of them are particularly important because they are used so frequently.

bridge

The `bridge` application connects two endpoints together.

Argument syntax: `<target_endpoint>[,<target_endpoint>][|<target_endpoint>]`

Endpoints separated by commas are dialed simultaneously. Endpoints separated by pipes are dialed sequentially. The first endpoint to answer receives the call, and dialing to all other endpoints is discontinued.

Examples:

```
<action application="bridge" data="user/1000"/>
<action application="bridge"
  data="sofia/gateway/my_gateway_name/$1"/>
```

See "Dialstring Formats" later in this chapter.

playback

The `playback` application simply plays an audio file to the caller. Files can be in many formats. The sound and music files included in FreeSWITCH are all `.wav` files.

Argument syntax: absolute path to a sound file or relative path to an installed sound file.

Examples:

```
<action application="playback" data="/absolute/path/to/sound.wav"/>
<action application="say" data="voicemail/vm-goodbye.wav"/>
```

say

The `say` application uses the built-in "say engine" to voice to the caller some piece of information. (This is not text-to-speech. See the `speak` application.)

Argument syntax: `<module_name> <say_type> <say_method> <text>`

The `module_name` is usually the language.

The `say_type` can be any of the following:

- number
- items
- persons

- messages
- currency
- time_measurement
- current_date
- current_time
- current_date_time
- telephone_number
- telephone_extension
- url
- ip_address
- e-mail_address
- postal_address
- account_number
- name_spelled
- name_phonetic
- short_date_time

The say_method can be any of the following:

- n/a (a method is not applicable)
- pronounced ("one hundred, twenty-three")
- iterated ("one two three")
- counted (special case, similar to "pronounced")

Examples:

```
<action application="say" data="en number pronounced 1234"/>
<action application="say" data="en number iterated 1234"/>
<action application="say" data="en currency pronounced 1234"/>
<action application="say" data="en items pronounced 1234"/>
```

play_and_get_digits

The play_and_get_digits application will play a sound file to the caller, while at the same time listening for digits dialed by the caller. This allows you to create interactive Dialplans without necessarily creating an entire IVR.

Argument syntax: <min> <max> <tries> <timeout> <terminators> <file>
  <invalid_file> <var_name> <regex>

Arguments:

- min — Minimum number of digits to collect
- max — Maximum number of digits to collect
- tries — Number of attempts to play the file and collect digits
- timeout — Number of milliseconds to wait between each digit
- terminators — Digits used to end input if less than `<min>` digits have been pressed (Typically #)
- file — Sound file to play while digits are fetched
- invalid_file — Sound file to play when digits don't match the `<regex>` argument
- var_name — Channel variable that digits should be placed in
- regex — Regular expression to match digits

Example:

```
<action application="play_and_get_digits" data="2 5 3 8000 #
  /path/to/sound_file.wav /path/to/invalid_sound.wav my_digits \d+"/>
<action application="log" data="User entered these digits:
  ${my_digits}"/>
```

This example executes `play_and_get_digits` with the following parameters:

- looks for a minimum of two digits
- maximum of five digits
- tries three times
- each time before playing it waits 8 seconds (8000ms) for the digits
- uses the # key as the terminator
- plays the sound file `/path/to/sound_file.wav` while collecting digits
- plays the sound file `/path/to/invalid_sound.wav` if invalid digits are dialed
- stores the dialed digits in the channel variable `my_digits`
- matches against the pattern `\d+`

ivr

The `ivr` application sends the caller to a predefined IVR.

Argument syntax: name of IVR to execute.

```
<action application="ivr" data="ivr_demo"/>
```

(See also the `ivr_demo` extension in `conf/dialplan/default.xml`.)

sleep

The `sleep` application pauses Dialplan execution for the specified number of milliseconds.

Argument syntax: number of milliseconds to sleep.

Example:

```
<action application="sleep" data="1000"/>
```

answer

The `answer` application "picks up the phone" as it was by establishing an audio path to the calling party.

Example:

```
<action application="answer"/>
```

hangup

The `hangup` application disconnects the audio path and ends the call.

Argument syntax: Optional hang up cause.

Examples:

```
<action application="hangup"/>
<action application="hangup" data="BUSY"/>
```

set

The `set` application sets a channel variable or processes an API command from within the Dialplan. (This latter feature is demonstrated in *Chapter 8, Advanced Dialplan Concepts.*)

Argument syntax: <variable_name=value>

Example:

```
<action application="set" data="my_chan_var=example value"/>
<action application="log" data="INFO my_chan_var contains
  ${my_chan_var}"/>
```

Dialstring formats

Before we leave our discussion of the Dialplan, it would be good to consider one more topic: Dialstrings. A **Dialstring** is exactly what it sounds like- a string of characters that defines a destination to be dialed by FreeSWITCH. All Dialstrings have a specific syntax. The syntax varies depending upon the type of endpoint being dialed. The most important types of Dialstring in FreeSWITCH are those for Sofia, because they represent how we dial SIP endpoints. However, as we will see there are several different kinds of Dialstrings. They are used primarily in two places, which are as follows:

1. Bridging an existing call leg in the Dialplan with the `bridge` application
2. Creating a new call leg at the CLI with the `originate` command

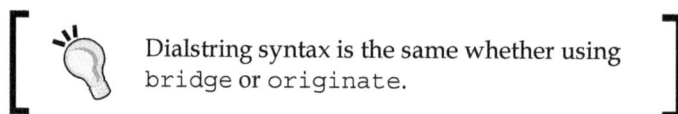

> Dialstring syntax is the same whether using `bridge` or `originate`.

Let's learn a bit more about Dialstrings by considering a few examples, starting with some sofia Dialstrings. The basic sofia Dialstring takes two different formats:

1. `sofia/<profile name>/<user@domain>`
2. `sofia/gateway/<gateway name>/<user>`

As we learned in *Chapter 4, The User Directory*, we can dial another SIP endpoint, either with or without a gateway. When using sofia to dial out through a profile, it is necessary to specify both the user and domain. However, when dialing out a gateway it is not necessary to include the domain because this is already defined in the gateway configuration. Therefore, the following is not allowed:

```
<!-- Wrong -->
<action application="bridge"
   data="sofia/gateway/my_gateway/user@1.2.3.4/">
```

The correct syntax is as follows:

```
<!-- Correct -->
<action application="bridge" data="sofia/gateway/my_gateway/user">
```

The equivalent for dialing out the `internal` profile would look like the following:

```
<!--Also correct -->
<action application="bridge" data="sofia/internal/ user@1.2.3.4/">
```

Knowing these two syntaxes will cover the vast majority of your SIP dialing needs. However, there are many edge cases. For a complete discuss on see `http://wiki.freeswitch.org/wiki/Dialplan_XML#SIP-Specific_Dialstrings`.

When dialing a user who is registered on your FreeSWITCH server there is a shortcut available:

```
user/<user id>[@domain]
```

This syntax makes it very easy to dial another phone registered on your system. In fact, the `Local_Extension` in `conf/dialplan/default.xml` uses this method to connect calls to registered users:

```
<action application="bridge"
  data="user/${dialed_extension}@${domain_name}"/>
```

The `@domain` is optional if you have only one domain defined on your FreeSWITCH server.

Following are a few more types of Dialstrings:

- `loopback/<destination number>`: Create a call leg and put it in the Dialplan at <destination_number>
- `openzap/<span>/<channel>/<phone number>`: Create a call leg on a telephony interface card (See `http://wiki.freeswitch.org/wiki/OpenZAP` for more information on using traditional telephone hardware with FreeSWITCH)
- `error/<error code>`: Simulate an error condition; useful for testing
- `group/<group name>[@domain]`: Call a group of users (see *Chapter 4, The User Directory*)

Feel free to try some of these. If you have a phone registered to your FreeSWITCH server, then use the `originate` command from `fs_cli`. The basic syntax of originate is:

```
originate <dialstring> <destination number>
```

Try the following and see what happens. Replace "1000" with the extension number of your phone:

```
originate loopback/9664 1000
originate user/1000 9664
originate error/USER_BUSY 1000
originate loopback/9192 1000
originate loopback/4000 1000
```

As you can see, FreeSWITCH has many tools for creating calls. There is virtually no scenario that it cannot handle or emulate.

Summary

Completing this chapter is an important milestone for the beginner. Understanding the concepts presented here is a large part of being able to configure and maintain a FreeSWITCH server. A number of topics were discussed. They are as follows:

- The basic hierarchy of the FreeSWITCH XML Dialplan:
    - The Dialplan consists of one or more contexts
    - Contexts consist of one or more extensions
    - Extensions contain one or more conditions
    - Conditions usually have one or more actions or anti-actions
- Regular expressions and pattern matching
- An introduction to the concept of channel variables
- How Dialplan parsing and processing works
- Creating our own custom extension
- A list of some of the more common and useful Dialplan applications

Having these basic skills, you should now be able to create truly useful extensions that do more than merely connect one telephone user to another. Although the Dialplan is very powerful and flexible, it is not in and of itself an IVR engine or a programming language. FreeSWITCH has modules that work with the Dialplan to add these more advanced features to your system.

In the next chapter, we will see how to use a programming language called Lua to create very flexible IVR applications.

6
Using the Built-in XML IVR Engine

The built-in IVR (Interactive Voice Response) engine is a powerful component of the FreeSWITCH system. It allows messages to be played and interactive responses (usually touch-tones) to be processed, in order to direct calls to particular destinations. It can ultimately allow callers to hear information without needing to speak to a live person, select options that enable/disable features, or enter data that can be used in account, billing, or other operations.

Most people are familiar with an IVR as an auto-attendant that answers a main number for your company and provides a list of options to reach people (that is, 'For sales press 1, for support press 2'). This avoids disruptions to unintended call recipients, and reduces or removes the need for a dedicated receptionist. More advanced IVRs can also be used for collecting information from a caller, such as a caller's account number or the PIN number for a conference bridge. In this chapter, we will explore utilizing the built-in IVR engine that FreeSWITCH provides natively. You will use the skills you learned in *Chapter 5, Understanding the XML Dialplan*, to route calls to an IVR application via the Dialplan, and we will build an IVR menu using the built-in XML configuration files native to FreeSWITCH.

The following topics will be discussed:

- IVR Engine Overview
- IVR XML Configuration File
- IVR Menu Definitions
- IVR Menu Destinations
- Routing Calls to Your IVR
- Nesting IVRs
- Using Phrases with IVRs
- Advanced Topics

IVR engine overview

Unlike many applications within FreeSWITCH which are built as modules, IVR is considered the core functionality of FreeSWITCH. It is used anytime a prompt is played and digits are collected. Even if you are not using the IVR application itself from your Dialplan, you will see IVR-related functions being utilized from various other applications. As an example, the `voicemail` application makes heavy use of IVR functionality when playing messages, while awaiting digits to control deleting, saving, and otherwise managing voicemails.

In this section, we will only be reviewing the IVR functionality that is exposed from within the `ivr` Dialplan application. This functionality is typically used to build an auto-attendant menu, although other functions are possible as well.

IVR XML configuration file

FreeSWITCH ships with a sample IVR menu, typically invoked by dialing 5000 from the sample Dialplan. When you dial 500, you will hear a greeting welcoming you to FreeSWITCH, and presenting your menu options. The menu options consist of calling the FreeSWITCH conference, calling the echo extension, hearing music on hold, going to a sub-menu, or listening to screaming monkeys. We will start off reviewing the XML that powers this example.

Open `conf/autoload_configs/ivr.xml` which contains the following XML:

```
<configuration name="ivr.conf" description="IVR menus">
  <menus>
    <!-- demo IVR, Main Menu -->
    <menu name="demo_ivr"
      greet-long="phrase:demo_ivr_main_menu"
      greet-short="phrase:demo_ivr_main_menu_short"
      invalid-sound="ivr/ivr-that_was_an_invalid_entry.wav"
      exit-sound="voicemail/vm-goodbye.wav"
      timeout="10000"
      inter-digit-timeout="2000"
      max-failures="3"
      max-timeouts="3"
      digit-len="4">
      <entry action="menu-exec-app" digits="1" param="bridge
        sofia/$${domain}/888@conference.freeswitch.org"/>
      <entry action="menu-exec-app" digits="2" param="transfer 9196
        XML default"/>
      <entry action="menu-exec-app" digits="3" param="transfer 9664
        XML default"/>
      <entry action="menu-exec-app" digits="4" param="transfer 9191
        XML default"/>
```

```
        <entry action="menu-exec-app" digits="5" param="transfer
          1234*256 enum"/>
        <entry action="menu-exec-app" digits="/^(10[01][0-9])$/"
          param="transfer $1 XML features"/>
        <entry action="menu-sub" digits="6" param="demo_ivr_submenu"/>
        <entry action="menu-top" digits="9"/>
      </menu>

      <!-- Demo IVR, Sub Menu -->
      <menu name="demo_ivr_submenu"
        greet-long="phrase:demo_ivr_sub_menu"
        greet-short="phrase:demo_ivr_sub_menu_short"
        invalid-sound="ivr/ivr-that_was_an_invalid_entry.wav"
        exit-sound="voicemail/vm-goodbye.wav"
        timeout="15000"
        max-failures="3"
        max-timeouts="3">
        <entry action="menu-top" digits="*"/>
      </menu>

    </menus>
  </configuration>
```

In the preceding example, there are two IVR menus defined. Let's break apart the first one and examine it, starting with the IVR menu definition itself.

IVR menu definitions

The following XML defines an IVR menu named `"demo_ivr"`.

```
<menu name="demo_ivr"
  greet-long="phrase:demo_ivr_main_menu"
  greet-short="phrase:demo_ivr_main_menu_short"
  invalid-sound="ivr/ivr-that_was_an_invalid_entry.wav"
  exit-sound="voicemail/vm-goodbye.wav"
  timeout="10000"
  inter-digit-timeout="2000"
  max-failures="3"
  max-timeouts="3"
  digit-len="4">
```

We'll use this menu's name later when we route calls to the IVR from the Dialplan. Following the name, various XML attributes specify how the IVR will behave. The following options are available when defining an IVR's options:

greet-long

The greet-long attribute specifies the initial greeting that is played when a caller reaches the IVR. This is different from the greet-short sound file which allows for introductions to be played, such as "Thank you for calling XYZ Company". In the sample IVR, the greet-long attribute is a Phrase Macro that plays an introductory message to the caller ("Welcome to FreeSWITCH...") followed by the menu options the caller may choose from.

Argument syntax: Sound filename (or path + name), TTS, or Phrase Macro.

Examples:

```
greet-long="my_greeting"
greet-long="phrase:my_greeting_phrase"
greet-long="say:Welcome to our company. Press 1 for sales, 2 for
    support."
```

greet-short

The greet-short attribute specifies the greeting that is re-played if the caller enters invalid information, or no information at all. This is typically the same sound file as greet-long without the introduction. In the sample IVR, the greet-short attribute is a Phrase Macro that simply plays the menu options to the caller, and does not play the lengthy introduction found in greet-long.

Argument syntax: Sound filename (or path + name), TTS, or Phrase Macro.

Examples:

```
greet-short="my_greeting_retry"
greet-long="phrase:my_greeting_retry_phrase"
greet-long="say:Press 1 for sales, 2 for support."
```

invalid-sound

The invalid-sound attribute specifies the sound that is played when a caller makes an invalid entry.

Argument syntax: Sound filename (or path + name), TTS, or Phrase Macro.

Examples:

```
invalid-sound="invalid_entry.wav"
invalid-sound="phrase:my_invalid_entry_phrase"
invalid-sound="say:That was not a valid entry"
```

exit-sound

The `exit-sound` attribute specifies the sound, which is played when a caller makes too many invalid entries or too many timeouts occur. This file is played before disconnecting the caller.

Argument syntax: Sound filename (or path + name), TTS, or Phrase Macro.

Examples:

```
exit-sound="too_many_bad_entries.wav"
exit-sound="phrase:my_too_many_bad_entries_phrase"
exit-sound="say:Hasta la vista, baby."
```

timeout

The `timeout` attribute specifies the maximum amount of time to wait for the user to begin entering digits after the greeting has played. If this time limit is exceeded, the menu is repeated until the value in the `max-timeouts` attribute has been reached.

Argument syntax: Any number, in milliseconds.

Examples:

```
timeout="10000"
timeout="20000"
```

inter-digit-timeout

The `inter-digit-timeout` attribute specifies the maximum amount of time to wait in-between each digit the caller presses. This is different from the overall timeout. It is useful to allow enough time to enter as many digits as necessary, without frustrating the caller by pausing too long after they are done making their entry. For example, if both 1000 and 1 are valid IVR entries, the system will continue waiting for the `inter-digit-timeout` length of time after 1 is entered, before determining that it is the final entry.

Argument syntax: Any number, in milliseconds.

Examples:

```
inter-digit-timeout="2000"
```

max-failures

The `max-failures` attribute specifies how many failures, due to invalid entries, to tolerate before disconnecting.

Argument syntax: Any number.

Examples:

```
xx-xx="too_many_bad_entries.wav"
xx-xx="phrase:my_too_many_bad_entries_phrase"
```

max-timeouts

The `max-timeouts` attribute specifies how many timeouts to tolerate before disconnecting.

Argument syntax: Any number.

Examples:

```
max-timeouts="3"
```

digit-len

The `digit-len` attribute specifies the maximum number of digits that the user can enter before determining the entry is complete.

Argument syntax: Any number greater than 1.

Examples:

```
digit-len="4"
```

tts-voice

The `tts-voice` attribute specifies the specific text-to-speech voice that should be used.

Argument syntax: Any valid text-to0speech voice.

Examples:

```
tts-voice="Mary"
```

tts-engine

The `tts-engine` attribute specifies the specific text-to-speech engine that should be used.

Argument syntax: Any valid text-to-speech engine.

Examples:

```
tts-engine="flite"
```

confirm-key

The `confirm-key` attribute specifies the key which the user can press to signify that they are done entering information.

Argument syntax: Any valid DTMF digit.

Examples:

```
confirm-key="#"
```

These attributes dictate the general behavior of the IVR.

IVR menu destinations

After defining the global attributes of the IVR, you need to specify what specific destinations (or options) are available for the caller to press. You do this with `<entry>` XML elements. Let's review the first five XML options used by this IVR:

```
<entry action="menu-exec-app" digits="1" param="bridge
   sofia/$${domain}/888@conference.freeswitch.org"/>
<entry action="menu-exec-app" digits="2" param="transfer 9196 XML
   default"/>
<entry action="menu-exec-app" digits="3" param="transfer 9664 XML
   default"/>
<entry action="menu-exec-app" digits="4" param="transfer 9191 XML
   default"/>
<entry action="menu-exec-app" digits="5" param="transfer 1234*256
   enum"/>
<entry action="menu-exec-app" digits="/^(10[01][0-9])$/"
   param="transfer $1 XML features"/>
```

Each preceding entry defines three parameters—an action to be taken, the digits the caller must press to activate that action, and the parameters that are passed to the action. In most cases you will probably use the `menu-exec-app` action, which simply allows you to specify an action and parameters to call just as you would from the regular Dialplan (`bridge`, `transfer`, `hangup`, and so on.). These options are all pretty simple—they define a single digit which, when pressed, either bridges a call or transfers the call to an extension.

There is one entry that is a bit different from the rest, which is the final IVR entry. It deserves a closer look.

```
<entry action="menu-exec-app" digits="/^(10[01][0-9])$/"
  param="transfer $1 XML features"/>
```

This entry definition specifies a regular expression for the digits field. This regular expression field is identical to the expressions you would use in the Dialplan. In this example, the IVR is looking for any four-digit extension number from 1000 through 1019 (which is the default extension number range for the predefined users in the directory). As the regular expression is wrapped in parenthesis, the result of the entry will be passed to the `transfer` application as the `$1` channel variable. This effectively allows the IVR to accept 1000-1019 as entries, and transfer the caller directly to those extensions when they are entered into the IVR.

The remaining IVR entry actions are a bit different. They introduce `menu-sub` as an action, which transfers the caller to an IVR sub-menu, and `menu-top`, which restarts the current IVR and replays the menu.

```
<entry action="menu-sub" digits="6" param="demo_ivr_submenu"/>
<entry action="menu-top" digits="9"/>
```

Several other actions exist that can be used within an IVR. The complete list of actions you can use from within the IVR include the following:

menu-exec-app

The `menu-exec-app` action, combined with a `param` field, executes the specified application and passes the parameters listed to that application. This is equivalent to using `<action application="app" data="data">` in your Dialplan. The most common use of `menu-exec-app` is to transfer a caller to another extension in the Dialplan.

Argument syntax: `application <params>`

Examples:

```
<entry digits="1" action="menu-exec-app" param="application param1
  param2 param3 ...">
<entry digits="2" action="menu-exec-app" param="transfer 9664 XML
  default">
```

menu-exec-api

The `menu-exec-api` action, combined with a `param` field, executes the specified API command and passes the parameters listed to that command. This is equivalent to entering API commands at the CLI or from the event socket.

Argument syntax: `api_command <params>`

Examples:

```
<entry digits="1" action="menu-exec-api" param="eval Caller Pressed
   1!">
```

menu-play-sound

The `menu-play-sound` action, combined with a `param` field, plays a specified sound file.

Argument syntax: valid sound file.

Examples:

```
<entry digits="1" action="menu-play-sound"
   param="screaming_monkeys.wav">
```

menu-back

The `menu-back` action returns to the previous IVR menu, if any.

Argument syntax: None.

Examples:

```
<entry digits="1" action="menu-back">
```

menu-top

The `menu-top` action restarts this IVR's menu.

Argument syntax: None.

Examples:

```
<entry digits="1" action="menu-top">
```

Take a look at the XML for the sample sub-menu IVR and see if you can figure out what it does. Also note how it is called above, when clicking 6 from the main menu.

```
<menu name="demo_ivr_submenu"
    greet-long="phrase:demo_ivr_sub_menu"
    greet-short="phrase:demo_ivr_sub_menu_short"
    invalid-sound="ivr/ivr-that_was_an_invalid_entry.wav"
    exit-sound="voicemail/vm-goodbye.wav"
```

```
        timeout="15000"
        max-failures="3"
        max-timeouts="3">
   <entry action="menu-top" digits="*"/>
  </menu>
```

Routing calls to your IVR

Routing calls to your IVR is simple and can be done from within the Dialplan. Simply add the following XML application to your Dialplan extension where you want to invoke an IVR:

```
<action application="ivr" data="demo_ivr"/>
```

This will cause FreeSWITCH to look for the IVR named demo_ivr and invoke it. Note that it is not possible to return from an IVR and continue processing Dialplan entries; the IVR must ultimately transfer, bridge, or hangup the caller.

The XML Dialplan entry for invoking the demo_ivr, which is included with the sample FreeSWITCH configuration files, is as follows:

```
<!-- a sample IVR  -->
<extension name="ivr_demo">
  <condition field="destination_number" expression="^5000$">
    <action application="answer"/>
    <action application="sleep" data="2000"/>
    <action application="ivr" data="demo_ivr"/>
  </condition>
</extension>
```

Note that in the preceding example, a sleep application appears before the IVR is executed. This is important as it allows for media to begin flowing between your caller and your FreeSWITCH instance, before the IVR's greeting begins playing. If the Dialplan does not do this, you may get complaints from some callers of IVRs to "clip" the beginning of the greeting.

Nesting IVRs

There are two ways to "nest" or otherwise combine IVRs.

The first way is to use the sub-menu system list, as mentioned. Simply create two or more IVR menus as if they were independent menus, with each one having a unique name. Then, from the main IVR, create an entry option with an action of menu-sub and a param containing the name of the child IVR.

```
<entry digits="1" action="menu-sub" param="child_ivr"/>
```

The advantage to creating your menus this way is that you gain the ability to use the menu-back action to allow callers to get to the previous IVR menu, useful if you might have multiple parents calling the same child menu.

The other way to use sub-menus is to assign each IVR a unique extension number and simply transfer the caller from one extension to another, in order to get to and from the parent and child menus. In this way, you can always guarantee that you can get from one specific IVR to another and back again, regardless of how an IVR was invoked.

Using phrases with IVRs

You may have noticed the greet-long and greet-short option in the examples use "phrase:demo_ivr_main_menu" as opposed to a specific sound filename and path. IVRs allow you to specify sound files using the phrase and text-to-speech macros. This is useful for several reasons, most notably the ability to chain together multiple sounds into one "phrase" and the ability to have different languages presented to the caller, based on the caller's information.

Calling Phrase Macros

Phrase Macros can be called from the Dialplan, from an IVR, or from Dialplan script. (The latter will be covered in the next chapter.) Phrase Macros can be used virtually anywhere that a sound filename can be used. (Phrase Macros are used only for playback purposes, so they cannot be used when specifying a filename for a recording operation.) We have already seen examples of using phrases in our XML IVR configuration files. Following are a few examples of using Phrase Macros from the Dialplan:

```
<action application="playback"
  data="phrase:myphrase:arg1:arg2:arg3"/>
<action application="play_and_get_digits" data="2 5 3 7000 #
  phrase:myphrase:arg1 /invalid.wav my_var \d+"/>
```

Note, too, that there is no requirement to have an argument. The following code is valid as well:

```
<action application="playback" data="phrase:myphrase"/>
```

Now let's look at some phrases to see what they can accomplish for you.

Phrase Macro examples: voicemail

The FreeSWITCH voicemail system is exemplary in its use of Phrase Macros to simplify the task of combining pre-recorded sound prompts in a reusable way. By looking at the Phrase Macros used in the FreeSWITCH voicemail implementation, we can learn virtually all there is to know about using these powerful tools.

Open `conf/lang/en/vm/sounds.xml` in a text editor and scan through the file. You will notice the familiar opening `<include>` tag and the subsequent `<macro>` tags. Just by looking at the definitions of these macros, you can get an idea of what some of them do. The basic syntax of a Phrase Macro looks like the following:

```
<macro name="<macro name>">
  <input pattern="<pattern>">
    <match>
      <action>

    </match>
    <nomatch>
      <action>

    </nomatch>
  </input>

  <input pattern="<pattern>">
    <match>
      <action>

    </match>
    <nomatch>
      <action>

    </nomatch>
  </input>
</macro>
```

The macro is defined by the contents within the `<macro>` and `</macro>` tags. The `input pattern` is a regular expression (pattern) that is matched against any arguments that are passed to the Phrase Macro. The actions inside of the `<match>` and `</match>` tags are executed if there is a positive match, otherwise the actions inside of `<nomatch>` and `</nomatch>` are executed. If a match is found, then the special regular expression capture variables (`$1`, `$2`, and so on) are available inside the `<match>` node. Note that you may have multiple input patterns. This functions in a way that is very similar to the way the XML Dialplan functions. (See the following code for an example of using multiple `input pattern` nodes.)

Let's review a few simple macros. Locate the `voicemail_goodbye` macro as follows:

```
<macro name="voicemail_goodbye">
  <input pattern="(.*)">
    <match>
      <action function="play-file" data="voicemail/vm-
        goodbye.wav"/>
    </match>
  </input>
</macro>
```

This macro is called by the voicemail system when the caller logs out. In this case the input pattern is "(.*)" which will always match any arguments, and in fact will match even if no arguments are passed. (This pattern is very common in Phrase Macros.) If there is a match, (and there always will be) then this macro plays the `vm-goodbye.wav` file. That is all it does. At first glance, it may not seem advantageous to have seven lines of code just to play a single sound file. However, using this Phrase Macro allows us to customize what happens when a caller logs out of voicemail, and we can do so without editing any source code. There are, though, other advantages.

Locate the `voicemail_enter_pass` macro:

```
<macro name="voicemail_enter_pass">
  <input pattern="(.*)">
    <match>
      <action function="play-file" data="voicemail/vm-
        enter_pass.wav"/>
      <action function="say" data="$1" method="pronounced"
        type="name_spelled"/>
    </match>
  </input>
</macro>
```

Note that this macro captures the arguments and places them in the special variable `$1`. In the default configuration, the `voicemail` module sends # as the argument. This macro is what controls the dialog when the caller is logging into voicemail. Specifically, it plays the sound file that says, "Please enter your password, followed by..." and then uses the `say` application to "say" the word "pound". The net effect, then, is that the caller hears "Please enter your password, followed by pound". This macro lets us customize what the caller hears when he or she is prompted to enter a password.

> Watch the `fs_cli` while logging into voicemail and checking messages. You can observe the phrases being parsed and executed.

At this point, we can already see that Phrase Macros are good for customization, and they stitch together various sound prompts to create meaningful sentences to play to the caller. A classic example of this is the IVR menu. The voicemail main menu really is just an IVR menu for a specific purpose. The voicemail main menu is a dialog that says to the caller, "To listen to new messages, press 1. To listen to saved messages, press 2. For advanced options, press 5. To exit, press pound". Let's look at this macro. Locate the macro `voicemail_menu`, listed as follows:

```
<macro name="voicemail_menu">
  <input pattern="^([0-9#*]):([0-9#*]):([0-9#*]):([0-9#*])$">
    <match>
      <!-- To listen to new messages -->
      <action function="play-file" data="voicemail/vm-
        listen_new.wav"/>
      <action function="play-file" data="voicemail/vm-press.wav"/>
      <action function="say" data="$1" method="pronounced"
        type="name_spelled"/>
      <action function="execute" data="sleep(100)"/>

      <!-- To listen to saved messages -->
      <action function="play-file" data="voicemail/vm-
        listen_saved.wav"/>
      <action function="play-file" data="voicemail/vm-press.wav"/>
      <action function="say" data="$2" method="pronounced"
        type="name_spelled"/>
      <action function="execute" data="sleep(100)"/>

      <!-- For advanced options -->
      <action function="play-file" data="voicemail/vm-advanced.wav"/>
      <action function="play-file" data="voicemail/vm-press.wav"/>
      <action function="say" data="$3" method="pronounced"
        type="name_spelled"/>
      <action function="execute" data="sleep(100)"/>

      <!-- To exit -->
      <action function="play-file" data="voicemail/vm-to_exit.wav"/>
      <action function="play-file" data="voicemail/vm-press.wav"/>
      <action function="say" data="$4" method="pronounced"
        type="name_phonetic"/>
    </match>
  </input>
</macro>
```

Most of this phrase is self-explanatory. The key piece of information is actually found in the pattern (highlighted). The voicemail module calls this macro with an argument list that looks like this: 1:2:5:#. The input pattern is simply a regular expression that parses out those values, so that $1 contains "1", $2 contains "2", $3 contains "5", and $4 contains "#".

> You may be wondering where the key presses are defined, that is, where you can tell the FreeSWITCH voicemail module that the caller should press *1* for new messages, press *2* for saved messages, and so on. The answer is in the file conf/autoload_configs/voicemail.conf. xml. Look in the <profiles> node for the default voicemail profile. Notice that many of the parameters have names ending with "-key". These are all customizable. The parameter "play-new-messages-key" defines which key the user presses to listen to new messages. The parameter "config-menu-key" is what the user presses to access the advanced options menu. Feel free to experiment with your own customizations. The FreeSWITCH developers recommend that you make a copy of the default voicemail profile, and then define your own custom profile if you wish to make changes to a production system.

Let's look at one more example of using Phrase Macros to solve what may otherwise be complicated IVR scenarios. The voicemail_message_count macro solves two distinct problems. First, we have two different types of voicemail messages, namely, new and saved. Second, we have the challenge of when to use "messages" (plural) or "message" (singular), when telling the caller how many messages are present. Notice how our voicemail_message_count macro elegantly solves both problems as follows:

```
<macro name="voicemail_message_count">
  <input pattern="^(1):(.*)$" break_on_match="true">
    <match>
      <action function="play-file" data="voicemail/vm-you_have.wav"/>
      <action function="say" data="$1" method="pronounced"
        type="items"/>
      <action function="play-file" data="voicemail/vm-$2.wav"/>
      <action function="play-file" data="voicemail/vm-message.wav"/>
    </match>
  </input>
  <input pattern="^(\d+):(.*)$">
    <match>
      <action function="play-file" data="voicemail/vm-you_have.wav"/>
      <action function="say" data="$1" method="pronounced"
        type="items"/>
```

```
        <action function="play-file" data="voicemail/vm-$2.wav"/>
        <action function="play-file" data="voicemail/vm-messages.wav"/>
    </match>
  </input>
</macro>
```

Again, much of this is self-explanatory, and like the previous example, the key to understanding this macro is in the input patterns (highlighted). The voicemail module calls this macro with an argument of "x:new" or "x:saved" representing the number of new or saved messages, respectively. The number of messages is captured in $1, and then type of messages (either "new" or "saved") will be stored in $2. The macro uses $2 to determine whether to play voicemail/vm-new.wav or voicemail/vm-saved.wav, so that problem is easily solved. However, what about saying "messages" versus "message"?

Notice that the first input has an extra attribute, namely, break_on_match. By setting this attribute to "true", we tell the macro to stop looking at the rest of the input patterns in the macro. If the user has a single new message, then the voicemail module will call this phrase with an argument of "1:new". (Likewise, it would call the argument with 1:saved for a single saved message.) The first pattern will match, and no more searching for matches will be performed. Then, the actions within the first <match> will be executed. In this case the Phrase Macro stitches together a phrase that says, "You have ... one ... new ... message". However, if there is more than one message (or zero messages), then the argument would be something like 2:new. In this case, the first input pattern match would fail, and then it would continue on to the second pattern, where it would match. The actions inside this <match> node would yield a phrase that says, "You have ... two ... new ... messages". By using a more specific input pattern first, along with setting break_on_match to "true", and by using the more general input pattern second, we have a simple and elegant way of handling the "plural problem" that is common among many languages.

Keep these principles in mind as we will put them to good use in *Chapter 7, Building IVR Applications with Lua*.

Advanced routing

IVRs are not just limited to menus. While you most likely want to program complex IVRs using a programming language, it's possible to use the built-in XML IVRs in other ways, too.

For example, let's say you wanted to require callers to enter a PIN number in order to reach a special answering service. You might create an IVR that contains the PIN number as the only available entry, and replace the sound files with a greeting, requesting the PIN number and the invalid entry sound with an invalid password message. The menu would be simple enough as follows:

```
<menu name="enter_pin"
      greet-long="phrase:enter_your_pin"
      invalid-sound="phrase:invalid_pin"
      exit-sound="phrase:invalid_pin"
      timeout="15000"
      max-failures="3"
      max-timeouts="3">
  <entry digits="1828" action="menu-exec-app" param="transfer
    after_hours XML default"/>
</menu>
```

This would effectively create a prompt, requesting a password as stated above, and disconnecting callers after three tries.

As another option, you might create an IVR that collects some data that is later used in your Dialplan. Let's say, you wanted the caller to enter the caller ID that they want appearing on their next outgoing call. You could create an IVR to collect ten digits, pass the result to another extension which sets the digits to the current caller ID, and then go to the final destination. Your IVR menu might look like the following:

```
<menu name="set_callerid"
      greet-long="phrase:enter_your_callerid"
      invalid-sound="phrase:invalid_callerid"
      exit-sound="phrase:invalid_callerid"
      timeout="15000"
      max-failures="99"
      max-timeouts="99">
  <entry digits="$(\d{10})" action="menu-exec-app"
    param="transfer $1 XML set_callerid"/>
</menu>
```

You would then create a special context in your Dialplan that might look like this:

```xml
<context name="set_callerid">
  <extension name="SetIt">
    <condition field="destination_number" expression="^(\d{10})$">
      <action application="set"
        data="effective_caller_id_number=$1"/>
      <action application="bridge"
        data="sofia/external/18005551212"/>
    </condition>
  </extension>
</context>
```

The combination of the preceding IVR and helper context would allow callers to enter their Caller ID, and have it set prior to the bridge application being called.

Summary

The IVR system within FreeSWITCH is a powerful, flexible tool for use when creating anything that gathers input from a caller. When combined with the various other applications in FreeSWITCH, the possibilities for routing callers using dynamic and creative call flows are endless. Now that we have considered the XML IVR system and the Phrase Macro system, let's turn our attention to an alternative means of control complex interaction with the caller, that is, Dialplan scripting with the Lua programming language.

7
Building IVR Applications with Lua

In the previous chapter, we discussed the basics of building Interactive Voice Response (IVR) applications using the built-in XML IVR engine. The XML IVR engine is useful for building simple IVR applications that are relatively static in nature. FreeSWITCH has other ways of building IVR applications that are more flexible and powerful than the built-in XML IVR engine. One way is by utilizing the various scripting languages that have been integrated into FreeSWITCH. FreeSWITCH supports the following scripting languages for building voice applications:

- JavaScript
- Lua
- Perl

Any of the preceding languages can be used for building IVR applications. In this chapter we will focus on using Lua, a lightweight scripting language that is designed to be embedded within other projects. (A famous example of which is *World of Warcraft*.)

> Each of the scripting languages has its own advantages and drawbacks. Lua is a good choice because it is fast, scalable, and easy to learn. All things being equal, Lua is a good choice for almost any voice application in FreeSWITCH.

As a part of our building voice applications with Lua, we will make extensive use of custom Phrase Macros in our examples.

Getting started with Lua

Enabling Lua (via `mod_lua`) is very similar to the process we used in *Chapter 2, Building and Installation*, where we enabled `mod_flite`. It is done in the following way:

1. Open `modules.conf` in the FreeSWITCH source directory and locate the following line:

   ```
   #languages/mod_lua
   ```
   Remove the # and save the file.

2. Open `modules.conf.xml` in the `conf/autoload_configs` directory and locate the following line:

   ```
   <!-- <load module="mod_lua"/> -->
   ```
   Remove the `<!--` and `-->` tags and save the file.

3. Build and compile `mod_lua` from the FreeSWITCH source directory:

   ```
   make mod_lua-install
   ```

4. Wait for the installation to finish, and then restart FreeSWITCH. Launch `fs_cli` and type `show application`. If Lua loaded successfully, then you will see that `lua` is now available as a Dialplan application as follows:

   ```
   lua,Launch LUA ivr,<script>,mod_lua
   ```

You are almost ready to write scripts in Lua.

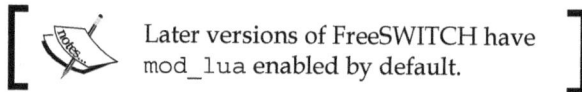

> Later versions of FreeSWITCH have mod_lua enabled by default.

Running Lua scripts from the Dialplan

The new `lua` Dialplan application is called from within `<action>` tags using the familiar syntax:

```
<action application="lua" data="my_script.lua arg1 arg2 arg3"/>
```

Arguments passed to the script are separated by spaces. To include an argument that contains a space, use single quote characters to delimit the argument as follows:

```
<action application="lua" data="my_script.lua 'arg 1' 'arg 2' 'arg 3'"/>
```

If you put your script in the `scripts` subdirectory under the main FreeSWITCH installation directory, then it is not necessary to specify the full path to your script file. If needed you can use an absolute path. For example, in Linux/Unix environments, do the following:

```
<action application="lua" data="/full/path/to/my_script.lua"/>
```

In Windows:

```
<action application="lua" data="C:\full\path\to\my_script.lua"/>
```

Before we start writing scripts, let's take a brief look at the syntax of the Lua language.

Basic Lua syntax

Lua has a simple syntax that is easy both to learn and to read. Following is a simple script:

```
-- This is a sample Lua script
-- Single line comments begin with two dashes

--[[
  This is a multi-line comment.
  Everything between the double square brackets
     is part of the comment block.
]]

-- Lua is loosely typed
var = 1          -- This is a comment
var = "alpha"    -- Another comment
var = "A1"       -- You get the idea...

--[[
  When the Lua script is called from the dialplan
  you have a few magic objects. A handy one is
  the 'freeswitch' object which lets you do things
  like this:
  freeswitch.consoleLog("INFO","This is a log line\n")

  Another important one is the 'session' object which
  Lets you manipulate the call:
  session:answer()
  session:hangup()
]]
```

```
-- Lua makes extensive use of tables
-- Tables are a hybrid of arrays and associative arrays
my_table = {
     key1 = val1,
     key2 = val2,
     "index 1",
     "index 2"
}
freeswitch.consoleLog("my_table key1 is '" .. my_table[key1] .. "'\n")
freeswitch.consoleLog("my_table index 1 is '" .. my_table[1] .. "'\n")


-- Access arguments passed in
arg1 = argv[1]        -- First argument
arg2 = argv[2]        -- Second argument

-- Simple if/then
if ( var == "A1" ) then
   freeswitch.consoleLog("INFO","var is 'A1'\n")
end

-- Simple if/then/else
if ( var == "A1" ) then
   freeswitch.consoleLog("INFO","var is 'A1'\n")
else
   freeswitch.consoleLog("INFO","var is not 'A1'!\n")
end

-- String concatenation uses ..
var = "This " .. " and " .. "that"
freeswitch.consoleLog("INFO","var contains '" .. var .. "'\n")

-- The end
```

Every Lua script that is executed from the Dialplan receives the session object, which represents the call leg that is being processed. The session object is the primary means of manipulating the call, and is used extensively in Lua scripting.

Building voice applications

Now that we have covered the basic Lua syntax, let's create a simple Lua script and the corresponding entry in the Dialplan. First, create a new Dialplan extension that will execute the Lua script when a user dials *9910*:

1. Open the `01_Custom.xml` file that we created in *Chapter 5, Understanding the XML Dialplan,* and add the following new extension:

```xml
<extension name="Simple Lua Test">
  <condition field="destination_number" expression="^(9910)$">
    <action application="lua" data="test1.lua"/>
  </condition>
</extension>
```

2. Save the file. Launch `fs_cli` and issue `reload_xml,` or press F6.

Our Dialplan is now ready to call the Lua script named `test1.lua`. Create this new script as follows:

1. Using your text editor, create `test1.lua` in the `freeswitch/scripts/` directory and add the following lines:

```lua
-- test1.lua
-- Answer call, play a prompt, hangup

-- Set the path separator
pathsep = '/'
-- Windows users do this instead:
-- pathsep = '\'

--Answer the call
session:answer()

--Create a string with path and filename of a sound file
prompt = "ivr" .. pathsep  .. "ivr-welcome_to_freeswitch.wav"

-- Print a log message
freeswitch.consoleLog("INFO","Prompt file is '" .. prompt .. "'\
n")

--Play the prompt
session:streamFile(prompt)

-- Hangup
session:hangup()
```

2. Save the file.

The preceding script is now ready for us to test. Using a phone that is registered on your FreeSWITCH server, dial *9910*. You will hear the sound prompt played, and then the system will disconnect the call.

> After editing and saving a Lua script, there is no need to execute `reloadxml`. As soon as the script file is saved, the `lua` call from the Dialplan will use the updated script.

Let's look at a few lines in this script and review their functions.

```
pathsep = '/'
```

This creates a variable named `pathsep`, whose value is a single forward slash (/) character. This is used as the path separator for Linux/Unix based systems. Windows users will, of course, need to use the backslash (\) character as the path separator.

```
session:answer()
```

The preceding line answers the call. Most scripts will answer the call as their first action.

```
prompt = "ivr" .. pathsep .. "ivr-welcome_to_freeswitch.wav"
```

The preceding line creates a variable named `prompt` that contains the relative path to one of the included sound files.

```
freeswitch.consoleLog("INFO","Prompt file is '" .. prompt .. "'\n")
```

The preceding command will print a line of information to the FreeSWITCH console. It is very handy for troubleshooting and debugging. If you watch the FreeSWITCH console while calling 9910 you should see a line like the following in the output:

```
2010-02-10 16:37:52.583000 [INFO] switch_cpp.cpp:1129 Prompt file is
'ivr/ivr-welcome_to_freeswitch.wav'
```

> Be sure to include a trailing newline sequence (\n) when using `freeswitch.consoleLog`.

```
session:streamFile(prompt)
```

The preceding line uses the session object's `streamFile` method to play the audio file to the caller. Keep in mind that when specifying a relative path name, FreeSWITCH will actually find the file that matches the sample rate of the call. In many cases, this will be 8000 because the sampling rate of 8000 Hz (8 kHz) is typical for a phone call. In this example, the actual path to the sound file is the following:

```
/usr/local/freeswitch/sounds/en/us/callie/ivr/8000/ivr-welcome_to_
freeswitch.wav
```

> A complete list of English sound files and their contents can be found in docs/phrase/phrase_en.xml, under the FreeSWITCH source directory.

```
session:hangup()
```

The preceding line simply hangs up the call, disconnecting the calling party.

Building simple scripts with Lua is not at all difficult. Now let's write a script that does some basic interaction with the caller.

Simple IVR—interacting with the caller

Most IVR applications require some sort of input from the caller. For example, it is quite common for an IVR application to prompt the caller to enter a PIN or an account number, and then act accordingly. Let's write a small script that demonstrates how to collect some dialed digits from the caller, and read them back, using two different pronunciation methods.

1. Open the `01_Custom.xml` file and add the following new extension:

   ```
   <extension name="Read Back Entered Digits">
     <condition field="destination_number" expression="^(9911)$">
       <action application="lua" data="read_back_digits.lua"/>
     </condition>
   </extension>
   ```

2. Save the file. Launch `fs_cli` and issue `reload_xml`, or press F6.

Our Dialplan is now ready to call the Lua script named `read_back_digits.lua`. Create this new script as follows:

1. Using your text editor create `read_back_digits.lua` in the `freeswitch/scripts/` directory and add the following lines:

   ```
   -- read_back_digits.lua
   ```

```
--Answer the call
session:answer()

-- Set the path separator
pathsep = '/'
-- Windows users do this instead:
-- pathsep = '\'

-- Set a variable that contains the sound prompt to play
prompt = "ivr" .. pathsep .. "ivr-please_enter_extension_followed_
by_pound.wav"

-- Set a variable that contains the invalid message to play
invalid = "ivr" .. pathsep .. "ivr-that_was_an_invalid_entry.wav"

-- Play file and collect digits
-- Variable 'digits' will contain the digits collected
-- Valid input is 3 digits min, 5 digits max
-- Caller presses # (pound or hash) to finish
digits = session:playAndGetDigits(3, 5, 3, 7000, "#", prompt,
invalid, "\\d+")

-- Read back digits iterated, then pause
-- "one two three four five"
session:execute("say", "en number iterated " .. digits)
session:sleep(1000)

-- Read back digits pronounced, then pause
-- "twelve thousand, three hundred forty-five"
session:execute("say", "en number pronounced " .. digits)
session:sleep(1000)

-- Politely hang up
thankyou = "ivr" .. pathsep .. "ivr-thank_you.wav"
goodbye  = "voicemail" .. pathsep .. "vm-goodbye.wav"
session:streamFile(thankyou)
session:sleep(250)
session:streamFile(goodbye)

-- Hangup
session:hangup()
```

2. Save the file.

This script is now ready for us to test. Dial *9911* and listen for the prompt, which will tell you to enter an extension. Key in several digits and then press #. The system will read back the digits in iterated format (one-two-three-four), then in pronounced format (one thousand, two hundred thirty-four), and will finally say, "Thank you, goodbye," before hanging up. The `playAndGetDigits` method will also handle invalid input for you. Try entering only two digits or a star to hear the invalid entry dialog. If the caller makes three invalid entries then `playAndGetDigits` will disconnect.

Conditions and looping

The previous examples demonstrate a basic dialog with the caller. Let's now examine a script that will use conditionals and looping. We will also apply what we learned in *Chapter 6, Using the Built-in XML IVR Engine*, to create a new Phrase Macro to assemble several individual sound files into a larger sound prompt.

Let's create the Phrase Macro first. We need a Phrase Macro that will stitch together individual sounds files into a prompt that says, "To continue, press one. To exit, press two". We will add a new macro to the `custom-phrases.xml` file that we created in *Chapter 6, Using the Built-in XML IVR Engine*.

1. Open the file `conf/lang/en/demo/custom-phrases.xml`. Add the following lines:

```xml
<macro name="read_digits2_phrase" pause="100">
  <input pattern="(.*)">
    <match>
      <action function="play-file" data="voicemail/vm-continue.
wav"/>
      <action function="play-file" data="voicemail/vm-press.wav"/>
      <action function="play-file" data="digits/1.wav"/>
      <action function="execute" data="sleep(250)"/>
      <action function="play-file" data="voicemail/vm-to_exit.
wav"/>
      <action function="play-file" data="voicemail/vm-press.wav"/>
      <action function="play-file" data="digits/2.wav"/>
      <action function="execute" data="sleep(250)"/>
    </match>
  </input>
</macro>
```

2. Save the file. Launch `fs_cli` and issue `reload_xml`, or press F6.

The Phrase Macro `read_digits2_phrase` is now ready to be used.

> Remember that any time you edit an XML configuration file, you need to issue the `reload_xml` command, or press F6 at the FreeSWITCH command line. It is good to get into the habit of reloading your XML configuration whenever you make a change because this will make it easier to locate the source of any errors or typos.

1. Open the `01_Custom.xml` file and add the following new extension:

```xml
<extension name="Read Back Entered Digits #2">
  <condition field="destination_number" expression="^(9912)$">
    <action application="lua" data="read_back_digits2.lua"/>
  </condition>
</extension>
```

2. Save the file. Launch `fs_cli` and issue `reload_xml`, or press F6.

Our Dialplan is now ready to call the Lua script named `read_back_digits2.lua`. Create the following new script:

1. Using your text editor create `read_back_digits2.lua` in the `freeswitch/scripts/` directory and add the following lines:

```lua
-- read_back_digits2.lua
-- Demonstrates while loop and session:ready()

--Answer the call
session:answer()

-- Set the path separator
pathsep = '/'
-- Windows users do this instead:
-- pathsep = '\'

-- Set a variable that contains the sound prompt to play
prompt = "ivr" .. pathsep .. "ivr-please_enter_extension_followed_
by_pound.wav"

-- Set a variable that contains the invalid message to play
invalid = "ivr" .. pathsep .. "ivr-that_was_an_invalid_entry.wav"

-- Set a flag for continuing or  exiting
continue = true

-- Initiate while loop
-- Loop continues until caller hangs up or chooses to exit
```

```
while( session:ready() == true and continue == true) do
    -- Play file and collect digits
    -- Variable 'digits' will contain the digits collected
    -- Valid input is 3 digits min, 5 digits max
    -- Caller presses # (pound or hash) to finish
    digits = session:playAndGetDigits(3, 5, 3, 7000, "#", prompt,
invalid, "\\d+")

    -- Read back digits iterated, then pause
    -- "one two three four five"
    session:execute("say", "en number iterated " .. digits)
    session:sleep(1000)

    -- Read back digits pronounced, then pause
    -- "twelve thousand, three hundred forty-five"
    session:execute("say", "en number pronounced " .. digits)
    session:sleep(1000)

    -- Ask caller to continue or exit
    digits = session:playAndGetDigits(1, 1, 2, 4000, "#", "phrase:
read_digits2_phrase", invalid, "\\d{1}")
    freeswitch.consoleLog("INFO","digits is '" .. digits .. "'\n")

    if (digits == "2") then
        continue = false
        freeswitch.consoleLog("INFO","Preparing to exit...\n")
    end
end

-- Politely hang up
thankyou = "ivr" .. pathsep .. "ivr-thank_you.wav"
goodbye  = "voicemail" .. pathsep .. "vm-goodbye.wav"
session:streamFile(thankyou)
session:sleep(250)
session:streamFile(goodbye)

-- Hangup
session:hangup()
```

2. Save the file.

We are now ready to test. At the FreeSWITCH command line issue the command /log 6 so that debug messages are not displayed. Watch the console while you call the new extension. Dial *9912* and enter in the value to be read back. After the value is read back, there will be a second prompt that will ask you to press *1* to continue, or to press *2* to exit. (Technically, any key other than *2* will continue the script.) Try both options and watch the console. You will see the console log messages from the script that print the digit you pressed.

Let's review the two highlighted lines from our script:

```
while( session:ready() == true and continue == 1) do
```

This line initiates the while loop. Notice that there are two conditions that must be true or the while loop will exit, namely, session:ready() must be true and the variable continue must also be true. The session:ready() method is a simple way to know that the caller has not hung up. When the caller hangs up session:ready() will be a non-true value. The other condition is a test on the variable continue, which is a simple flag that we created and set to true, until the caller dials **2** when prompted to continue or exit.

```
if (digits == "2") then
```

The preceding line quite simply checks to see if the caller pressed *2* in order to exit. If digits contains "2" then the script sets the value of continue to false, which causes the while loop to exit.

This example demonstrates some simple ways to use conditionals to your advantage. The session:ready() method is an important tool to use when you need to break out of your script's main control loop, when the caller hangs up.

Let's take what we have learned thus far and create a simple utility script that lets the caller make recordings. The script will prompt the user for a series of digits, which it will use for the filename, allow the caller to record a prompt, give the caller a choice to accept or re-record, and finally let the caller choose to record another prompt or exit the script. It will also introduce the concept of functions and using setInputCallback to handle certain key presses. Finally, we will create two new Phrase Macros and reuse an existing Phrase Macro. The basic call flow looks like the following:

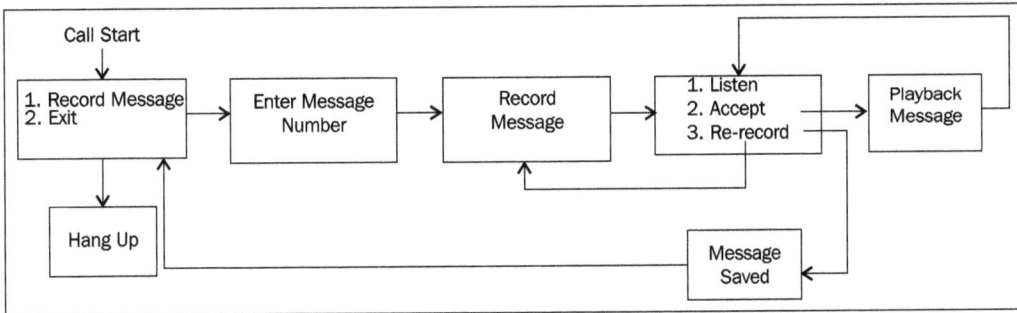

Start by adding the extension to the Dialplan as follows:

1. Open the `01_Custom.xml` file and add the following new extension:

```
<extension name="Record Sound Files Utility">
  <condition field="destination_number" expression="^(9913)$">
    <action application="lua" data="record_sound_files.lua"/>
  </condition>
</extension>
```

2. Save the file. Launch `fs_cli` and issue `reload_xml`, or press F6.

Our Dialplan is now ready to call the Lua script named `record_sound_files.lua`. Next, let's create some Phrase Macros. The first Phrase Macro tells the caller, "To record a greeting, press one. To exit, press two". Note that this Phrase Macro is almost identical to the `read_digits2_phrase` macro that we created in the previous example. The other Phrase Macro will tell the user to enter the message number (that is, the filename) and press pound. Add the two new Phrase Macros as shown in the following snippet:

1. Open the file `conf/lang/en/demo/custom-phrases.xml`. Add these lines:

```
<macro name="record_greeting_or_exit" pause="100">
  <input pattern="(.*)">
    <match>
      <action function="play-file" data="voicemail/vm-
        record_greeting.wav"/>
      <action function="play-file" data="voicemail/vm-press.wav"/>
      <action function="play-file" data="digits/1.wav"/>
      <action function="execute" data="sleep(250)"/>
      <action function="play-file" data="voicemail/vm-to_exit.
wav"/>
      <action function="play-file" data="voicemail/vm-press.wav"/>
```

```
        <action function="play-file" data="digits/2.wav"/>
        <action function="execute" data="sleep(250)"/>
      </match>
    </input>
  </macro>

  <macro name="enter_message_number" pause="100">
    <input pattern="(.*)">
      <match>
        <action function="play-file" data="voicemail/vm-press.wav"/>
        <action function="play-file" data="voicemail/vm-
          message_number.wav"/>
        <action function="execute" data="sleep(250)"/>
        <action function="play-file" data="currency/and.wav"/>
        <action function="play-file" data="voicemail/vm-press.wav"/>
        <action function="play-file" data="digits/pound.wav"/>
        <action function="execute" data="sleep(250)"/>
      </match>
    </input>
  </macro>
```

2. Save the file. Launch `fs_cli` and issue `reload_xml`, or press F6.

The Phrase Macros `record_greeting_or_exit` and `enter_message_number` are now ready to be used. Finally, create the new script in the following way:

1. Using your text editor create `record_sound_files.lua` in the `freeswitch/scripts/` directory and add the following lines:

```
-- record_sound_files.lua
-- Lets user record one or more sound files
-- Sounds are stored in ${sounds_dir}

-- Input Callback to handle digits dialed during the recording
function onInput (s, type, obj)
    if ( type == 'dtmf' ) then
        return "break"  -- This ends the recording
    end
end

--Answer the call
session:answer()

-- Set the path separator
pathsep = '/'
-- Windows users do this instead:
```

```
-- pathsep = '\'

-- Set a variable that contains the sound prompt to play
prompt = "ivr" .. pathsep .. "ivr-please_enter_extension_followed_
by_pound.wav"

-- Set a variable that contains the invalid message to play
invalid = "ivr" .. pathsep .. "ivr-that_was_an_invalid_entry.wav"

-- Set a flag for continuing or exiting
continue = true

-- Specify what to do when caller dials digits during the
recording
session:setInputCallback("onInput", "")

-- Initiate while loop
-- Loop continues until caller hangs up or chooses to exit
while( session:ready() and continue ) do
    -- First menu:
    -- 1 = Record
    -- 2 = Exit
    digits = session:playAndGetDigits(1, 1, 3, 7000, "#",
      "phrase:record_greeting_or_exit", invalid, "\\d{1}")
    if (digits == "2") then
        continue = false
        freeswitch.consoleLog("INFO","Preparing to exit...\n")
    else
        -- Collect message number from caller
        -- Variable 'digits' will contain the digits collected
        -- Valid input is 3 digits min, 5 digits max
        -- Caller presses # (pound or hash) to finish
        msgnum = session:playAndGetDigits(3, 5, 3, 7000, "#",
          "phrase:enter_message_number", invalid, "\\d+")

        -- Read back the message number
        session:execute("say", "en number iterated " .. msgnum)
        session:sleep(1000)

        -- New loop: accepted or not
        accepted = false
        while ( not accepted ) do
            -- Record record file
            session:streamFile("phrase:voicemail_record_message")
            -- Play a "bong" tone prior to recording
```

```
session:streamFile("tone_stream://v=-7;%(100,0,941.0,1477.0);v=-
7;>=2;+=.1;%(1000, 0, 640)")
            filename = session:getVariable('sounds_dir') ..
pathsep
            .. msgnum .. ".wav"
            session:recordFile(filename,300,100,10)

            -- New loop: Ask caller to listen, accept, or re-
record
            listen = true
            while ( listen ) do
                session:streamFile(filename)
                -- Use handy record_file_check macro courtesy of
the
                  voicemail module
                local digits = session:playAndGetDigits(1, 1, 2,
4000, "#", "phrase:voicemail_record_file_check:1:2:3", invalid,
"\\d{1}")
                if ( digits == "1") then
                    listen = true
                    accepted = false
                    session:execute("sleep","500")
                elseif ( digits == "2" ) then
                    listen = false
                    accepted = true
                    -- Let the caller know that the message is
saved
                    -- NOTE: you could put these into a Phrase
Macro as well
                    session:streamFile("voicemail/vm-message.wav")
                    session:execute("sleep","100")
                    session:execute("say", "en number iterated "
.. msgnum)
                    session:execute("sleep","100")
                    session:streamFile("voicemail/vm-saved.wav")
                    session:execute("sleep","1500")
                elseif ( digits == "3" ) then
                    listen = false
                    accepted = false
                    session:execute("sleep","500")
                end -- if ( digits == "1" )
            end -- while ( listen )
        end -- while ( not accepted )
    end -- if ( digits == "2" )
end -- while ( session:ready() )
```

```
-- Let's be polite
thankyou = "ivr" .. pathsep .. "ivr-thank_you.wav"
goodbye  = "voicemail" .. pathsep .. "vm-goodbye.wav"
session:streamFile(thankyou)
session:sleep(250)
session:streamFile(goodbye)

-- Hangup
session:hangup()
```

2. Save the file.

Test the script by dialing 9913. The first menu simply says, "To continue, press one. To exit, press two". Press *1*. The system will then ask for a message number followed by the pound sign. Key in 1234#. Next, you will be prompted to record a message. Record a message and then press any digit to finish. The recording will be played back, and then you will be in the last menu with some options, namely, listen, accept, and re-record. Try each one to see how the script operates. You may record as many files as you need.

> To see the sounds directory go to `fs_cli` and issue the following command: `eval ${sounds_dir}`. Also note that the `recordFile` method will overwrite any existing files without warning, so be careful!

Let's review a few key parts of this script in the following way, starting with the `onInput` function:

```
function onInput (s, type, obj)
    if ( type == 'dtmf' ) then
        return "break"  -- This ends the recording
    end
end
```

This function simply tests the type of input and returns a value of "break" if the user dialed a DTMF digit. When, though, is this function executed? It is closely related to this line of code found later in the script:

```
session:setInputCallback("onInput", "")
```

The `setInputCallback` method specifies what to do when the caller dials a digit. Whenever a digit is dialed, the function specified here is called. (Note that this does not apply when executing `session:playAndGetDigits`, which handles digits on its own.) In our script, the function `onInput` is called whenever the caller dials a digit.

The script simply returns "break", which stops both recording and playback. So, not only can you stop recording by pressing a digit, you can also skip past the playback of various prompts. Dial *9913* again and when you get to the voice prompt that says, "Record your message at the tone", press a digit to skip past it.

Notice that we nested a pair of while loops inside of the main while loop. The main while loop continues to execute until the caller hangs up or dials 2 to exit. The middle while loop continues until the variable accepted is true. The inner while loop continues until the variable listen is false. The inner while loop allows the caller to listen to his or her recording as often as desired before accepting it, and the middle while loop allows the caller to re-record the file as many times as desired. The outer while loop lets callers record as many different sound files as they wish.

The script records all sound files as .wav files. You can change the file type by choosing a different file extension, such as .ul or .gsm. However, the FreeSWITCH developers recommend using .wav files, unless there is an extremely compelling reason not to.

There is one other curious line of code, which is as follows:

```
session:streamFile("tone_stream://v=-7;%(100,0,941.0,1477.0);v=-
7;>=2;+=.1;%(1000, 0, 640)")
```

The preceding line uses the built-in **Tone Generation Markup Language (TGML)** to create the "bong" tone played to the caller just prior to recording. FreeSWITCH allows you to create and playback a wide array of tones. See http://wiki.freeswitch.org/wiki/TGML for more information.

Using a combination of playing sound files and accepting caller input via touch-tones, as well as recording the caller's voice, you can easily build custom voice applications.

Up to this point, what we have accomplished with Lua is similar to what we did with the XML IVR engine. Let's now consider some advanced concepts that explicitly show the advantages of using a scripting language.

Advanced IVR concepts

In addition to important programming constructs like conditionals and looping, there are other things that are possible by utilizing a scripting language. One of the advanced functions of a really useful IVR is the ability to interact with a third-party database. In some cases, this is a simple Web lookup function. In other cases, it involves asking the caller for an account or ID number and a PIN code, and then polling a database. Let's consider simple examples of each method.

Connecting to a database with LuaSQL

The LuaSQL interface implements a simple interface between Lua and a DBMS. (The LuaSQL interface is provided by the Kepler project. More information is available at http://www.keplerproject.org/luasql/.)

> The examples in this section require some working knowledge of databases and the ability to compile LuaSQL, for the target database type to which you will be connecting. It is beyond the scope of this book to describe all the possible installation scenarios. The examples presented here were done on a 32-bit CentOS 5.3 installation using PostgreSQL 8.1.8.

Set up your database to use the examples presented in the following section:

1. Create a database user named `freeswitch`.

2. Create a database named `testdb`.

3. Create a table named `users`.

   ```
   CREATE TABLE users (
       name character varying(20),
       pin integer,
       acct integer,
       balance numeric(9,2),
       PRIMARY KEY(acct)
   );
   ```

4. Add some data as follows:

   ```
   INSERT INTO users(name, pin, acct, balance) VALUES('Anthony',
   7654,9898, 123.45);
   INSERT INTO users(name, pin, acct, balance) VALUES('Michael',
   9642,1771, 0.00);
   INSERT INTO users(name, pin, acct, balance) VALUES('Darren',
   3756,2316, 15.75);
   ```

Test to make sure that you can log in to your database with your username, otherwise the Lua script will not be able to communicate with your database.

Next add a new extension in the following way:

1. Open the `01_Custom.xml` file and add the following new extension:

   ```
   <extension name="Simple db connection">
     <condition field="destination_number" expression="^(9914)$">
       <action application="lua" data="db_connect.lua"/>
     </condition>
   </extension>
   ```

2. Save the file. Launch `fs_cli` and issue `reload_xml`, or press F6.

Our Dialplan is now ready to call the Lua script named db_connect.lua. Our script will demonstrate the basic concepts of connecting to the database and performing an SQL query. We will accept an account number and PIN from the caller, query the database, check the PIN, and if it is correct the script will read the customer's balance. Let's create our script in the following way:

1. Using your text editor create db_connect.lua in the freeswitch/scripts/ directory and add the following lines:

```
-- db_connect.lua
-- Connects to a database, checks PIN, reads balance

-- Load the LuaSQL
require "luasql.postgres"

-- A hangup function makes the code a bit cleaner
function hangup_call ()
    session:streamFile("ivr/ivr-thank_you.wav")
    session:sleep(250)
    session:streamFile("voicemail/vm-goodbye.wav")
    session:hangup()
end

-- Clean up if necessary
function close_db_conn()
    cur:close()
    con:close()
    env:close()
end

-- Create database environment object
env = assert (luasql.postgres())

-- Create database connection object
con = assert (env:connect("testdb","freeswitch","freeswitch","loca
lhost"))

-- Set invalid entry file
invalid = "ivr/ivr-that_was_an_invalid_entry.wav"

-- Greet caller
session:answer()
session:streamFile("ivr/ivr-hello.wav")

tries = 0
while (tries < 3) do
-- Collect account number
    acct = session:playAndGetDigits(3, 5, 3, 7000, "#", "phrase:
enter_message_number", invalid, ".+")

    -- Pull account from database
    cur = assert(con:execute("SELECT * FROM users WHERE acct = '"
.. acct .. "'"))
```

```
-- Get the results, indexed alphanumerically by column names
row = cur:fetch ({}, "a")

-- Confirm that we received the record
if (cur:numrows() == 1) then
    -- We have an account, now collect PIN and check
    tries = 0
    while (tries < 3) do
        pin = session:playAndGetDigits(3, 5, 3, 7000, "#",
"ivr/ivr-please_enter_pin_followed_by_pound.wav", invalid, "\\d+")
        if (pin == row.pin) then
            bal = row.balance
            user_repeat = true
            while(user_repeat == true) do
                session:streamFile("voicemail/vm-you_have.
wav")
                session:execute("sleep",200)
                session:execute("say", "en currency pronounced
" .. bal)
                session:execute("sleep",200)
                digits = session:playAndGetDigits(1,1,3,7000,"
#","ivr/ivr-to_repeat_these_options.wav",invalid,"\\d+") -- repeat
y/n
                freeswitch.consoleLog("INFO","User entered '"
.. digits .. "'\n")
                if (digits == "1") then
                    user_repeat = true
                else
                    close_db_conn()
                    hangup_call()
                    break
                end
            end
        else
            -- Caller entered wrong PIN
            session:streamFile("ivr/ivr-that_was_an_invalid_
entry.wav")
            tries = tries + 1;
        end
    end
    if (tries > 2) then
        -- Too many failed attempts to enter PIN
        session:streamFile("voicemail/vm-abort.wav")
        close_db_conn()
        hangup_call()
        break
    end
else
    -- We did not find this account
    session:streamFile(invalid)
```

```
            tries = tries + 1;
        end
    end -- while (tries < 3)

    if (tries > 2) then
        session:streamFile("voicemail/vm-abort.wav")
        close_db_conn()
        hangup_call()
    end
```

2. Save the file.

Test the new extension by dialing *9914*. Enter in a four-digit account number that is found in the database and press #. In our example, you could enter *1771*. Enter the corresponding PIN number for the account and press #. The system will do a database lookup and then read back the account balance. Try different combinations of valid and invalid account numbers, and PIN numbers to see how the script handles errors.

Let's review the important new features presented in this script. You will notice first of all that we used a pair of functions. These are not required. However, they make the code more readable. Function `hangup_call` simply ends the call. Function `close_db_conn` closes the database connection that we opened. These functions are called in various places in our script so that we can exit the script cleanly.

The database connectivity occurs with several lines in particular, which are highlighted:

```
require "luasql.postgres"
```

This line simply loads the `luasql.postgres` module. Depending on your database environment it could be `luasql.mysql`, `luasql.odbc`, or even `luasql.oci8` for Oracle databases.

```
env = assert (luasql.postgres())
```

This line creates a database environment object for us to use.

```
con = assert (env:connect("testdb","freeswitch","freeswitch",
"localhost"))
```

This line does a little more work. It actually creates a connection object which allows us to talk to our database. The arguments to `connect` are as follows:

- Database name
- Username
- Password
- Host name or IP address

If the connection is successful, then the connection object allows us to perform SQL queries on the target database.

```
cur = assert(con:execute("SELECT * FROM users WHERE acct = '" .. acct
.. "'"))
```

This line actually performs a SQL SELECT on the users table in the target database. It returns a **cursor** object. The cursor object represents the results of the SQL statement performed on the target database. Our example uses the cursor object to return a row of data as follows:

```
row = cur:fetch ({}, "a")
```

The fetch method takes two arguments, namely, a Lua table name (optional), and either "a" or "n" to represent the kind of indices the row object will have.

- "a" means alphanumeric indices: the columns will be accessed by the name of the column.
- "n" (default) means numeric indices: the columns will be accessed by the numeric index of the field positions in the row.

The table is an optional argument which will populate a Lua table with the row data. In our example, we pass in empty braces ({}) to indicate that we will not be using a Lua table. The fetch method will return a row of data or nil if no more data is found. Note that a SELECT can return zero, one, or more rows of data. The fetch method allows the programmer to cycle through the results one row at a time. In our example, we selected a row of data based on the acct field, which is a primary key, so our result would be either no records or one record. We double-check our results as follows:

```
if (cur:numrows() == 1) then
```

The PostgreSQL, MySQL, and Oracle LuaSQL drivers all support the numrows() method. In our example, we want to know if we received back exactly one row of data, which corresponds to the account number that the caller entered. We make the assumption that if the query did not return exactly one row of data then the caller entered an invalid account number. Once it is established that a valid account has been entered we then check to see if the caller entered the correct PIN as follows:

```
if (pin == row.pin) then
```

This check makes sure that the caller entered the PIN that is read from the database. If not, the caller is prompted again to enter the PIN. Three wrong attempts will cause the script to exit.

> More information about connection and cursor objects can be found at the following website: http://www.keplerproject.org/luasql/manual.html

Connecting to databases is relatively straightforward using LuaSQL. Now let's consider an alternate method of connecting to an external data source.

Making a web call with curl

Sometimes it is useful to make a Web call from your script. There are varied applications where this is used, such as checking a news or weather feed, or integrating a voice application with a Web application. In this example, we will do a very simple web call to get the UTC time from the U.S. Navy website, which returns the data in an easily parseable manner. We will also introduce a few new concepts, including, using the freeswitch.API object, passing arguments to a Phrase Macro, and using Lua's string manipulation functions to do pattern-matching and data extraction.

The first step is to install mod_curl, which we can do just like we did with mod_lua at the beginning of the chapter in the following way:

1. Open modules.conf in the FreeSWITCH source directory and locate the following line:

    ```
    #applications/mod_curl
    ```
    Remove the # and save the file.

2. Open modules.conf.xml in the conf/autoload_configs directory and locate the following line:

    ```
    <!-- <load module="mod_curl"/> -->
    ```
    Remove the <!-- and --> tags and save the file.

3. Build and compile mod_lua from the FreeSWITCH source directory:

    ```
    make mod_curl-install
    ```

4. Wait for the installation to finish and then restart FreeSWITCH. Launch fs_cli and type help. If mod_curl loaded successfully, then you will see that curl is now available as an API command as follows:

    ```
    curl,curl url [headers|json] [get|head|post [url_encoded_
    data]],curl API,mod_curl
    ```

Next, add a new extension to the Dialplan as follows:

1. Open the `01_Custom.xml` file and add the following new extension:

```xml
<extension name="Web Lookup">
  <condition field="destination_number" expression="^(9915)$">
    <action application="lua" data="web-lookup.lua"/>
  </condition>
</extension>
```

2. Save the file. Launch `fs_cli` and issue `reload_xml`, or press F6.

Our Dialplan is now ready to call the Lua script named `web-lookup.lua`. Now let's create a new Phrase Macro that will accept an `hh:mm:ss` argument and read back the time as follows:

1. Open the file `conf/lang/en/demo/custom-phrases.xml`. Add the following lines:

```xml
<macro name="simple_time" pause="50">
  <input pattern="(\d\d):(\d\d):(\d\d)">
    <match>
      <action function="execute" data="sleep(250)"/>
      <action function="say" data="$1" method="pronounced"
      type="number"/>
      <action function="execute" data="sleep(50)"/>
      <action function="say" data="$2" method="pronounced"
      type="number"/>
      <action function="execute" data="sleep(50)"/>
      <action function="play-file" data="currency/and.wav"/>
      <action function="execute" data="sleep(50)"/>
      <action function="say" data="$3" method="pronounced"
      type="number"/>
      <action function="execute" data="sleep(50)"/>
      <action function="play-file" data="time/seconds.wav"/>
      <action function="execute" data="sleep(250)"/>
    </match>
  </input>
</macro>
```

2. Save the file. Launch `fs_cli` and issue `reload_xml`, or press F6.

The Phrase Macro `simple_time` is now ready to be used. It accepts the time argument in hh:mm:ss format and applies the input pattern of `(\d\d):(\d\d):(\d\d)`, to receive the variables `$1`, `$2`, and `$3` which contain the hour, minutes, and seconds respectively. Finally, create the new Lua script as follows:

1. Using your text editor create `web-lookup.lua` in the `freeswitch/scripts/` directory and add the following lines:

```lua
-- web-call.lua
-- Makes a curl call to http://tycho.usno.navy.mil/cgi-bin/timer.pl
-- Extracts time information and reads back to caller

-- Set a variable with the target URL
web_url = "http://tycho.usno.navy.mil/cgi-bin/timer.pl"

-- Number of times we've read time to caller
num_reads = 0

-- Get a FreeSWITCH API object
api = freeswitch.API()

session:answer()

while(session:ready() == true and num_reads < 10) do
    freeswitch.consoleLog("INFO","URL:   " .. web_url .. "\n")
    raw_data = api:execute("curl", web_url)
    freeswitch.consoleLog("INFO","Raw data:\n" .. raw_data .. "\n\n")

    -- Look for line that matches <BR>MMM. dd, hh:mm:ss UTC
    date_time = string.match(raw_data,"<BR>.-UTC",1)
    if (date_time == nil) then
        freeswitch.consoleLog("INFO","UTC date and time not found\n")
    else
        freeswitch.consoleLog("INFO","UTC date and time is '" .. date_time .. "'\n")

    -- Now parse out the individual elements into smaller strings
        time = string.gsub(date_time,".-(%d+:%d+:%d+).+","%1")
        freeswitch.consoleLog("INFO","Time is '" .. time .. "'\n")
        session:streamFile("phrase:simple_time:" .. time)
    end

    num_reads = num_reads + 1
    session:execute("sleep","1000")
end

session:hangup()
```

2. Save the file.

Dial *9915* and listen. The script will perform the web lookup using the FreeSWITCH `curl` API. If the call is successful, the raw data is parsed to extract the hour, minutes, and seconds, after which those values are passed into the `simple_time` Phrase Macro. The macro then reads back the time to the caller. After ten cycles the script will exit. You may hang up at any time.

> Be sure that your FreeSWITCH server has Internet access, otherwise the web-lookup.lua script will fail.

Let's review the new concepts presented in this example. Notice the following two related lines of code:

```
api = freeswitch.API()
raw_data = api:execute("curl", web_url)
```

The first line creates a FreeSWITCH API object which allows us to send API commands from our script. (Remember, API commands are those that are sent from the FreeSWITCH command line.) The second line actually executes the `curl` command and captures the result. The script prints the raw data from the `curl` call, which generally looks like the following:

```
<!DOCTYPE HTML PUBLIC "-//W3C//DTD HTML 3.2 Final"//EN>
<html>
  <body>
    <TITLE>What time is it?</TITLE>
    <H2> US Naval Observatory Master Clock Time</H2> <H3><PRE>
    <BR>Feb. 28, 06:39:03 UTC        Universal Time
    <BR>Feb. 28, 01:39:03 AM EST     Eastern Time
    <BR>Feb. 28, 12:39:03 AM CST     Central Time
    <BR>Feb. 27, 11:39:03 PM MST     Mountain Time
    <BR>Feb. 27, 10:39:03 PM PST     Pacific Time
    <BR>Feb. 27, 09:39:03 PM AKST    Alaska Time
    <BR>Feb. 27, 08:39:03 PM HAST    Hawaii-Aleutian Time
    </PRE></H3><P><A HREF="http://www.usno.navy.mil"> US Naval
    Observatory</A>
  </body>
</html>
```

This data all comes in a single string of text. The following line of code extracts the line of text with the UTC time:

```
date_time = string.match(raw_data,"<BR>.-UTC",1)
```

The `date_time` variable now contains `<BR>Feb. 28, 06:39:03 UTC`. The `string.match` function applies a pattern-match on the `raw_data` string. The pattern we match against is `<BR>.-UTC`. There are two meta-characters in this pattern, namely, the period and the dash. The other characters are literal. In plain language this pattern reads, "Match a string of text beginning with '<BR>' and any subsequent characters until 'UTC' is found". The `.-` means, "Match as few characters as possible".

[Lua string manipulation functions are documented online at `http://www.lua.org/manual/5.1/manual.html#5.4`.]

Now that we have a single line of text, we need to extract the hour, minute, and second of the time:

```
time = string.gsub(date_time,".-(%d+:%d+:%d+).+","%1")
```

This line uses the `string.gsub` function to perform a "match and modify" on a particular string. The arguments to `string.gsub` are the string to match, the pattern to match against, and the "replacement" value. In our example, we want to extract the `hour:minute:second` information from the string. The `string.gsub` function works by matching part or all of the input string and then returning a replacement value. This is somewhat different from many other languages' string handling and pattern-matching. However, it is just as effective. The pattern that we use in this case is as follows:

```
.-(%d+:%d+:%d+).+
```

This pattern matches, from the beginning of the string, as few characters as possible until it gets to the time. It "captures" the time value (`hh:mm:ss`), and then continues matching until the end of the string. The `hh:mm:ss` value is represented by `%1`. Putting `%1` as the "replacement" argument causes `string.gsub` to return only the captured data, which is precisely what we want. Now that we have the time information we can pass it to our Phrase Macro in the following way:

```
session:streamFile("phrase:simple_time:" .. time)
```

The time value in the format `hh:mm:ss` is passed into the Phrase Macro, where it is matched against the `input pattern` as follows:

```
<input pattern="(\d\d):(\d\d):(\d\d)">
```

The hour, minute, and second values get captured in $1, $2, and $3 respectively and are read back to the caller. The script then repeats nine more times and hangs up unless the caller hangs up first.

In some cases, it is necessary to encode and decode string data. For reference, following are some functions that you can use to URL-encode and URL-decode strings as needed in your web calls:

```
function urldecode (s)
 return (string.gsub (string.gsub (s, "+", " "),
         "%%(%x%x)",
         function (str)
           return string.char (tonumber (str, 16))
           end ))
end

function urlencode (s)
 return (string.gsub (s, "%W",
         function (str)
           return string.format ("%%%02X", string.byte (str))
         end))
end
```

By now it is probably apparent that retrieving external data (via a database connection or web lookup) is relatively straightforward. The real work is in handling the possible exceptions and acting upon the retrieved data.

Lua patterns versus regular expressions

Technically speaking, Lua does not natively support regular expressions. However, the Lua pattern-matching syntax has many similarities to traditional Perl-compatible regular expressions (PCRE). The following table shows Lua patterns and the PCRE equivalents:

Lua Metacharacter	PCRE Metacharacter
.	.
+	+
-	*?
*	*
%	\
Lua Character Class	**PCRE Character Class**
%d	\d
%w	\w
%s	\s

Complete Lua pattern syntax documentation can be found online at
http://www.lua.org/manual/5.1/manual.html#5.4.1

With a little practice, anyone familiar with regular expressions will be able to write effective Lua patterns.

Scripting tips

There are a few things to keep in mind when doing Lua scripts from the Dialplan. They are as follows:

- When a Lua script is finished, the call automatically hangs up. If you wish for the Dialplan to continue processing, be sure to execute `session:setAutoHangup(false)`. Consider the following Dialplan snippet:

```
<condition>
    <action application="lua" data="my_script.lua"/>
    <!--the following is not executed unless setAutoHangup is
        false -->
    <action application="transfer" data="$1 XML default"/>
</condition>
```

  In some cases, you will wish to continue executing the Dialplan after the Lua script has finished processing. In those cases be sure to execute `session:setAutoHangup(false)` in the script.

- The proper way to exit a Lua script is for the script to run out of commands. There is no explicit `exit()` command.

- Keeping the previous point in mind, note that calling `session:bridge()` or `session:transfer()` may not work as you expect. The `bridge` or `transfer` will not occur until the script exits. Consider the following code snippet:

```
freeswitch.consoleLog("INFO","Before transfer...\n")
session:transfer("9999 XML default")
freeswitch.consoleLog("INFO","After transfer...\n")
```

  The `transfer` will not occur until after the second `consoleLog` call and any subsequent lines of code are executed. If you wish to use `bridge` or `transfer` then be sure that they occur at the logical end of your script.

- Do not use Lua (or any other scripting language) as a replacement for the Dialplan. The XML Dialplan is extremely efficient at routing calls that no scripting language can compete. Use Lua for interacting with the caller, or, to perform functions that are not easily executed in the Dialplan. A good rule of thumb is that if you *can* do it in the Dialplan, you *should* do it in the Dialplan.

- Do not overuse scripts called from the Dialplan. If you find that you are trying to build elaborate scripts to control calls, do inline billing, third-party call control, and so on. Then it is most likely you need to use the event socket. *Chapter 9, Controlling FreeSWITCH Externally*, details some of the amazing things that are possible using the event socket.

Summary

Lua is a great choice for building simple and elegant voice applications for interacting with callers. It is very lightweight, and is therefore scalable. It has a simple syntax that is easy to learn and there is ample online documentation.

In this chapter, we accomplished a number of objectives as follows:

- Built `mod_lua` and enabled it to be loaded by default
- Became acquainted with basic Lua syntax and control structures
- Wrote several scripts that demonstrate how to interact with a caller, including answering, hanging up, playing sound files, playing Phrase Macros, and accepting input from the caller
- Learned how to use the `freeswitch` object to send log messages to the console, and to execute API commands
- Installed LuaSQL and demonstrated how to connect to a PostgreSQL database from within a Lua script
- Built `mod_curl` and enabled it to be loaded by default
- Demonstrated the use of `curl` requests to perform web calls from within a Lua script
- Became familiar with Lua's pattern-matching syntax

Now that we have a basis for writing scripts to interact with a caller, it is time to move on to one of the most powerful features of any telephony software available today: *Controlling FreeSWITCH externally with the event socket.*

8
Advanced Dialplan Concepts

In the preceding chapters you learned a bit about the power of the XML configuration files used in FreeSWITCH. Specifically, you learned about Dialplan entries and using XML to set general configuration settings. In this chapter, we will dive deep into the general structure of Dialplans, features of the XML Dialplan processing system, and how you can use what appear to be very basic features to achieve very complex results.

Some items in this chapter may appear to be repetitive, but we want to go back over some basic Dialplan functionality talked about elsewhere, and be sure we explain the how's and why's of the Dialplan system. It is quite common for people to use the XML Dialplan in FreeSWITCH without really understanding it, hampering efforts to extend the system or debug complex problems. This chapter aims to make you an expert at exactly how and why things operate the way they do within the Dialplan.

In this chapter, we will presume you have some basic understanding of how FreeSWITCH routes and processes calls, and have seen some XML configurations. Configuring and placing some phone calls on a demo FreeSWITCH installation would work to your benefit prior to reading this chapter.

We will discuss the following topics:

- Dialplan overview
- General Dialplan concepts
- Hunting and executing
- XML Dialplan module
- XML Dialplan pre-processing
- Utilizing global variables
- Utilizing channel variables
- Testing variables with regular expressions

- Passing variables to other legs
- Macros in Dialplans
- Pitfalls to avoid
- Multiple extensions on the same pass
- Time of day routing
- Special attributes of the XML extensions
- Alternatives to XML

Dialplan overview

The Dialplan engine in FreeSWITCH is an incredibly flexible piece of software. If you have a background of using other switching systems, you are probably used to the Dialplan being tied to a somewhat flat, static set of logic statements — you pre-program a set of decisions in the switch's native language (that is, answer calls, play files, collect digits, and transfer calls) and this happens for every call. Anything that cannot be done using the pre-built commands and logic statements available in that switch, well, just cannot be done.

In FreeSWITCH, Dialplan processing is actually done by the loadable module. The logic in this module is called every time a call is handled, and you can even load multiple Dialplan modules so as to process calls in a different way, depending on the logic you need. This is a very important distinction between FreeSWITCH and other systems, and it is often overlooked. By making Dialplan processing modular, a new form of freedom is introduced to the way that calls are routed. You can write your own module or use alternative modules to open up new subsets of commands for processing your Dialplan. This freedom is comparable to other switches that allow you to invoke external scripts to handle your Dialplan, except that FreeSWITCH gives you tighter integration by keeping everything in C and allowing you to utilize its internal APIs and/or linked libraries (if necessary), as opposed to external calls to scripting languages. This allows processing to take place with a much lower cost for resources on your system.

Why make Dialplan processing modular? It is important to first understand why we have a Dialplan. If we forget about programming for a while and just focus on what people want to get out of their switching system, the answer is simple: people want a flowchart-style way of designing switching logic. No matter what you are trying to do, if you charted out your entire decision-making process into a flowchart, you have just designed your Dialplan. Inherently, you have also envisioned the requirements of decisions a Dialplan module must be able to handle.

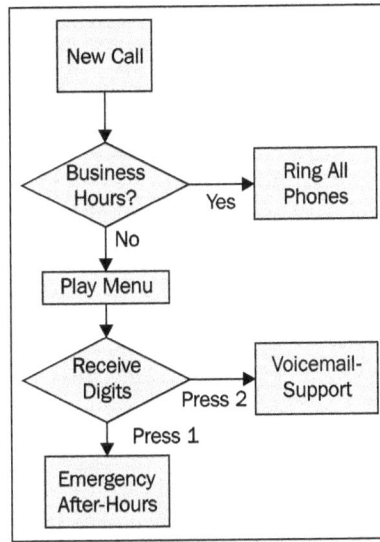

Let us take an example and break it apart. On close examination of the example shown here, we understand that this flowchart makes a lot of assumptions about pieces of information and logic that the Dialplan must be able to process. For example, in order to make a decision about whether or not you are currently open for business, the Dialplan processor must have access to the system's date and time and you should be able to compare it with the time of day you are open or closed. To make the decision about whether your caller is pressing 1, the Dialplan processor must have the ability to interpret touch-tones. Based on the conditions being compared, you must then be able to do something with the call — transfer it, play a file, hang up, and so on. All these requirements make up the logic and syntactical commands that the Dialplan will utilize. In many systems, the ability to handle these decisions is done by writing somewhat cryptic configuration code that can lead to certain limitations and drive you nuts. In FreeSWITCH, the logic can exist in different languages, or you can write your own language.

The technical advantages to having loadable Dialplan modules are numerous. Firstly, the switching system itself can now provide links to any existing external libraries (such as SQL libraries, YAML libraries, CURL HTTP libraries, and so on) in order to retrieve your Dialplan configuration and turn it into the expected style of logic that FreeSWITCH needs for processing the call. Secondly, because the Dialplan processing module can rely on other event-driven pieces of the system, you can do things like attempting to load a Dialplan module from a remote web server — and if it fails, fall back to your local Dialplan. This creates a somewhat redundant Dialplan system, and while FreeSWITCH currently implements this code elsewhere via XML CURL hooks, nothing can stop you from creating redundancy in your own Dialplan module manually.

A further advantage is being able to customize logic inside a loadable module to route calls explicitly based on logic you hardcode in the C programming language (native to FreeSWITCH). This allows you to make up your own Dialplan processing routines rather than rely on the ones built into FreeSWITCH. Your own routines can tie together libraries you have linked (like SQL) with C-based logic APIs exposed by FreeSWITCH. For example, you could easily query an SQL database to find out if a user wants to have their call *proxied*, and then directly invoke the FreeSWITCH API to turn on proxying, all from within your Dialplan processor, with just a few lines of C code. This creates a huge advantage because you gain great flexibility without having to spawn expensive third-party processes and threads to process your Dialplan (such as invoking a shell script or a PHP script just to do a simple true/false test of a value in an SQL database). This allows FreeSWITCH to handle much higher call volumes.

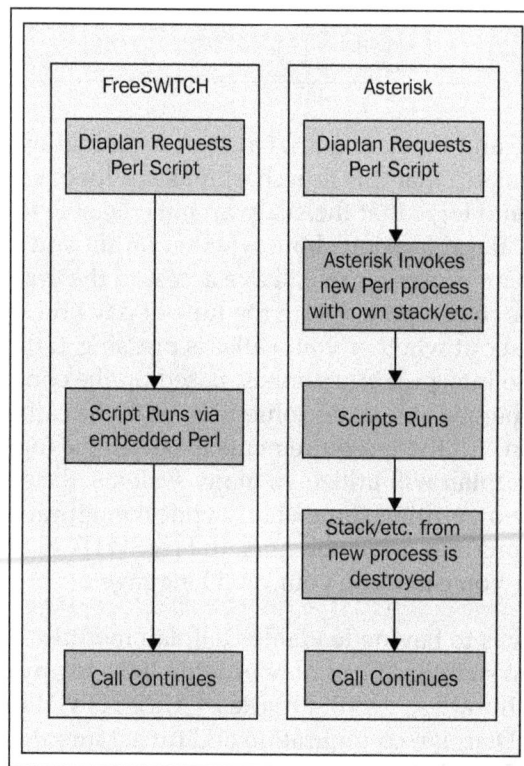

FreeSWITCH	Asterisk
Diaplan Requests Perl Script	Diaplan Requests Perl Script
	Asterisk Invokes new Perl process with own stack/etc.
Script Runs via embedded Perl	Scripts Runs
	Stack/etc. from new process is destroyed
Call Continues	Call Continues

There is a common misconception that the FreeSWITCH Dialplan is based on, and requires, XML. That is simply not true. If you prefer flat files, you could use them to store your Dialplan configuration. If you prefer YAML, you could use that, too. You just need to load the correct C-based Dialplan module to interpret your stored logic for the particular type of configuration file you want FreeSWITCH to utilize.

This aside, the most common (and currently, the most robust) Dialplan processing mechanism in FreeSWITCH is still the XML-based Dialplan module. Most Dialplan examples that are shipped with FreeSWITCH, or those scattered on the Web are in XML, therefore, they will remain the focus of this chapter. Creating your own C modules is beyond the scope of this book, but it is important that you understand that this functionality exists. As you get more and more advanced in using FreeSWITCH, you may find that the built-in XML Dialplan processor will not handle your needs for all cases, and you should remember that you are not limited to using just XML! There are other avenues to achieve what you want to accomplish in terms of call routing.

Before we dig into the specifics of the XML Dialplan, let us review and expand on some basic concepts about Dialplans in general.

General Dialplan concepts

In general, a Dialplan helps generate a list of actions to take so that a caller can reach the person or people they want to talk to. A Dialplan module implements the decision-making process that powers this. While a Dialplan module is free to implement any concept it wants for organizing how calls are routed, three concepts, in particular, are generally used when processing a call. These three concepts can be broken down by asking the same three questions for every call:

- **Contexts**: Where do we look for a general list of destinations (or features) that the current caller is allowed to reach?
- **Conditions**: Whom, specifically, is the caller trying to reach?
- **Actions**: What actions need to be taken to reach that party?

These three questions are generally answered by breaking routing decisions into three concepts—caller context, condition matching, and actions. These concepts are not necessarily unique to FreeSWITCH. We'll explore each of these concepts individually in this section.

The end result of any Dialplan's decision making is a series of actions. Every Dialplan module must return a list of actions that, when executed one after the other, results in party A reaching party B successfully.

Contexts

We discussed contexts briefly in *Chapter 5*, but let us dig into them a bit deeper.

When we talk about context, we are really referring to a list of individual destinations that a caller is allowed to reach. These parties don't have to be individual people; they can be groups of people or interactive features (for example, voicemail) but ultimately, a caller wants to be connected to *someone or something*. A **context** is a collection of rules that helps determine who a caller is trying to reach, and whether they are allowed to reach that destination or not.

You can think of a caller's context as the overall grouping of logic statements for a general set of destinations that can be called. The most commonly used contexts are the "internal" and the "public" contexts. The "internal" context generally refers to calls being made by users who are internal, or inside the walls of the switching system (such as people sitting inside an office building). These people can call each other with four-digit dialing, or dial *9* and call an outside number. The "public" context usually refers to people outside the system calling in. These people can usually only reach a small subset of destinations within the system, such as employee desk phones, but can't reach a destination like a lobby phone directly.

Why have a group of destinations at all? Why not just have internal and public numbers? Most places need more flexibility than that. For a better example, let's take a common example of phones at a hotel. If we looked at all the use cases at a hotel, we might break them into three general contexts — internal staff, internal guests, and external callers. For the purposes of this discussion, we'll nickname those use cases as "staff", "guests", and "external".

For external callers, the reason to group who they can call together is simple — we want external callers to be able to reach front desk staff and the hotel restaurant by calling one of two main phone numbers. We do not, however, want outside callers to be able to call rooms or use the in-house hotel features (for example, our phone system's wake-up call service) directly. Therefore, we'll put together a list of externally accessible numbers in the context "external" and route all outside callers to this context for processing.

Hotel guests, on the other hand, should be able to call each other's rooms, use the wake-up call services, and call the front desk staff. Again, this group of numbers is different from those of the external callers — so they get their own context with those destinations.

Finally, staff have special functions, such as being able to flag a person's phone as "checked out", restricting calls from that phone while a room is empty (for safety, in order to prevent toll fraud). These functions aren't accessible to guests, and certainly not to outside callers, so staff get their own context as well.

Visually, the logic you're creating ends up looking something like this:

		Caller (Context)		
		Internal Guest	*Internal Staff*	*External Caller*
Calling To	Front Desk	√	√	√
(Destination)	Restaurant	√	√	√
	Hotel Rooms	√	√	X
	Wake-up Call	√	X	X
	Set checked-out flag	X	√	X

Thus the need for contexts. The preceding list shows that each individual type of caller has specific constraints on whom they can (and are allowed to) call.

Note carefully that the concept of a context is not for calling a specific party, but only for creating a container listing of who can be called. The actual decisions on whom we want to reach are handled by conditions, described further in this section.

Conditions

Once the system has figured out the *general list* of who is *allowed* to be reached, it must figure out precisely who is being asked for and how to reach them. This is done using conditions.

Conditions are one or more logic statements that are used to figure out where the call should go. They typically involve comparing information about a caller (such as what number they dialed or their caller ID) with a set of rules. This information is gathered from Dialplan variables (we will discuss them later) and matched against regular expressions, strings, or other variables.

Conditions are most commonly used to match the dialed number with a specific destination that maps to a specific phone. For example, we might be testing to see if a person dialed a specific number, say, 415-886-7949. If they did, we would provide a list of actions that would connect to the user at extension 7949.

Sometimes destination matching works on fields other than the dialed number. For example, you might check the calling party's caller ID, and if it's your mother, for example, you might play a busy signal. There are many combinations of field and value pairs you might check in order to determine where to send a call. You can even check for technical- or database-driven settings, such as whether someone is behind NAT or whether they have a call-forwarding entry saved in a database table.

It is also possible to set up the Dialplan in such a way that multiple conditions match, triggering multiple actions in the same call. Such an example might be carried out to connect a caller to someone, and when they hang up, continue the call only if they are calling from a specific area code and play a survey for them. Multiple conditions can exist in various ways depending on your Dialplan processor.

Using our hotel example discussed earlier, you might end up with three contexts that each check various conditions to determine different destinations, as follows:

"Internal Guest" Context	"Internal Staff" Context	"External" Context

Did they dial 0?
  - Go to front desk
	Did they dial 0?
	  - Go to front desk	

Did they dial 2929?
  - Go to restaurant
	Did they dial 2929?
	  - Go to restaurant
		Did they dial 646-222-2929?
		  - Go to restaurant

Did they dial 3000-3999?
  - Ring room 3000-3999
	Did they dial 3000-3999?
	  - Ring room 3000-3999	

Did they dial *5? - Go to wakeup call		
	Did they dial *6? - Set checked out flag	

> By default, and in most use cases, the Dialplan is processed until a match is found.

Actions

Actions are steps to take when a condition matches. This is where the Dialplan generates a list of things the switch will need to do to actually get the caller to the destination party. Actions include "answering", "bridging", and so on.

It is very important to understand that the Dialplan module only creates a list of actions to perform — **it does not actually execute those actions real-time!** There are some exceptions to this rule, but the general premise of the original Dialplan structure revolves around staying modular and not requiring the module to do any of the heavy lifting to actually connect the call and perform the actions.

To clarify this further, think of the Dialplan as generating a to-do list for what needs to happen on the call. A to-do list might consist of:

- Answer
- Play welcome file
- Transfer to user "john doe"
- Hang up

That list would be handed back to FreeSWITCH to perform on its own.

The Dialplan is not intended to be interactive during the actual flow of the call. If you need complete interaction while a call is in progress, you should utilize a scripting language linked to FreeSWITCH. You can learn about this in *Chapter 7*.

Putting it all together

The time at which FreeSWITCH actually processes all the conditions, actions, and contexts you've specified is during the ROUTE phase. Every call goes through the ROUTE state. The routing state is when FreeSWITCH passes control of the call to the Dialplan module in use and the previous three concepts are put into action to develop a list of actions.

The process generally looks like this:

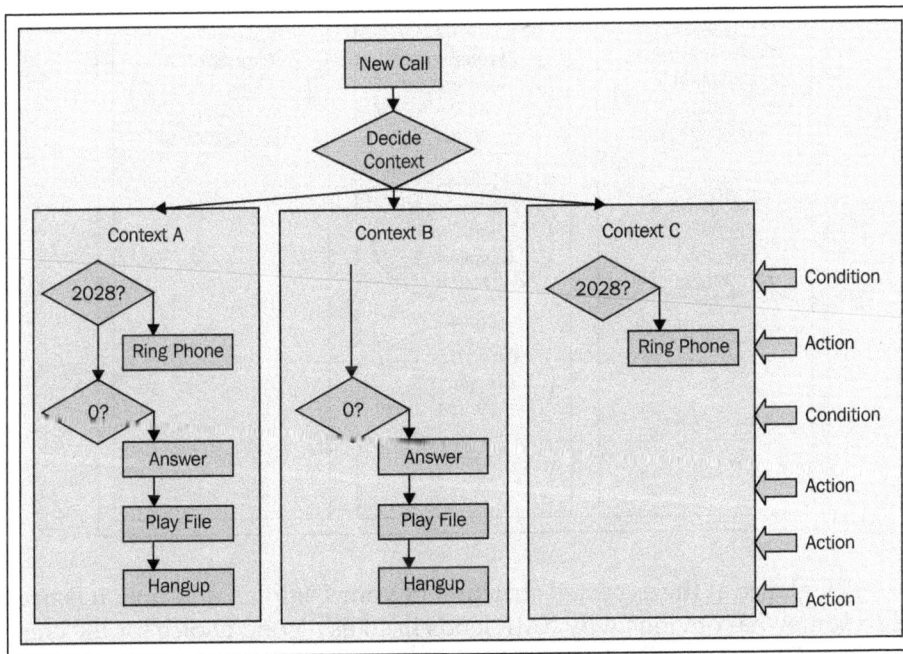

A list of resulting actions is finally returned to FreeSWITCH, such as:

- EXECUTE answer
- EXECUTE play `file.wav`
- EXECUTE hangup

XML Dialplan module review

As we discussed in *Chapter 5*, the XML Dialplan module is the most popular way to configure FreeSWITCH. At the time of writing this book it is also the most robust. It supports contexts which contain lists of extensions, with each extension containing one or more conditions, and each condition containing a list of actions to execute. Let's review a few concepts to make sure that you are fully comfortable with them.

The searching and processing of Dialplan entries is based on an expected layout that looks something like a multi-dimensional tree.

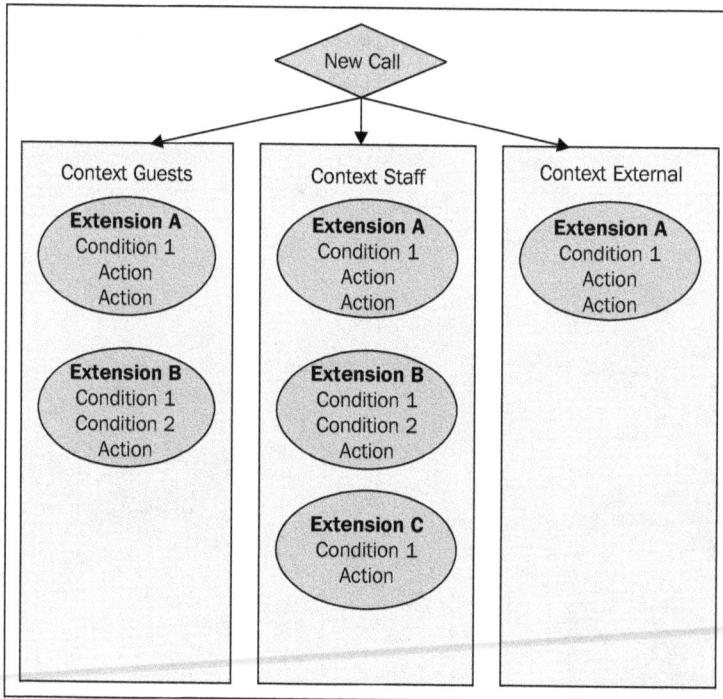

After a quick glance at the expected structure of your Dialplan and how it is used, it should be somewhat obvious why XML lends itself as a good choice for the creation of a Dialplan. The nesting attributes of XML are a perfect fit for the scenario shown. FreeSWITCH relies on a tree of configuration options in a Dialplan, and XML is naturally a limitless tree-like structure that allows for embedding values within each leaf on the tree. In addition, you can add custom tags and attributes at any time—even ones that are ignored by FreeSWITCH, but are useful for your own software when reading/writing to XML. It is a great match.

At this point, you should be well versed with contexts, extensions, conditions, and actions. Let us dig a bit deeper into the XML Dialplan to see how these different Dialplan features can behave.

Extensions

Extensions are simply XML containers that group conditions and actions together. Note that the name "extensions" can be a bit misleading. Most people are used to an extension being something you attempt to reach by dialing it, such as "2900" or "3000", but extensions in FreeSWITCH are not related to what you dial at all, they are simply named subsections of the Dialplan. For example, to reach someone by dialing 2900, you might actually be hitting an extension named "darren", like this:

```
<extension name="darren">
  <condition field="destination_number" expression="^2900$">
    <action application="bridge" data="user/darren"/>
  </condition>
</extension>
```

As you can see from this example, the extension is named "darren", but dialing 2900 is how you reach Darren, thanks to the condition.

Extensions have a variety of behaviors that can be modified. By default when FreeSWITCH finds an extension that has matching conditions, it stops looking for additional extensions. For example, if you have an extension that modifies your Caller ID, followed by an extension that actually routes the call, FreeSWITCH will never reach the second extension by default. As an example, this will fail to reach anyone:

```
<extension name="set_callerid">
  <condition field="destination_number" expression="^2900$">
    <action application="set"
            data="effective_callerid_number=4158867900"/>
  </condition>
</extension>
<extension name="darren">
  <condition field="destination_number" expression="^2900$">
    <action application="bridge" data="user/darren"/>
  </condition>
</extension>
```

In the preceding example, the second extension will never run. If you want to allow additional extensions to run after a successful match, you must use the `continue` flag. If we modify the previous example, the Dialplan now operates as expected:

```
<extension name="set_callerid" continue="true">
  <condition field="destination_number" expression="^2900$">
    <action application="set"
            data="effective_callerid_number=4158867900"/>
  </condition>
</extension>
<extension name="darren">
  <condition field="destination_number" expression="^2900$">
    <action application="bridge" data="user/darren"/>
  </condition>
</extension>
```

Note we have added `continue="true"` only to the first extension, indicating to keep processing even if that extension matches. We do not add it to the second extension because we do not want to continue processing the Dialplan after the second match (where the call is actually connected).

Conditions

Conditions allow for testing regular expressions against variables. Conditions exist within extension tags. We will discuss the different types of variables available a bit later in this chapter.

Conditions can be used to test one or more expressions. By default, and at their most basic level, one or more conditions can be specified, with a group of actions executed when all conditions evaluate to true.

As an example, let us look at the following code snippet.

```
<extension name="test_three_things">
  <condition field="network_addr" expression="^192\.168\.1\.1$"/>
  <condition field="destination_number" expression="^2900$">
    <action application="playback" data="i-know-you.wav"/>
  </condition>
</extension>
```

In this example, there are two conditions listed. Note carefully the `/>` at the end of the first XML tag. While there are no actions contained within the first condition, it is still tested and, if it fails, the entire extension is skipped. However, if both conditions pass, meaning the caller is dialing 2900 and their network IP address is 192.168.1.1, then the actions will run. This effectively creates AND logic between the two conditions — both must match before the playback action is specified.

Why does this work? The secret is in the `break` flag. Every condition statement has a `break` flag associated with it that determines what should happen if a particular evaluation method fails. The default behavior for the `break` flag is "on-false", meaning that we break out of, or stop processing conditions and extensions as soon as we encounter a false or negative result during evaluation.

You can set the `break` parameter to one of four values:

- `on-false` — stop searching after the first unsuccessful match. (default behavior)
- `on-true` — stop searching conditions after the first successful match
- `always` — stop at this condition regardless of a match or non-match
- `never` — continue searching regardless of a match or non-match

You can even create a pseudo if/then/else processing section using conditions. Let us examine the use of one of these attributes further: the `never` flag.

Let's say you want to create an extension that processes calls only from a particular IP address and checks if the user dialed *72 or *73. You could do this as two separate extensions, as follows:

```
<extension name="extension_72">
  <condition field="network_addr" expression="^192\.168\.1\.1$"/>
  <condition field="destination_number" expression="^\*72$">
    action application="playback" data="forward-on.wav"/>
  </condition>
</extension>
<extension name="extension_73">
  <condition field="network_addr" expression="^192\.168\.1\.1$"/>
  <condition field="destination_number" expression="^\*73$">
    <action application="playback" data="forward-off.wav"/>
  </condition>
</extension>
```

You could also use the power of the `break` flag to consolidate this into a single extension, as follows:

```
<extension name="extension_72_or_73">
  <condition field="network_addr" expression="^192\.168\.1\.1$"/>
  <condition field="destination_number" expression="^\*72$"
          break="on-true">
    <action application="playback" data="forward-on.wav"/>
  </condition>
  <condition field="destination_number" expression="^\*73$">
    <action application="playback" data="forward-off.wav"/>
  </condition>
</extension>
```

As you can see, by adding the `break="on-true"` to the first condition, we stop processing *only* when the condition evaluates to `true`. Otherwise, we continue processing. Think of this as an if/then/elseif statement, if the first condition matches, run it and stop processing, otherwise run the second condition if it matches.

As another example, consider the concept of using an if/then followed by another if/then. You could simulate this logic by using the `break="never"` flag. While actions inside failing conditions will not be added to the list of execution steps, the subsequent conditions will still be processed. Consider the example where we want to check two different network parameters in the same extension block:

```
<extension name="decide_routing">
  <condition field="network_addr" expression="192\.168\.1\.1$"/
          break="never">
    <action application="set" data="inhouse=true"/>
  </condition>
  <condition field="source" expression="PortAudio"/>
    <action application="set" data="portaudio=true"/>
  </condition>
</extension>
```

The preceding XML would test to see if a user is calling from 192.168.1.1 and set a variable if yes. It would continue, in all cases, to the second condition as well and test whether the user was using `portaudio` or not, and set a variable if true. This represents an effective if/then followed by another if/then.

A condition must exist inside every extension tag, even if you intend for the condition to, always, be true. The following code snippet is not valid:

```
<extension name="set_callerid">
  <action application="set"
          data="effective_callerid_number=4158867900"/>
</extension>
```

No condition exists, so this extension will be ignored and the actions will never be run.

Conditions cannot be nested. The following XML is not valid:

```
<extension name="InvalidExtension">
  <condition field="testfield" expression="true">
    <condition field="testfield2" expression="false">
      ...
    </condition>
  </condition>
</extension>
```

Special condition variables

While most conditions you will encounter utilize variables and expressions, some conditions can be written to utilize special condition variables in order to make processing simpler and more flexible.

The following variables are available for use as attributes in your XML condition tags:

- `context`: The current Dialplan context
- `rdnis`: Redirected Number, the directory number to which the call was last presented
- `destination_number`: Called number, the number this call is trying to reach
- `Dialplan`: Name of the Dialplan module in use (that is XML, YAML)
- `caller_id_name`: Name of the caller, if available
- `caller_id_number`: Number of the party who called, if available
- `ani`: Automatic Number Identification of the calling party
- `aniii`: The type of device placing the call, if available (that is payphone)
- `uuid`: Unique identifier of the current call
- `source`: Name of the FreeSWITCH module that received the call (for example, `PortAudio`)
- `chan_name`: Name of the current channel (Example: PortAudio/1234)
- `network_addr`: IP address of the signaling source for a call
- `year`: Calendar year, 0-9999
- `yday`: Day of year, 1-366
- `mon`: Month, 1-12 (Jan = 1, for example.)
- `mday`: Day of month, 1-31
- `week`: Week of year, 1-53
- `mweek`: Week of month, 1-6
- `wday`: Day of week, 1-7 (Sun = 1, Mon = 2, for example.)
- `hour`: Hour, 0-23
- `minute`: Minute (of the hour), 0-59
- `minute-of-day`: Minute of the day, (1-1440) (midnight = 1, 1am = 60, noon = 720, for example.)

These condition variables can be used like this:

```
<extension name="holiday_example" continue="true">
  <condition mday="1" mon="1">
    <action application="set" data="open=false"/>
  </condition>
</extension>
```

This example would set a variable named open to false on New Year's Day. Note the condition line, which utilizes the mday and mon condition variables.

Inline execution

The original design of FreeSWITCH was to forbid actions from occurring during the routing/Dialplan phase. This had the intended side effect of discouraging people from evaluating and manipulating variables and call flow from within the Dialplan itself, leaving that for the various embedded scripting languages FreeSWITCH plugs into. The theory was simple—rather than design a possibly obscure and limiting set of commands that can be used within the Dialplan to evaluate variables and create logic, FreeSWITCH would instead link to various scripting languages that could be executed via the Dialplan and complex logic could be performed from there. This not only expands the possibilities of what can be performed, it also avoids having to train people on the ins and outs of the XML processing system.

As FreeSWITCH evolved, however, more and more people desired the ability to handle call flow processing in the native XML Dialplan language. One of the most basic features that was noticeably absent during Dialplan routing was the ability to set, and later test (and possibly override) a variable. After some amount of nagging to the core developers, the inline flag was added to XML Dialplan processing.

The inline flag allows for some (but not all) commands to be executed *during* the Dialplan phase, breaking many of the rules previously stated. While its use is discouraged, it is sometimes necessary to achieve additional functionality or just make code more naturally readable.

As an example of why we need inline execution, let us look at the following code snippet:

```
<extension name="check_for_user" continue="true">
  <condition field="${callerid}" expression="2035551212">
    <action application="set" data="user=yes"/>
  </condition>
</extension>
<extension name="route_users_only">
  <condition field="${user}" expression="yes">
```

```xml
      <action application="answer" />
      <action application="playback" data="tada.wav" />
      <action application="hangup" />
    </condition>
  </extension>
```

The preceding code snippet defines two extensions that rely on each other — the first extension is supposed to set a variable named "user" to "yes" if someone is calling from 203-555-1212, and the second snippet is supposed to route all calls with the user variable set to a message playing `tada.wav`. The snippet does not work this way, though. Let us examine why not.

Recall that conditions are evaluated first before any action is ever executed. In the previous example, `set` is an action. Therefore, it will not run until after all conditions are evaluated. This means that the condition that looks at the variable `${user}` will always fail, because the code that sets that variable has yet to run. Hence the need for inline processing.

If the XML action is changed to read:

```xml
<action application="set" data="user=yes" inline="true"/>
```

The XML Dialplan processor will actually execute the `set` command as soon as it is encountered. Now the XML snippet works as expected.

To avoid abuse of this feature, and for various other technical reasons, the `inline` flag is only available to applications that run quickly and get or set some variable(s). Inline functions must also not access or modify the state of the current session.

The list of actions available for inline processing includes:

- `check_acl`: Check Access Control Lists
- `eval` : Execute an internal API or simply log some text to the console
- `event`: Fire arbitrary events
- `export`: Set a variable on the channel that will survive on B legs/transfers
- `log`: Create a log entry manually
- `presence` – Sends PRESENCE_IN and PRESENCE_OUT events
- `set` – Set a variable on the channel
- `set_global`: Set a global variable
- `set_profile_var`: Set the users profile we want to use
- `set_user`: Set the current user and add all their channel variables to the active leg

- `sleep`: Pause processing
- `unset`: Unset a variable
- `verbose_events`: Be verbose on events being sent
- `cidlookup`: Sets the `caller_id_name` field via CNAM lookups
- `curl`: make an http request and receive the response
- `easyroute`: database-driven DID routing engine
- `enum`: Perform `enum` lookups or related services
- `lcr`: Least cost routing decisions
- `nibblebill`: Bill accounts on a per-minute basis
- `odbc_query`: Perform manual ODBC queries

The details on each of these commands are documented on the FreeSWITCH Wiki.

Actions and anti-actions

Another available call control mechanism is the `action` and `anti-action` tags. Unlike conditions, these tags allow you to failover to an alternate set of actions if a `condition` fails. This is another version of if/then/else, but can be easier to read and manage, especially when trying to queue multiple actions within the same `condition`.

Let us take an example to see how this works:

```
<condition field="${inhouse}" expression="true">
  <action application="log" data="This is an in-house call"/>
  <anti-action application="log" data="Not in-house call"/>
</condition>
```

The preceding example would output "This is an in-house call" to the log if the variable `${inhouse}` is set to "true," otherwise it would output "Not in-house call" to the log. This is much easier to read than splitting the if/then/else logic into two separate `condition` statements.

Pitfalls to avoid

There are two major places where the Dialplan design can confuse new users of FreeSWITCH—especially those with a background using Asterisk. The first is in understanding how variables are handled during conditional processing, and the second is in interpreting the logs.

Keeping in mind that the Dialplan is a hunting phase of a module prior to any commands actually executing, let us again look at the example given as shown that does *not* work as intended. This time around, we will do what many people try to do when debugging their XML – we will add the info application to the XML to obtain a printout on the console of what variables are set on a channel.

```
<extension name="check_for_user" continue="true">
  <condition field="${callerid}" expression="2035551212">
    <action application="set" data="user=yes"/>
    <action application="info"/>
  </condition>
</extension>
<extension name="route_users_only">
  <condition field="${user}" expression="yes">
    <action application="answer" />
    <action application="playback" data="tada.wav" />
    <action application="hangup" />
  </condition>
</extension>
```

When this code snippet runs, the info command will output all variables set on the channel to the screen, and the user will see that the variable "user" is in fact set to "yes." Yet the following condition, which tests the variable user, did not run. Many users will think FreeSWITCH is broken, but in fact, they are misreading the output they are seeing. After careful examination, you will note in your logs that the set command executed after all the conditions were tested, and the info application ran subsequently, showing that the variable had been set, but the conditional testing had been completed long back. This can lead to many hours of frustration, if you are not careful when reading the logs.

The log will show whether or not individual Dialplan entries were matched, which can confuse people into thinking those sections of the Dialplan were actually executed. In fact, you must scroll lower down in the log to discover what actions were actually taken. Get used to looking for the EXECUTE log statements and paying more attention to those to see what is actually happening. If items are not being executed as expected, then your conditions are not set correctly.

XML Dialplan commands

While we would love to go through all the available Dialplan commands, the list far exceeds the space we have for this chapter. Therefore, we will limit our discussion of available Dialplan commands to three areas—Dialplan tools, Sofia connectivity, and general API commands. These Dialplan commands are provided by `mod_dptools`, `mod_sofia`, and `mod_commands` respectively.

- `mod_dptools`: `mod_dptools` is a collection of Dialplan management tools. There are many, many commands available from within the Dialplan. You have already learned how basic commands like `answer`, `hangup`, `bridge`, and `set` work. Let us go over a few of the more advanced commands.

- `bind_meta_app`: `bind_meta_app` binds an application to the specified call leg(s). During a bridged call, the DTMF sequence on the bound call leg will trigger the execution of the application. The call leg that is not bound will not hear the DTMF sequence being dialed. You can only bind a single digit, and the binding is always proceeded with a *.

  As an example, let us say you want to allow *2 to begin a call recording. When the calling party presses *2, the recording would begin. In this case, you could utilize the following Dialplan snippet. Notice the `bind_meta_app` highlighted:

```
<action application="bind_meta_app" data="2 a s record_session::
recording.wav"/>
```

```
<action application="bridge"
        data="sofia/sipprovider/+14158867900">
```

  Pressing *2 on the calling end (the A leg, which is the second parameter) would invoke call recording on the same leg (the third parameter s indicates same leg).

  Notice the format of the `bind_meta_app` parameters:

```
<action application="bind_meta_app" data="KEY LISTEN_TO RESPOND_ON
                                    APPLICATION[::PARAMETERS]"/>
```

  ○ `KEY` = The key to listen for.

  ○ `LISTEN_TO` = Which call leg to listen for the keypress on. Acceptable parameters are a, b, or ab.

  ○ `RESPOND_ON` = Which call leg to respond to the keypress on. For example, when playing a file as the response command, which leg will hear the playback. Acceptable parameters are s for same leg as the key was pressed on, or o for the opposite leg.

- ○   APPLICATION = What application to run.

- ○   PARAMETERS = Parameters to pass to the application. Note that you separate applications and parameters using double colons (APPLICATION::PARAMS).

> Once bound to a call leg, the application binding will persist for the lifetime of the call leg.

- **eavesdrop**: The eavesdrop command allows you to listen in on other channels. As an example, the following Dialplan command would allow you eavesdrop on a UUID placed in $1.

```
<action application="eavesdrop" data="$1"/>
```

You can replace $1 with any UUID you wish, or retrieve the UUID from the database, like this:

```
<action application="eavesdrop" data="${db(select/spymap/
${extension})}"/>
```

In this example, the variable extension is utilized, which can be set prior in the Dialplan, and used as a search parameter to look into the database for a UUID associated with an extension. In this scenario, if you recorded the extension number and UUID of all active calls in the database under the table spymap, you could later retrieve that information for eavesdropping here.

- **execute_extension**: You can execute an extension from within another extension with this Dialplan application. The purpose would be to route a call temporarily to another extension, then return back to the same place we left. This is similar to the loopback function found in other switches.

execute_extension executes an extension like a macro, and then returns. This is different from transfer, which goes to the new extension instantly and does not return. execute_extension will keep the current scope and build a one-time extension, execute it, and return right back to where it was called.

```
<action application="execute_extension" data="destination_number
[Dialplan] [context]"/>
```

If you do not specify the Dialplan and context, it defaults to the current one.

> Use `execute_extension` only when you need to execute a command and return to Dialplan processing where you left off. When you do not need to do anything else, use the `transfer` application. If you are a programmer, then this analogy is fitting: `execute_extension` is like `gosub` whereas `transfer` is like `goto`.

- `send_display`: You can send a customized info packet to a phone, which (on some models of phones) will display the message on the phones display.

  An example of usage:

  ```
  <action application="send_display" data="Support Call"/>
  ```

  This could be used to display a department or message on the phone that indicates who the call is for, or what department was called initially.

- **Other Dialplan commands**: There are many more commands available for review on the FreeSWITCH wiki at: `http://wiki.freeswitch.org/wiki/Mod_dptools`.

- `mod_sofia`: `mod_sofia` is generally responsible for all things SIP. This includes acting as an endpoint for sending and receiving SIP calls and managing SIP registrations and contact information. Various commands exist within `mod_sofia` that help manage not only initiation and receiving of calls, but also the management and deconstruction of endpoint information such as a device's registered IP address and whether the device is behind NAT.

  While Sofia itself does not provide applications that you utilize from the Dialplan directly, it is used in so many command parameters that it is important to go through it more specifically here.

  Sofia is generally accessed when bridging SIP calls. **Bridging** refers to connecting an A leg to a newly initiated B leg. When bridging calls, the general format is as follows:

  ```
  <action application="bridge"
          data="sofia/profile/endpoint [@domain] ">
  ```

  Let us analyze the data portion of this command.

As the `bridge` command is a general purpose command that does not exclusively bridge SIP calls, you must specify the `sofia/` parameter first to indicate you are working with a SIP call. Following the `sofia/` parameter, you must specify what gateway or SIP profile is to be used for connecting the call. If you specify a gateway that you have configured in your SIP configuration, the domain name of the receiving server is already known and does not need to be added at the end of the dial string (that is you can leave off `[@domain]`). If you specify a profile name as the second parameter, you are simply telling Sofia, which IP address, port, and parameters to utilize when connecting the call. In this case, you must specify a domain or IP address at the end of your Sofia `bridge` command. Finally, the endpoint parameter specifies the username to send to the remote system. This is often a DID or extension number, so that the remote end knows what party on their system to connect to.

Here are some examples of different ways you might bridge a call. In the following examples, let us assume we have a service provider gateway named `supersip` and a Sofia profile named `external`.

```
<action application="bridge" data="sofia/supersip/+14158867900">
```

This would bridge a caller to (415) 886-7900 using the `supersip` provider information.

```
<action application="bridge" data="sofia/external/+14158867900@
sip.supersip.com">
```

This would bridge a caller to (415) 886-7900 using the `supersip` provider, except in this case we have explicitly specified that we wish to call via the profile `external` (using whatever IP address and port are contained within that profile) and that we are routing the call via a server at `sip.supersip.com`.

```
<action application="bridge" data="sofia/external/someuser@
otheroffice.com:5080">
```

This would bridge a caller to the user `someuser` located on the server `otheroffice.com` via port 5080. It is good to note that nothing is stopping you from bridging calls between FreeSWITCH, Asterisk or other types of servers via this method — including other servers on your local network. You have complete control of the username, server, port, and routing of a call via this command when used in this way.

Now consider a more complex example. Sofia accepts parameters at the end of a dial string to specify advanced options on how a call should behave. As an example, let us say we want to send a call using TCP instead of the default UDP transport protocol. Adding a semi-colon at the end of a dial string allows you to attach Sofia options at the end of the dial-string. In this case, we want to add the option `transport=tcp` to the end of a dial-string. It can be done like this:

```
<action application="bridge" data="sofia/external/+14158867900@
sip.supersip.com;transport=tcp">
```

The purpose and importance of reviewing these examples is to expose the power that is contained within the Sofia system that is accessible via the Dialplan. Commands are not limited to basic bridging options based on defined profiles—you can connect calls to anywhere you need to via creative use of variables, options, and Dialplan functions.

- `mod_commands`: `mod_commands` provides commands on the CLI to the administrator of the system. Sometimes, those commands may be useful within FreeSWITCH call processing too. While generally CLI commands differ from applications called from the Dialplan, you can explicitly run any CLI command you wish by wrapping the command into an evaluation string.

As an example, the CLI command `hupall(NORMAL_CLEARING)` normally resets (hangs up on) all active calls and terminates them with the reason NORMAL_CLEARING. This command is normally run only from the command line. If you wanted it to be available via the Dialplan when dialing *999*, you could define an extension like this:

```
<extension name="Make API call from Dialplan">
  <condition field="destination_number" expression="^(999)$">
    <action application="set" data="api_result=${hupall(normal_
clearing)}"/>
  </condition>
</extension>
```

Note the highlighted line. We have wrapped the CLI command `hupall` in an expression as `${hupall(normal_clearing)}` and placed it within an extension. In addition, the results of the command will be stored in the variable `api_result`, since we placed the expression in the set command.

While this example is not very practical, the point of the exercise is to show that any CLI command can be executed from the Dialplan and its results utilized.

For a complete list of CLI commands, review the FreeSWITCH wiki at `http://wiki.freeswitch.org/wiki/Mod_commands`.

Hunting versus executing

While it has been mentioned previously, the concept of hunting versus executing really deserves a closer look. It is important to understand that the Dialplan processor is different from the actual execution of the Dialplan. Furthermore, you can tweak this behavior to blur the line between this distinction to gain extra power, but at the expense of some added complexity.

To understand hunting versus executing you must first understand that FreeSWITCH breaks calls up into various states for processing. Every call in FreeSWITCH goes through these states – beginning a new channel, routing of the call, executing actions on the call, ending the call, reporting on the call, and finally killing the channel and all associated memory. The two specific states of the call relevant to this chapter are ROUTE and EXECUTE. Route refers to the stage when FreeSWITCH is looking for Dialplan actions to take based on the information about a call and your loaded Dialplan module. The ROUTE state is where a list of actions to take should be collected. EXECUTE is the state in which each Dialplan application is executed in succession.

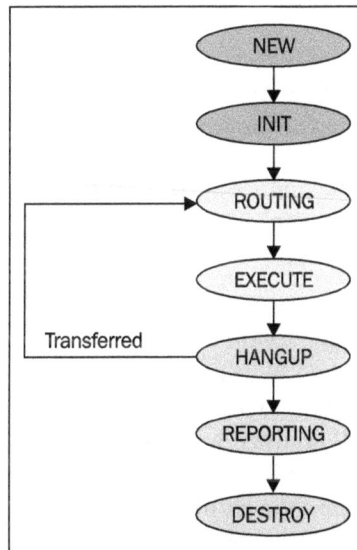

When calls hit the ROUTE state, the relevant Dialplan module is invoked. In this example we will look at the XML Dialplan processor and its output during a test call.

Say we have the following definition in our XML Dialplan — three phone numbers reachable via context external:

```
<context name="external">
    <extension name="number_A">
            <condition field="destination_number"
expression="^4158867997">
                    <action application="answer" />
                    <action application="playback" data="welcome-to-the-
party.wav" />
                    <action application="hangup" />
            </condition>
    </extension>
    <extension name="number_B">
            <condition field="destination_number"
expression="^4158867998">
                    <action application="answer" />
                    <action application="playback" data="not-in-service.
wav" />
                    <action application="hangup" />
            </condition>
    </extension>
    <extension name="number_C">
            <condition field="destination_number"
expression="^4158867999">
                    <action application="answer" />
                    <action application="playback" data="test-msg.wav" />
                    <action application="hangup" />
            </condition>
    </extension>
</context>
```

This XML Dialplan snippet results in a call to (415) 886-7999 being answered and a greeting being played. We will analyze what actually happens behind the scenes to make this happen by looking at an incoming caller who is trying to actually reach this number. The full log of someone trying to reach this number looks like this:

```
New Channel sofia/sipinterface_1/sip1@127.0.0.1 [f560901c-f5dc-4208-
8bcd-31e8bf1244b9]
(sofia/sipinterface_1/sip1@127.0.0.1) Running State Change CS_NEW
(sofia/sipinterface_1/sip1@127.0.0.1) State NEW
Channel sofia/sipinterface_1/sip1@127.0.0.1 entering state
[received] [100]
    . . .
(sofia/sipinterface_1/sip1@127.0.0.1) State Change CS_NEW -> CS_INIT
Send signal sofia/sipinterface_1/sip1@127.0.0.1 [BREAK]
```

```
(sofia/sipinterface_1/sip1@127.0.0.1) Running State Change CS_INIT
(sofia/sipinterface_1/sip1@127.0.0.1) State INIT
sofia/sipinterface_1/sip1@127.0.0.1 SOFIA INIT
(sofia/sipinterface_1/sip1@127.0.0.1) State Change CS_INIT -> CS_
ROUTING
Send signal sofia/sipinterface_1/sip1@127.0.0.1 [BREAK]
(sofia/sipinterface_1/sip1@127.0.0.1) State INIT going to sleep
(sofia/sipinterface_1/sip1@127.0.0.1) Running State Change CS_ROUTING
(sofia/sipinterface_1/sip1@127.0.0.1) State ROUTING
sofia/sipinterface_1/sip1@127.0.0.1 SOFIA ROUTING
sofia/sipinterface_1/sip1@127.0.0.1 Standard ROUTING
Processing Darren->4158867999 in context external
Dialplan: sofia/sipinterface_1/sip1@127.0.0.1 parsing [external-
>number_A] continue=false
Dialplan: sofia/sipinterface_1/sip1@127.0.0.1 Regex (FAIL) [number_A]
destination_number(4158867999) =~ /^4158867997/ break=on-false
Dialplan: sofia/sipinterface_1/sip1@127.0.0.1 parsing [external-
>number_B] continue=false
Dialplan: sofia/sipinterface_1/sip1@127.0.0.1 Regex (FAIL) [number_B]
destination_number(4158867999) =~ /^4158867998/ break=on-false
Dialplan: sofia/sipinterface_1/sip1@127.0.0.1 parsing [external-
>number_C] continue=false
Dialplan: sofia/sipinterface_1/sip1@127.0.0.1 Regex (PASS) [number_C]
destination_number(4158867999) =~ /^4158867999/ break=on-false
Dialplan: sofia/sipinterface_1/sip1@127.0.0.1 Action answer()
Dialplan: sofia/sipinterface_1/sip1@127.0.0.1 Action playback(test-
msg.wav)
Dialplan: sofia/sipinterface_1/sip1@127.0.0.1 Action hangup()
(sofia/sipinterface_1/sip1@127.0.0.1) State Change CS_ROUTING -> CS_
EXECUTE
Send signal sofia/sipinterface_1/sip1@127.0.0.1 [BREAK]
(sofia/sipinterface_1/sip1@127.0.0.1) State ROUTING going to sleep
(sofia/sipinterface_1/sip1@127.0.0.1) Running State Change CS_EXECUTE
(sofia/sipinterface_1/sip1@127.0.0.1) State EXECUTE
sofia/sipinterface_1/sip1@127.0.0.1 SOFIA EXECUTE
sofia/sipinterface_1/sip1@127.0.0.1 Standard EXECUTE
EXECUTE sofia/sipinterface_1/sip1@127.0.0.1 answer()
sofia/sipinterface_1/sip1@127.0.0.1 receive message [ANSWER]
  ...
Channel [sofia/sipinterface_1/sip1@127.0.0.1] has been answered
sofia/sipinterface_1/sip1@127.0.0.1 receive message [AUDIO_SYNC]
EXECUTE sofia/sipinterface_1/sip1@127.0.0.1 playback(test-msg.wav)
EXECUTE sofia/sipinterface_1/sip1@127.0.0.1 hangup()
Channel sofia/sipinterface_1/sip1@127.0.0.1 entering state
[completed] [200]
```

```
Hangup sofia/sipinterface_1/sip1@127.0.0.1 [CS_EXECUTE] [NORMAL_
CLEARING]
Send signal sofia/sipinterface_1/sip1@127.0.0.1 [KILL]
Send signal sofia/sipinterface_1/sip1@127.0.0.1 [BREAK]
(sofia/sipinterface_1/sip1@127.0.0.1) State EXECUTE going to sleep
   ...
```

A little overwhelming at first, so let us take this log apart piece by piece.

In this log snippet, the caller trying to reach our test number (415-886-7999) is first setup and then proceeds to the ROUTE state of the call. Note that the call was received and entered a state of ROUTE (first highlight). Our Dialplan is configured to route inbound calls to the XML modules context named "external" and search through various conditions looking for a match. You can see that we are in context external by reviewing the highlighted log entry:

```
(sofia/sipinterface_1/sip1@127.0.0.1) Running State Change CS_ROUTING
(sofia/sipinterface_1/sip1@127.0.0.1) State ROUTING
sofia/sipinterface_1/sip1@127.0.0.1 SOFIA ROUTING
sofia/sipinterface_1/sip1@127.0.0.1 Standard ROUTING
Processing Darren->4158867999 in context external
```

After we are in context external, the Dialplan module checks to see if the caller dialed one of the three specific numbers defined earlier in our XML Dialplan. Note the field being compared appears in parenthesis on the left and the field we are trying to match against is on the right. The result appears at the end – either FAIL or PASS.

```
Dialplan: sofia/sipinterface_1/sip1@127.0.0.1 parsing [external-
>number_A] continue=false
Dialplan: sofia/sipinterface_1/sip1@127.0.0.1 Regex (FAIL) [number_A]
destination_number(4158867999) =~ /^4158867997/ break=on-false
Dialplan: sofia/sipinterface_1/sip1@127.0.0.1 parsing [external-
>number_B] continue=false
Dialplan: sofia/sipinterface_1/sip1@127.0.0.1 Regex (FAIL) [number_B]
destination_number(4158867999) =~ /^4158867998/ break=on-false
Dialplan: sofia/sipinterface_1/sip1@127.0.0.1 parsing [external-
>number_C] continue=false
Dialplan: sofia/sipinterface_1/sip1@127.0.0.1 Regex (PASS) [number_C]
destination_number(4158867999) =~ /^4158867999/ break=on-false
Dialplan: sofia/sipinterface_1/sip1@127.0.0.1 Action answer()
Dialplan: sofia/sipinterface_1/sip1@127.0.0.1 Action playback(test-
msg.wav)
Dialplan: sofia/sipinterface_1/sip1@127.0.0.1 Action hangup()
```

```
(sofia/sipinterface_1/sip1@127.0.0.1) State Change CS_ROUTING -> CS_
EXECUTE
Send signal sofia/sipinterface_1/sip1@127.0.0.1 [BREAK]
(sofia/sipinterface_1/sip1@127.0.0.1) State ROUTING going to sleep
```

The XML Dialplan module is comparing the number dialed with the numbers the system knows about until it finds a match. Note the (FAIL) next to each comparison until 4158867999, where the result of the condition matching is (PASS). While you do not see any actions being taken at that point, the Dialplan module saves the actions to perform in order to reach 4158867999 in the lines that follow the (PASS) entry. These lines are prefaced with Action toward the end of the log lines. They are being queued and saved for later.

Now the call moves on to the EXECUTE phase, as indicated by the following highlighted log line:

```
(sofia/sipinterface_1/sip1@127.0.0.1) Running State Change CS_EXECUTE
(sofia/sipinterface_1/sip1@127.0.0.1) State EXECUTE
sofia/sipinterface_1/sip1@127.0.0.1 SOFIA EXECUTE
sofia/sipinterface_1/sip1@127.0.0.1 Standard EXECUTE
```

In the execute phase each action queued during the Dialplan processing phase is executed, in order. You can see both the action as it was requested, unparsed, followed by the log entries of the action actually executing, including any log entries that are output by the action that was executed.

```
EXECUTE sofia/sipinterface_1/sip1@127.0.0.1 answer()
sofia/sipinterface_1/sip1@127.0.0.1 receive message [ANSWER]
    . . .
Channel [sofia/sipinterface_1/sip1@127.0.0.1] has been answered
sofia/sipinterface_1/sip1@127.0.0.1 receive message [AUDIO_SYNC]
EXECUTE sofia/sipinterface_1/sip1@127.0.0.1 playback(test-msg.wav)
EXECUTE sofia/sipinterface_1/sip1@127.0.0.1 hangup()
Channel sofia/sipinterface_1/sip1@127.0.0.1 entering state
[completed] [200]
Hangup sofia/sipinterface_1/sip1@127.0.0.1 [CS_EXECUTE] [NORMAL_
CLEARING]
Send signal sofia/sipinterface_1/sip1@127.0.0.1 [KILL]
Send signal sofia/sipinterface_1/sip1@127.0.0.1 [BREAK]
(sofia/sipinterface_1/sip1@127.0.0.1) State EXECUTE going to sleep
```

Note as shown how the executed actions are interleaved with the results of each action. Anytime you see EXECUTE at the beginning of a log line, you know that the action was queued from the Dialplan phase and is now actually occurring in real-time. In this example, compare the EXECUTE statements to the XML we created in the example at the beginning of the section:

```
<extension name="number_C">
        <condition field="destination_number"
expression="^4158867999">
                <action application="answer" />
                <action application="playback" data="test-msg.wav" />
                <action application="hangup" />
        </condition>
</extension>
```

As you can see, each application was run in the EXECUTE phase as shown, in the same order as specified in the XML.

Utilizing variables

Up to this point we have considered the basic use of channel variables. FreeSWITCH has more advanced ways of using variables, including global variables. Let's round out our understanding of variables by looking at some of these.

Testing variables with regular expressions

We have already discussed the purpose and basic use of the condition XML tag. Now we will discuss the different elements you can actually test to help make decisions about call handling.

FreeSWITCH offers three general categories of variables that you can test – caller profile fields, channel variables, and global variables. In addition, you can utilize macros and API functions and utilize their output in your conditions as well. We will review each of these in detail.

Caller profile fields

Caller profile fields are variables that are retrieved when a caller is authenticated. The variables are set within the directory and can include things like the caller's area code, codec preferences, and so on. You can utilize caller profile fields within conditions when processing the Dialplan, like this:

```
<condition field="caller_profile_field">
```

The variables get set within your directory, like this:

```
<user id="bob">
    <variables>
          <variable name="caller_profile_field" value="1234"/>
    </variables>
</user>
```

In this example, when bob authenticates or is set as the current caller profile, all the variables contained within his profile are accessible via the as shown listed method for conditional testing.

The user directory was covered in detail in Chapter 4.

Channel variables

Every channel in FreeSWITCH can have a number of variables associated with it to track state, settings, and other information about a call. Channel variables are utilized in the format:

```
${variable}
```

Channel variables may be set in the Dialplan, application, or directory. They affect progress or settings for the call. They can be used almost anywhere variable processing is invoked, such as in Dialplan conditions, application commands and so on.

```
<condition field="${channel_variable}">
```

Channel variables are perhaps the most utilized and most important aspect of processing a call within FreeSWITCH. There are many, many channel variables available on any single call and even more which can be set to modify the behavior of a call. You can review the complete list of channel variables available online at `http://wiki.freeswitch.org/wiki/Channel_Variables`.

Channel variables and call setup

You can utilize channel variables when setting up calls or legs of a call, such as when originating a new call with the `originate` command or when bridging an A leg of a call to a B leg via the `bridge` command. In these instances there are two ways to set channel variables – curly brackets {} and square brackets []. Each work differently and are useful when bridging or originating a call to multiple parties at the same time.

Curly brackets are used "globally" for the duration of a call. Take the following example where we are bridging a call to Darren's cell phone, 203-829-3150. We only want to ring the phone for 20 seconds, to avoid hitting voicemail.

```
<application action="bridge" data="{call_timeout=20}sofia/my_
provider/2038293150">
```

The variable in brackets is utilized on the newly setup channel, `sofia/my_ provider/2038293150`.

Now, let's add in calling Darren's office phone. We want the office phone to ring for 30 seconds, but still leave the cell phone at 20 seconds. We can achieve this with square brackets before each leg of the bridge, like this:

```
<application action="bridge" data="[call_timeout=20]sofia/my_provider/
2038293150,[call_timeout=30]sofia/my_provider/4158867901">
```

By placing the variables in square brackets, they apply to each leg of the specific call.

> Curly braces are only valid at the very beginning of a dial string.

You can also "clobber" variables set with curly braces by using square brackets later. You must set a flag to make this work, named `local_var_clobber`. We can recreate the exact same example just specified by setting the "default" timeout to 30 for all legs and overriding the timeout to 20 seconds only for the cell phone, like this:

```
<application action="bridge" data="{local_var_clobber=true,call_
timeout=30}[call_timeout=20]sofia/my_provider/2038293150,sofia/my_
provider/4158867901">
```

Setting multiple variables can be accomplished by comma-delimiting. For example, you can specify:

```
{call_timeout=20,sip_secure_media=true}
```

to specify two variables for all channels, or:

```
[call_timeout=20,sip_secure_media=true]
```

for individual channels.

Global variables

When FreeSWITCH first starts up, it loads your entire XML configuration into memory. During this process, it looks for the following code:

```
<X-PRE-PROCESS cmd="set" data="domain=127.0.0.1"/>
```

This code defines global variables.

Global variables are expanded during this initial load process when FreeSWITCH starts up. The X-PRE-PROCESS tag designates a command to be processed during the actual XML load. When you set a variable during this phase, that variable is considered global automatically and becomes accessible throughout the application as $${variable} elsewhere in the XML.

Note also that when you utilize $${variable} in your XML, it is also replaced during XML load-time with the variable that was set during the X-PRE-PROCESS tag processing. For example, the following XML code:

```
<X-PRE-PROCESS cmd="set" data="domain=127.0.0.1"/>
<param name="domain" value="$${domain}"/>
```

would literally be compiled and seen by FreeSWITCH as one single line:

```
<param name="domain" value="127.0.0.1"/>
```

This behavior is a feature of the XML parser – not FreeSWITCH itself. The pre-processing of global variables happens prior to the XML file being utilized by any FreeSWITCH process or event.

FreeSWITCH outputs the compiled XML file to disk. You can review this file to see what happened to your pre-processor commands and global variable declarations. It is usually located in /usr/local/freeswitch/log/freeswitch.xml.fsxml.

You can utilize global variables in your conditions, your variable and parameter declarations, pretty much anywhere, like this:

```
<condition field="$${global_variable}">
```

Dialplan functions

Dialplan functions are small pieces of functionality that run real-time when processing Dialplan conditions. They can be used to gain a little more control and flexibility when writing your condition statements.

Dialplan functions can actually be used elsewhere – not just in the Dialplan. They are also not related to XML – they can be used anywhere that a FreeSWITCH string processor is invoked. Examples of other places they may appear include external scripts that execute and set variables, `bridge` and `transfer` statements, and so on. The general format for Dialplan functions is:

```
${api_func(api_args ${var_name})}
```

where `api_func` is the name of the Dialplan function, `api_args` is the name of the arguments to pass to the function, and `${var_name}` is an optional variable name to pass to the function. The format and expected parameters for `api_args` vary depending on the function being used. Each available Dialplan function is explained as follows in more detail.

Real-time condition evaluation

You can perform conditional evaluations within a condition expression using the `cond` function.

The general format of the condition functions is:

```
${cond(<expr> ? <true val> : <false val>)}
```

An example of using the condition function:

```
${cond(5 > 3 ? true : false)}
```

This expression would return true. The allowed comparison operators are:

```
== Equality
!= Not equal
> Greater than
>= Greater than or equal to
< Less than
<= Less than or equal to
```

Note that you can compare strings with strings and numbers with numbers, but if you compare a string to a number, they will be compared as `strlen(string)` and the number.

String conditioning

You can select a portion of a variable's value, (just like a `substr` function in many programming languages) by wrapping the variable in ${var:offset:length} tags. The arguments are:

- `var` — A string variable. Can be a literal string or a variable such as ${caller_id}.
- `offset` — The location to start copying data. 0 indicates the first character.
- `length` — The number of characters to look for. Optional. If omitted, the remainder of the string is copied.

  Some examples:

  ```
  var = 1234567890
  ${var:offset:length}
  ${var:0:1}   // 1
  ${var:1}     // 234567890
  ${var:-4}    // 7890
  ${var:-4:2}  // 78
  ${var:4:2}   // 56
  ```

An example of utilizing this API call to capture the first three numbers (U.S. area code) in an outgoing caller's Caller ID, stored in a variable named ${callerid}, via the Dialplan is as follows:

```
<application name="set" data="areacode=${callerid:0:3}">
```

Using anything less than or equal to 0 as the length will return from the specified position to the end of the string.

Database queries

You can arbitrarily `insert`, `delete`, `select` and `update` values from the database. The general format for database commands is:

```
${db(select/music/${caller_id_number})}
```

Database commands can be `insert`, `select`, or `delete`, followed by the table or realm, followed by a key and a value pair.

As an example, we could program specific hold music based on a caller's Caller ID:

```
<action application="playback" data="${db(select/music/${caller_id_
number})}"/>
```

As another example, we could `insert` data into the database. In this example we `insert` the current caller's UUID into a table named `spymap`, utilizing the caller's caller ID as the record key. Someone could later retrieve the last UUID based on a specific caller ID.

```
<action application="db" data="insert/spymap/${caller_id_number}/
${uuid}"/>
```

SIP contact parameters

You can retrieve the contact string and parameters of a registered Sofia contact (and manipulate them) using the `sofia_contact` command. The general format for this command is:

```
${sofia_contact(profile/foo@bar.com)}
```

This is useful for multiple reasons. At its simplest use, it can be used to retrieve the string and detect parameters such as whether NAT was detected on the registered user, or whether the user is registered at all. As a more complex example, you can use this feature to strip the contact string for pieces you wish to utilize and then manipulate them further.

The following XML snippet will look up a user named `foo@my.server.com` and get the user's domain name or IP address and contact parameters at the time of registration from the contact string. It will strip the username from the front of the user's contact record.

```
<condition field="\${sofia_contact($user_id@\$\${forced_domain})}"
expression="^[^\@]+(.*)">
  <action application="set" data="to_domain=$1"/>
</condition>
```

After you have stripped out the username, you could replace it with a new username. This is often done when routing DIDs to a customer's PBX – you could replace the recipient's username with the DID being called, like this:

```
<condition field="\${sofia_contact($user_id@\$\${forced_domain})}"
expression="^[^\@]+(.*)">
  <action application="bridge" data="sofia/external/${DID_
number}@$1"/>
</condition>
```

In this example, if a variable was set in the `${DID_number}` field, it would be combined with the user's IP address and contact routing information. So if a user was registered as `frank@72.44.12.28`, it might be replaced in this example with `2035551212@72.44.12.28`.

Set, export, and legs

When performing a `bridge` to connect two different call legs, you may find that you have a channel variable in the originating leg (the A leg) that you wish to be available also in the B leg. Sometimes you have a value that you want only to appear in one leg or the other. The techniques presented in this section will explain how to accomplish these tasks.

Set versus export

There are two general API commands available to set and modify information about calls and the way the switch will process calls. These commands are named `set` and `export`.

The `set` command sets variables on a channel, for use during the duration of the channel. These variables can then be accessed by applications (such as CDR) or by Dialplan condition testing. You have seen the `set` command used several times in examples throughout this book.

The `export` command takes `set` a step further. It sets variables on the current channel but also saves the variable for use in any future channels created that stem from the current channel or Dialplan context. In other words, `export` sets variables on both the A leg of a call and on any future B legs that get set up.

The difference between the two commands can be subtle until you start needing to access information on B legs (transferred calls). `export` then becomes very useful for ensuring consistency in variables that may be needed in multiple legs of calls. Consider these examples:

```
<!--Variable "foo" is set on both legs -->
<action application="export" data="foo=bar"/>
<action application="bridge" data="/user/1001"/>
<!--Variable "foo" is set on b leg only -->
<action application="export" data="nolocal:foo=bar"/>
<action application="bridge" data="/user/1001"/>
```

In some cases you may want to have the variable `foo` available in both call legs. There are other times, such as when processing CDRs, when you may wish to have a particular value present in only the B leg.

Passing variables via call headers

Sometimes it is useful to add your own custom headers to outbound calls. The SIP stack is the most common place to do this.

You can add arbitrary headers to outbound SIP calls by using the same set and export commands listed as shown but prefixing the variable names with the string 'sip_h_'. For example, to add the header CallerLikesTacos=1 to a call you could add a set command prior to a bridge command, like this:

```
<action application="set" data="sip_h_X-CallerLikesTacos=1"/>
<action application="bridge" data="sofia/mydomain.com/1000@example.
com"/>
```

If you wish to add headers to a BYE request you will need to use the prefix sip_bye_h_ on the channel variable.

> While not required, you should prefix your headers with "X-" to avoid issues with interoperability with other SIP stacks. X- headers are generally seen as custom headers and are ignored in the SIP world if not recognized.

XML Dialplan cookbook

We present here a few common scenarios that you may need to refer to from time-to-time because they are relatively common. The examples presented in this section are in the mold of the tradition "cookbook" full of "recipes" for the reader to try. Feel free to use and modify these recipes in your custom Dialplans.

Match by IP address and call a number

In the example as follows, the particular extension will be selected only if the IP address of the calling endpoint is 192.168.1.1. In the second condition, the dialed number is extracted in variable $1 and put in the data of the bridge application, in order to dial out to IP address 192.168.2.2

```
<extension name="Test1">
  <condition field="network_addr" expression="^192\.168\.1\.1$"/>
  <condition field="destination_number" expression="^(\d+)$">
    <action application="bridge" data="sofia/
profilename/$1@192.168.2.2"/>
  </condition>
</extension>
```

The first condition field is terminated by a slash. The last condition field which contains the `action` and `anti-action` is terminated by a regular `</condition>` tag. Also note that the as shown example is *not* the same as as follows:

```
<extension name="Test1Wrong">
  <condition field="destination_number" expression="^(\d+)$"/>
  <condition field="network_addr" expression="^192\.168\.1\.1$">
    <action application="bridge" data="sofia/
profilename/$1@192.168.2.2"/>
  </condition>
</extension>
```

The `Test1Wrong` example will not route the call properly, because the variable `$1` will not have any value, since the destination number was matched in a different condition field.

You can also solve the `Test1Wrong` example by setting a variable in the first `condition` which you then use inside the second condition's action:

```
<extension name="Test1_2">
  <condition field="destination_number" expression="^(\d+)$">
    <action application="set" data="dialed_number=$1"/>
  </condition>
  <condition field="network_addr" expression="^192\.168\.1\.1$">
    <action application="bridge" data="sofia/profilename/${dialed_
number}@192.168.2.2"/>
  </condition>
</extension>
```

You cannot use a variable set inside an extension for further conditions/matches as the extension is evaluated when the action is called.

If you need to do different actions based on a variable set inside an extension, you need to either use `execute_extension` or transfer the call for the variable to be set.

Match IP address and Caller ID

In this example we need to match a called number beginning with the prefix 1 **and** match the incoming IP address at the same time.

```
<extension name="Test2">
  <condition field="network_addr" expression="^192\.168\.1\.1$"/>
  <condition field="destination_number" expression="^1(\d+)$">
    <action application="bridge" data="sofia/
profilename/$0@192.168.2.2"/>
  </condition>
</extension>
```

Here, although we match with the rule `1(\d+)$` we don't use the variable `$1` which would contain only the rest of the dialed number with the leading 1 stripped off. Instead, we use the variable `$0` which contains the original destination number.

Match number and strip digits

In this example we need to match a called number beginning with 00 but we also need to strip the leading digits. Assuming that FreeSWITCH receives the number `00123456789` and we need to strip the leading `00` digits, then we can use the following extension:

```
<extension name="Test3.1">
  <condition field="destination_number" expression="^00(\d+)$">
    <action application="bridge" data="sofia/
profilename/$1@192.168.2.2"/>
  </condition>
</extension>
```

On the other hand, if you anticipate receiving non-digits, or you want to match on more than just digits, use ".+" instead of "\d+" because "\d+" matches numeric digits only, whereas a ".+" will match all characters from the current position to the end of the string:

```
<extension name="Test3.2">
  <condition field="destination_number" expression="^00(.+)$">
    <action application="bridge" data="sofia/
profilename/$1@192.168.2.2"/>
  </condition>
</extension>
```

> Technically we are not "stripping off" the digits we do not want but rather we are "capturing" the digits that we do want. Remember, the value matched inside the first set of parentheses is stored in $1. Semantics aside, the net result is that we have the digits we want in a variable that we can use for whatever purpose we need.

Match number, strip digits, and add prefix

In this example we need to strip the leading digits as as shown, but we also need to place a new prefix before the called number. Assuming that FreeSWITCH receives the number 00123456789 and we need to replace the 00 with 011, we can use the following extension:

```
<extension name="Test4">
  <condition field="destination_number" expression="^00(\d+)$">
    <action application="bridge"
      data="sofia/profilename/011$1@x.x.x.x"/>
  </condition>
</extension>
```

Call registered device

This example shows how to bridge to devices that have registered with your FreeSWITCH box. In this example we assume that you have set up a Sofia profile called local_profile and your phones are registering with the domain example.com. Note the '%' instead of '@' in the dial string:

```
<extension name="internal">
  <condition field="source" expression="mod_sofia" />
  <condition field="destination_number" expression="^(4\d+)">
    <action application="bridge" data="sofia/local_profile/$0%example.
com" />
  </condition>
</extension>
```

The use of % instead of @ is a FreeSWITCH-specific feature. Using the form user%domain tells FreeSWITCH that user is registered with domain, and that domain is being serviced by the FreeSWITCH directory.

Try party A, then party B

The following example shows how it is possible to call another action if the first action fails.

If the first action is successful the call is bridged to 1111@example1.company.com and will exist until one of the parties hangs up. After this, no other processing will be done because the caller's channel is closed. (In other words, 1111@example2.company.com is not called.)

If the initial call to 111@example1.company.com was not successful the channel will not be closed and the second action will be called.

```
<extension name="find_me">
  <condition field="destination_number" expression="^1111">
    <action application="set" data="hangup_after_bridge=true"/>
    <action application="set" data="continue_on_fail=true"/>
    <action application="bridge" data="sofia/local_profile/1111@
example1.company.com" />
    <action application="bridge" data="sofia/local_profile/1111@
example2.company.com" />
  </condition>
</extension>
```

Check for authenticated user

The following example requests that the caller authenticate if they are calling extension 9191. Note carefully that the only "action" here is actually an anti-action, meaning that only if the condition fails will the call be rejected with a 407 (that is "proxy authentication required").

```
<extension name="9191">
  <condition field="destination_number" expression="^9191$"/>
  <condition field="${sip_authorized}" expression="true">
    <anti-action application="reject" data="407"/>
  </condition>
</extension>
```

Route DIDs to extensions

To route incoming calls which come in to a certain DID via the context `public` to a fixed extension in the context `inhouse`, do something like the following:

```
<context name="public">
   <extension name="test_did">
      <condition field="destination_number" expression="^\d{6}(\
d{4})$">
         <action application="transfer" data="$1 XML inhouse"/>
      </condition>
   </extension>
</context>
```

This will capture only the last four digits of a ten-digit number and transfer the caller to that number via the `inhouse` context. Note the parentheses around `\d{4}` that allow us to capture only the last four digits.

Try a local extension, failback to voicemail

This extension calls a number for 20 seconds and, if no answer, fails over to `voicemail`. Note carefully that if the `bridge` fails immediately or altogether, the caller will not hear ringing for twenty seconds but will immediately go to voicemail. This is because `call_timeout` only applies if the `bridge` command is successful in attempting to initiate a call and ring a destination.

```
<extension name="Local_Extension">
  <condition field="destination_number" expression="^(\d{4})$">
    <action application="ring_ready"/>
    <action application="set" data="call_timeout=20"/>
    <action application="set" data="hangup_after_bridge=true"/>
    <action application="set" data="continue_on_fail=true"/>
    <action application="bridge" data="user/$1@$${domain}"/>
    <action application="answer"/>
    <action application="sleep" data="1000"/>
    <action application="voicemail" data="default $${domain} $1"/>
  </condition>
</extension>
```

Alternate outbound gateways

In this example we send ten-digit outbound calls from Office A to gateway 1 and from Office B to gateway 2. This assumes Office A and Office B are both using the same FreeSWITCH box but need different routing for outbound calls. It assumes both offices have four digit extensions, and that Office A's extensions start with 2 and Office B's extensions start with 3.

```xml
<extension name="officeA_outbound">
  <condition field="caller_id_number" expression="^2\d{3}$">
  <condition field="destination_number" expression="^(\d{10})$">
      <action application="set" data="effective_caller_id_
number=8001231234"/>
      <action application="set" data="effective_caller_id_
name=Office A"/>
      <action application="bridge" data="sofia/gateway/myswitch.
com/$1"/>
  </condition>
</extension>
<extension name="officeB_outbound">
  <condition field="caller_id_number" expression="^3\d{3}$">
  <condition field="destination_number" expression="^(\d{10})$">
      <action application="set" data="effective_caller_id_
number=8001231235"/>
      <action application="set" data="effective_caller_id_
name=Office B"/>
      <action application="bridge" data="sofia/gateway/otherswitch.
com/$1"/>
  </condition>
</extension>
```

Alternatives to XML

We have mentioned that XML is the primary, and most popular, Dialplan parser used in FreeSWITCH but there are some other modules that people have committed that you can also use, such as YAML.

YAML

`mod_yaml` provides a YAML interface to Dialplan configuration. This Dialplan module can be used in place of the XML Dialplan interface. While the module is not currently in development anymore due to lack of interest, the C code provides an interesting look into how one might write their own Dialplan processing routines.

If you are interested in creating your own Dialplan configuration processing engine, you could analyze components of the YAML Dialplan system.

The history behind `mod_yaml` is an interesting anecdote that highlights both the power and flexibility of the FreeSWITCH platform as well as Anthony's iron-like determination to prove that the FreeSWITCH developers are not whimsical when it comes to making important decisions about FreeSWITCH development, including what file types to use to store configuration information.

Several years ago a new FreeSWITCH user suggested that XML had shortcomings that YAML does not, and that it would make a better layout for storing things like Dialplan configurations. We explained to him that we did not have any special bias towards the use of XML—it simply met all of our necessary requirements, not the least of which is that it is rather well-known. Since no single file format is a perfect fit for every possible use case it was decided that XML was the least imperfect fit and thus it was chosen.

However, this individual implied that the FreeSWITCH development team was being "closed-minded" about the grand possibilities of the use of YAML. Anthony accepted this as a challenge, and in a three-hour period he read over the YAML specifications (as he was completely unfamiliar with the format) *and* wrote `mod_yaml`! At the end of the experience he said that using YAML for the Dialplan was painful and that he was more convinced than ever that XML was the best choice. Also, no one could claim that the FreeSWITCH developers are unwilling to try new things. Finally, the fact that an entirely new Dialplan application could be developed in such a short period of time illustrates the sheer brilliance of the FreeSWITCH architecture, as well as its chief architect.

Asterisk Dialplan

If you are used to the Asterisk Dialplan, some basic functionality is provided by the Asterisk Dialplan module, although it is not nearly as feature-rich as the XML engine. You can process contexts and route calls to phones using the Asterisk Dialplan. This module, again, is more of a sample on how to build an alternate Dialplan processing module and should not be utilized as a full, feature-rich Dialplan system.

Summary

In this chapter we delved very deeply into the operation of the FreeSWITCH Dialplan. Building upon the foundation laid in Chapter 5, we discussed many advanced Dialplan concepts:

- How Dialplan parsing works
- Using global variables and channel variables
- Advanced use of regular expressions
- Time of day routing and other advanced routing concepts

The Dialplan system in FreeSWITCH is one of the most important concepts you can learn. The power of FreeSWITCH is truly unleashed within the Dialplan system itself, and understanding the complexities of using various functions within FreeSWITCH is key to ensuring FreeSWITCH performs exactly the way you want.

Controlling FreeSWITCH Externally

9

The FreeSWITCH Event System is one of the most exciting components of FreeSWITCH. You have already learned how FreeSWITCH operates when it utilizes various static configuration files and scripting languages. The event system allows for tremendous real-time dynamic behavior and control of FreeSWITCH. Utilizing the event system is when FreeSWITCH really comes alive.

The event system allows external software programs to act as listeners regarding activity happening on the system. This allows for real-time interaction with telephony operations on the telephony softswitch in conjunction with externally running software or hardware. Almost everything that happens within the FreeSWITCH system causes some sort of **event message** to be generated. These events can be watched by external entities. This is similar to the publish/subscribe (or "pub-sub") system used by common message queuing software solutions, although it is specifically tailored for FreeSWITCH events.

The event system is bi-directional: In addition to allowing external programs to listen to events, external programs can also send events to the system. You can send and/or receive events in real-time from your own programs. This combination allows you to use FreeSWITCH in almost any way you can imagine.

In this chapter, we will discuss the following:

- General overview of the event system
- Event system architecture
- Accessing the event socket
- Event socket library
- Example ESL program in PHP
- Creating a conference manager using the event system

General overview

The **event system** is the nerve center of FreeSWITCH, allowing both internal and external software to subscribe to a stream of activity happening inside the switching system. In FreeSWITCH, almost everything that happens generates (or "fires") an event. Receiving a new phone call results in an event. Ending a call results in an event. Committing a log entry to disk results in an event. Even speaking or going silent can generate an event. Each event becomes part of an event stream, tagged with an event type, event category, and various other details about the event. Other pieces of software can then listen for these events and act on them in any way they wish, such as streaming them to you via a TCP socket connection in plain text.

Events provide yet another way to extend functionality within FreeSWITCH. Events are different from hooks or modules (which can affect the actual processing and handling of calls in real-time). Events provide an asynchronous (or non-blocking/queued) method of keeping track of activity on the system. They are generated by one part of the software in one place, then they are consumed by another part of the software. In practice, this is useful in scenarios where you may have more activity happening on the switch than you can actually process in an external program. As an example, you may suddenly have a large spike in call volume which generates new call events. You may also be attempting to consume these events via a web browser, but the web browser cannot immediately keep up with the number of new calls that happen. By using a queued event system you avoid blocking the core switching engine (and thus, blocking the calls themselves) from being handled while you wait for the web browser to catch up to the volume that is occurring. In addition, you get additional safety mechanisms in the system if the event queue fills up—new events can simply be dropped, but call processing can continue. (This is very rare, but it is possible.)

In this chapter, we will review all the different aspects of the event system—from receiving and processing events to sending events to FreeSWITCH from external programs. We will cover the modules that enable the event system externally, the types of events that can be generated, and the ways in which you might utilize events. Finally, we will consider a sample scenario and code to help you get started in creating your own programs to control FreeSWITCH.

Event system architecture

The event subsystem in FreeSWITCH was designed to maximize throughput and prioritize events depending on their type and the system load. There are two layers within event system itself of the FreeSWITCH. The first layer provides internal event handling routines and an interface for absorbing (or "consuming") events within FreeSWITCH itself. The second layer is provided by the modular architecture and provides the client-facing access to those events. By keeping these two pieces of functionality separate, the availability of a publish/subscribe style event system becomes apparent.

Within the internal event layer, FreeSWITCH provides core functionality that handles events occurring both on a system-level and a channel-level. Events can be published or broadcasted by any part of the system, including modules. Two core types of events generally exist—system events and logging events. System events are generated by the core subsystem components or by modules. They include everything from the system's internal timer heartbeat to conference subsystem events, such as a party joining or leaving a conference room. Logger events are generated every time a log entry is attempted to the FreeSWITCH log file. These subsystems actually consist of three event queues, each with its own thread and priority level: zero, one, or two. If a queue fills up, the system fails over to the next queue until the entire event system is full. As calls or system functions progress, events are produced and stored in memory via these backend threads while they await pickup from internal subscribers. Once a message has been picked up by all subscribed modules and subsystems, the event message is destroyed. This allows the event system to scale better as events that are thrown do not cause a call to block while waiting for event consumers to pick up queued events.

FreeSWITCH uses its modular architecture to make events available to external software. An event handling module can subscribe to internal event messages, format them and send them to an external program. Such modules are called, appropriately, event handlers. There are not a lot of event handlers bundled with FreeSWITCH, but the ones that do exist are quite rich in their abilities, mostly because the underlying event system is so rich to start with. We will review these modules and how to utilize them next.

Event-based modules

There are three different modules for handling events. They are as follows:

1. mod_event_socket
2. mod_event_multicast
3. mod_erlang_event

mod_event_socket is by far the most used of the event handler modules, so we will be discussing it in detail. The other two modules are designed for more specific use cases and we will discuss them briefly.

mod_event_socket

mod_event_socket is the most common module in FreeSWITCH for sending and receiving events via third-party programs. This module provides a TCP socket which you can connect to from external software programs. Once authenticated, you can send and receive plain-text event information that is easy to understand and parse. It allows for bi-directional communication for both consuming events from and sending events to FreeSWITCH.

Utilizing event sockets is generally easy. First, you connect from an external program to a preconfigured socket which is configured for mod_event_socket. You authenticate to the system, then you begin sending event messages to FreeSWITCH. You can also initiate a request to receive events, at which point mod_event_socket will attach event listeners to the event system, queue event messages, and send them to you as fast as you can process them.

The mod_event_socket module exposes an interface where you can request to receive plain-text, serialized copies of events and generate events of your own. You can optionally request to receive data formatted as XML. The module includes an event filtering mechanism, allowing you to subscribe only to the event types that are of interest to you. For example, your program may be designed only to operate on conferences; therefore, you need only to receive conference-related events. The module itself is ultimately responsible for capturing events from the internal event system, and echoing them to each active TCP connection it has established. It does the work of setting up and maintaining an individual queue for each individual TCP connection, as each of the connections are likely to consume events at a different rate. The queuing itself however, is part of the core operation of FreeSWITCH.

Configuring event socket settings

You enable the event socket system simply by loading mod_event_socket in your modules.conf.xml configuration file. Once loaded, mod_event_socket is configured by editing the event_socket.conf.xml configuration file. The following parameters are available:

- **listen-ip**: The IP address to listen on, for event socket connections. External programs would connect to this IP address. The default settings allow socket connections only from the local host. You can specify a specific IP address or use 0.0.0.0 to listen on all local IP addresses.

  ```
  <param name="listen-ip" value="127.0.0.1"/>
  ```

- **listen-port**: The TCP port to listen on for inbound connections.

  ```
  <param name="listen-port" value="8021"/>
  ```

- **password**: The authentication password that is required when connecting to this port.

  ```
  <param name="password" value="ClueCon"/>
  ```

- **apply-inbound-acl**: **Access Control List (ACL)** is used to know about the connections to this port. This allows you to have a fine-grained control over who is actually able to connect to the port/IP combination specified previously. You can either use a known access control list name (as specified in `conf/autoload_configs/acl.conf.xml`) or you can use an actual IP address range.

  ```
  <param name="apply-inbound-acl" value="<acl_list|cidr>"/>
  ```

  Examples:

  ```
  <param name="apply-inbound-acl" value="known_machines"/>
  <param name="apply-inbound-acl" value="10.20.0.0/16"/>
  ```

Note that multiple `apply-inbound-acl` parameters will not work.

Reading events

When reading events from `mod_event_socket`, the data will be in the format of name/value pairs, separated by a colon. An event message is terminated with two end-of-line (EOL) sequences. FreeSWITCH uses the traditional DOS/Windows EOL sequence of carriage-return linefeed (CRLF) characters. Your external program should connect to the event socket and read as many characters as you can, up until two linefeeds are encountered. Following is an example of a single key/value pair line:

```
Event-Name: CHANNEL_EVENT
```

Some key/value pairs contain multiple line breaks within the value itself. In this scenario, FreeSWITCH still wants to present the value as a single "line" to you. To do this, FreeSWITCH will URL encode the data so it still appears as one line. Following is an example of a multi-line value response:

```
variable_switch_r_sdp: v%3D0%0D%0Ao%3DUAC%206407%206867%20IN%2
0IP4%20192.168.27.72%0D%0As%3DSIP%20Media%20Capabilities%0D%0
Ac%3DIN%20IP4%2061.231.8.102%0D%0At%3D0%200%0D%0Am%3Daudio%2
012916%20RTP/AVP%200%2018%20101%0D%0Aa%3Drtpmap%3A0%20PCMU/
8000%0D%0Aa%3Drtpmap%3A18%20G729/8000%0D%0Aa%3Dfmtp%3A18%20annexb%3Dno
%0D%0Aa%3Drtpmap%3A101%20telephone-event/8000%0D%0Aa%3Dfmtp%3A101%200-
15%0D%0Aa%3Dmaxptime%3A20%0D%0A
```

The preceding example is a URL Encoded SDP header from a call that FreeSWITCH is processing. It originally looked like the following:

```
variable_switch_r_sdp: v=0
o=UAC 6407 6867 IN IP4 192.168.27.72
s=SIP Media Capabilities
c=IN IP4 61.231.8.102
t=0 0
m=audio 12916 RTP/AVP 0 18 101
a=rtpmap:0 PCMU/8000
a=rtpmap:18 G729/8000
a=fmtp:18 annexb=no
a=rtpmap:101 telephone-event/8000
a=fmtp:101 0-15
a=maxptime:20
```

If one of the name/value pairs is a `Content-Length` header, you need to read exactly that many bytes from the socket after the initial headers and two CRLF's are encountered. Once you have read all the bytes in the content length, the next packet will start on the subsequent byte. When you have an event containing the `Content-Length` header, this is an indication that additional content is generated with the event, which is not in the key/value form and may contain its own native formatting.

As an example, following is an event notifying of a change in a channel's state.

```
Content-Length: 646
Content-Type: text/event-plain
Channel-State: CS_EXECUTE
Channel-State-Number: 4
Channel-Name: sofia/default/1006%4010.0.1.250%3A5060
Unique-ID: 74775b0d-b112-46e2-95af-c28258650b1b
Call-Direction: inbound
Answer-State: ringing
Event-Name: CHANNEL_STATE
Core-UUID: 2130a7d1-c1f7-44cd-8fae-8ed5946f3cec
FreeSWITCH-Hostname: localhost.localdomain
FreeSWITCH-IPv4: 10.0.1.250
FreeSWITCH-IPv6: 127.0.0.1
Event-Date-Local: 2007-12-16%2022%3A33%3A18
Event-Date-GMT: Mon,%2017%20Dec%202007%2004%3A33%3A18%20GMT
Event-Date-timestamp: 1197865998931097
Event-Calling-File: switch_channel.c
Event-Calling-Function: switch_channel_perform_set_running_state
Event-Calling-Line-Number: 620
```

Minimum event information

Every event you receive from FreeSWITCH via `mod_event_socket` will contain a minimum amount of information, regardless of the event type. The fields provided for any event are made available to help you understand not only what event type to expect, but also to help you understand when the event actually happened and on which server. In a multi-server environment, these fields are particularly useful as the `Core-UUID` can be used to understand which system generated the event, while the timestamps ensure that events can be reconstructed and handled in the proper order.

The fields you will also receive in any event are illustrated by the following event:

```
Event-Name: CHANNEL_EVENT
Core-UUID: 689fd828-e85b-ca43-a219-39332bc55860
Event-Date-Local: 2007-05-09%2018%3A48%3A59
Event-Date-GMT: Wed,%2009%20May%202007%2016%3A48%3A59%20GMT
Event-Calling-File: switch_channel.c
Event-Calling-Function: switch_channel_set_caller_profile
Event-Calling-Line-Number: 840
```

The preceding information is always included, no matter which event is being received. That means that every event will be tagged with the following:

- `Event-Name` — The event's name, which is a description of the type of event it is
- `Core-UUID` — The UUID of the current instance of the FreeSWITCH core
- `Event-Date-Local` — The date/time of the event according to the system clock
- `Event-Date-GMT` — The date/time of the event in GMT (that is, UTC) time
- `Event-Calling-File` — The C source file from which the event was fired
- `Event-Calling-Function` — The name of the function that fired this event
- `Event-Calling-Line-Number` — The exact line number of the C source file where this event was fired

The last three events are particularly useful for testing and troubleshooting.

After the preceding information, event-specific information will be included depending on the type of event being sent. There is no line-break or spacing between the mentioned event key/value pairs and the event-specific key/value pairs.

Sending events

You can send events into the FreeSWITCH core via `mod_event_socket` over the same TCP connection you receive events over (the connection is bi-directional). All commands are formatted with a command name and arguments. Some commands require additional fields after the command itself. The formatting for additional fields when you send events is similar to the format you use when you receive events. You send FreeSWITCH a list of key/value pairs specifying the event name and specific flags related to the event, and FreeSWITCH injects the message into the event subsystem for modules or the FreeSWITCH core to handle.

An example of a basic command is as follows:

```
api sleep 5000
```

This would run the API command `sleep` and pass it the argument `5000`, causing the system to sleep for five seconds.

A more complicated example might be injecting messages directly into the FreeSWITCH event queue system. You can inject events into the FreeSWITCH system with the `sendevent` command, followed by associated parameters.

An example of the `sendevent` command is as follows:

```
sendevent NOTIFY
profile: internal
content-type: application/simple-message-summary
event-string: check-sync
user: 1005
host: 192.168.10.4
content-length: 5
hello
```

This would send a `NOTIFY` event with associated information. In this case, we are requesting that a `NOTIFY` message be sent to user `1005@192.168.10.4` on Sofia's `internal` profile. If `mod_sofia` is loaded and listening for these types of messages, it will generate the appropriate SIP packet to user 1005 for the requested `NOTIFY` message and include the `content-type` and `event-string` in the SIP message, along with the content itself, which in this case is "hello".

Note that all event messages you send into FreeSWITCH must be terminated by two CRLF character sequences.

The full list of event commands you can send to FreeSWITCH is detailed later in this chapter in the section FreeSWITCH Event System Commands.

Events from the Dialplan

`mod_event_socket` provides a Dialplan application named **socket** that allows for outbound TCP connections to be made to an IP and port, where the other end can stream commands for execution back to FreeSWITCH. This is similar to the network-based fast-agi (FAGI) of Asterisk, but it operates in full asynchronous mode, allowing commands to be issued and control to be returned immediately in anticipation of additional events or responses.

When you call outbound socket, FS automatically puts the call in PARK. You can watch calls go into the PARKed state by watching the event stack for the CHANNEL_PARK event.

The syntax for calling `socket` from the Dialplan is `<ip>:<port> [<keywords>`.

Following are examples of how to use it in the Dialplan.

```
<action application="socket" data="127.0.0.1:8084"/>
<action application="socket" data="127.0.0.1:8084 async"/>
<action application="socket" data="127.0.0.1:8084 full"/>
<action application="socket" data="127.0.0.1:8084 async full"/>
```

The optional keywords `async` and `full` modify the behavior as follows:

- `async`: The `async` keyword indicates that all commands will return instantly making it possible to monitor the socket for events while the stack of commands are executing.

  If the `async` keyword is absent, then all calls will block until the command has finished.

- `full`: The `full` keyword indicates that the other end will have the full command set for event socket. This is the same command set an inbound event socket connection has so you can execute API commands, get global events, and so on.

  If the `full` keyword is absent, then the command set and events are limited to that particular call. In other words, if `full` is not specified, then the commands sent on this socket connection can affect only the channel currently being processed. Likewise, the socket connection will only receive events related to this particular channel.

mod_event_multicast

mod_event_multicast is very similar to mod_event_socket. It allows for sending and receiving events via network multicasts to third-party programs and other FreeSWITCH instances using plain-text event information. Other hosts can be configured to listen for events and parse them, potentially triggering events on those hosts.

Event headers are the same as typical events except that all original headers are prefixed with 'Orig-' and the event is of CUSTOM type with a subtype of multicast:: event. A Multicast-Sender header is also added. Here is an example of a packet received outside of FreeSWITCH that was sent by mod_event_multicast:

```
Event-Name: CUSTOM
Core-UUID: 12938281-57ce-11de-9be6-99a22d850f40
FreeSWITCH-Hostname: SYS1
FreeSWITCH-IPv4: 192.168.1.12
FreeSWITCH-IPv6: %3A%3A1
Event-Date-Local: 2010-01-16%2018%3A15%3A10
Event-Date-GMT: Tue,%2016%20Jun%202009%2022%3A15%3A10%20GMT
Event-Date-Timestamp: 1245190510366825
Event-Calling-File: mod_event_multicast.c
Event-Calling-Function: mod_event_multicast_runtime
Event-Calling-Line-Number: 313
Event-Subclass: multicast%3A%3Aevent
Multicast: yes
Orig-Event-Name: CUSTOM
Orig-Core-UUID: 8784372-5ecc-4eaa-9002-9992b7ab7c4d
```

You configure mod_event_multicast by editing the conf/autoload_configs/ event_multicast.conf.xml configuration file. This file has four parameters to configure. They are as follows:

Port/address

It configures the address to send events to.

For example:

```
<param name="address" value="225.1.1.1"/>
<param name="port" value="4242"/>
```

Bindings

Bindings specify what events you want to send to the multi-cast addresses. This follows the same format as event `<arg>` `<arg>`, as specified earlier in this chapter. For example:

```
<param name="bindings" value="PRESENCE_IN CUSTOM sofia::register
   CUSTOM multicast::event"/>
```

TTL

You can specify the TTL (Time To Live) for packets so that packets get dropped if not delivered in a timely manner. This is dependent on your LAN/WAN switching equipment for following this setting. The value is the number of "hops" to allow.

```
<param name="ttl" value="1"/>
```

mod_erlang_event

mod_erlang_event provides native event data to and from Erlang-based software programs. This module allows for very tight integration with Erlang applications with very little overhead, as native Erlang API calls are utilized to interact with Erlang. Native Erlang data types are utilized to transmit information, so no parsing and conversion is necessary while processing the events.

You can read more about mod_erlang_event on the FreeSWITCH wiki (http://wiki.freeswitch.org/wiki/Mod_erlang_event). You would probably want to be familiar with the Erlang programming language before using this module.

FreeSWITCH event system commands

The following is a list of commands available for use from any event-based utility you use to connect to FreeSWITCH. You can use these commands from ESL (the FreeSWITCH Event Socket Library), via mod_event_socket and via any other standard interface that FreeSWITCH provides for accessing the event system. The syntax is the same from one access method to the next, although there may be variations in formatting and encoding, introduced by individual modules.

auth <password>

When you first connect to the FreeSWITCH event system via the mod_event_socket module, you must authenticate. This command allows you to pass your authentication parameters.

```
auth ClueCon
```

api

The `api` command allows any command to be sent, that would otherwise be accessible via the FreeSWITCH command-line interface. This executes the corresponding command in blocking mode, which means that the control will not return to the open event socket and no other commands will be allowed to execute until this one finishes.

Syntax: `api <command> <arg>`

Examples:

```
api originate sofia/mydomain.com/4158867999@telco.com 1000
```

This will initiate a call to (415) 886-7999 via `telco.com`, and connect it to local extension `1000`.

```
api sleep 5000
```

This would execute a sleep command for five seconds (`5000` milliseconds).

bgapi

The `bgapi` command will let you execute a job in the background and return a UUID with reference to the background job. When the command actually executes and completes, the result will be sent as an event with a UUID to match the one initially given.

The `bgapi` command accepts the same arguments for commands as the `api` command explained recently. The only difference is that the server returns immediately and is available for processing more commands.

Syntax: `bgapi <command> <arg>`

Examples:

```
bgapi originate sofia/example/300@foo.com 8600
Content-Type: command/reply
Reply-Text: +OK Job-UUID: c7709e9c-1517-11dc-842a-d3a3942d3d63
```

When the command is done executing, FreeSWITCH will fire an event with the same UUID in the `Job-UUID` field. The event type of the response message will be `BACKGROUND_JOB`, so you must be subscribed to receive those types of events in order to see the response. A sample response might look like the following:

```
Content-Length: 625
Content-Type: text/event-plain

Job-UUID: c7709e9c-1517-11dc-842a-d3a3942d3d63
```

```
Job-Command: originate
Job-Command-Arg: sofia/default/300%20foo.com
Event-Name: BACKGROUND_JOB
Core-UUID: 42bdf272-16e6-11dd-b7a0-db4edd065621
FreeSWITCH-Hostname: ser
FreeSWITCH-IPv4: 192.168.1.104
FreeSWITCH-IPv6: 127.0.0.1
Event-Date-Local: 2008-05-02%2007%3A37%3A03
Event-Date-GMT: Thu,%2001%20May%202008%2023%3A37%3A03%20GMT
Event-Date-timestamp: 1209685023894968
Event-Calling-File: mod_event_socket.c
Event-Calling-Function: api_exec
Event-Calling-Line-Number: 609
Content-Length: 41

+OK 7f4de4bc-17d7-11dd-b7a0-db4edd065621
```

Note that in the response of the background job, the original job ID is listed in Job-UUID, while the UUID of the call that the originate created (that is, the result of the originate command) is in the extra content data, in this case +OK 7f4de4bc-17d7-11dd-b7a0-db4edd065621. If you are building an application that needs to communicate asynchronously with FreeSWITCH, then be sure to use bgapi to submit commands and subscribe to BACKGROUND_JOB events. Use the Job-UUID value to match a bgapi command with its corresponding BACKGROUND_JOB event. The BACKGROUND_JOB event will contain the "final" results of the command that were sent via bgapi.

event

The event command starts or stops the streaming of events. Events are streamed via the module that is executing the event command (that is, mod_event_socket TCP connection, mod_erlang_event, and so on). You can subscribe to specific event class types, or you can subscribe to all event types.

Subsequent calls to 'event' will override and disable previously requested event sets.

Syntax: event plain <list of event types | all>

Examples:

```
event plain ALL
```

This requests a copy of all events.

```
event plain CUSTOM conference::maintenance
```

This requests a copy of CUSTOM events, specifically the `conference` module's maintenance events.

```
event plain CHANNEL_CREATE CHANNEL_DESTROY CUSTOM
    conference::maintenance sofia::register sofia::expire
```

Requests a copy of events that have to do with the creating or destroying of channels, and all custom events from the `conference` module's maintenance system and Sofia's register and expire system.

divert_events

The `divert_events` switch allows events which an embedded script would expect to get in the input call-back to be diverted to the event socket. This means that a running script in FreeSWITCH that needs input can actually receive it from an outside connecting program which sends the event responses via an event socket connection.

An input call-back can be registered in an embedded script using `setInputCallback()`. (We considered an example of using `setInputCallback()` in *Chapter 7, Building IVR Applications with Lua*.) Setting `divert_events` to "on" can be used for chat messages like a Gtalk channel, automatic speech recognition (ASR) events, and others.

Syntax: `divert_events <on|off>`

Examples:

```
divert_events on
divert_events off
```

filter

Specify event types to listen for. Multiple filters on a socket connection are allowed. Note that this command is a "filter in", not a filter out. Set multiple filters to narrow the types of events you wish to see.

Syntax: `filter <EventHeader> <ValueToFilter>`

Examples:

The following example will subscribe to all events.

```
events plain all
Content-Type: command/reply
Reply-Text: +OK event listener enabled plain
```

To receive only events of type CHANNEL_EXECUTE and HEARBEAT:

```
filter Event-Name CHANNEL_EXECUTE

Content-Type: command/reply
Reply-Text: +OK filter added. [filter]=[Event-Name CHANNEL_EXECUTE]

filter Event-Name HEARTBEAT

Content-Type: command/reply
Reply-Text: +OK filter added. [Event-Name]=[HEARTBEAT]
```

You can filter on any of the event headers.

To filter for a specific channel you would filter by uuid:

```
filter Unique-ID d29a070f-40ff-43d8-8b9d-d369b2389dfe
```

Use a combination of filters to narrow down the events you wish to receive on the socket.

filter delete

Specify the event filters that you wish to cancel. This can be used if you are accidentally (or intentionally) filtering too much data and wish to receive additional events.

Syntax: filter delete <EventHeader> <ValueToFilter>

Examples:

```
filter delete Event-Name HEARTBEAT
filter delete Unique-ID d29a070f-40ff-43d8-8b9d-d369b2389dfe
```

This deletes the filter which is applied for the given Unique-ID. After this, you will not receive any events for this Unique-ID.

```
filter delete Unique-ID
```

This deletes all the filters which are applied based on the Unique-ID.

sendevent

Send an event into the event system (multiline input for headers).

Syntax: sendevent <event-name>

This generates an event within the internal FreeSWITCH event system. Any of the modules or system processes that have subscribed to this event type will get the event.

If you issue `sendevent` without specifying an event type, and include an `Event-Name` header with the desired event name, you can specify any event type you want. For example:

```
sendevent SOME_NAME
Event-Name: CUSTOM
Event-Subclass: albs::Section-Alarm
Section: 33
Alarm-Type: PIR
State: ACTIVE
```

An example of the `sendevent` command is as follows:

```
sendevent NOTIFY
profile: internal
content-type: application/simple-message-summary
event-string: check-sync
user: 1005
host: 192.168.10.4
content-length: 5
hello
```

sendmsg <uuid>

Send a message to the call of given UUID (`call-command execute` or `hangup`). Use this command to control the behavior of specific in-progress calls. You need to provide a UUID for the call.

In order to control calls using send message, the calls should be parked. A parked call means the channel is sitting in a sort of limbo state, allowing you to execute applications on the channel without interrupting other applications already executing (Note: a parked call will not receive any media, including music-on-hold.).

You can `originate` a call directly to `park` by using the `&park()` syntax:

```
originate sofia/example/300@foo.com &park()
```

There are two types of core actions you can do to a channel — `execute` and `hangup`. These two actions are described in detail in the following section.

execute

The `execute` command is used to execute Dialplan applications. You can put an application name and application arguments into the execute request, and loop the command multiple times if you wish. A simple example might include playing a `.wav` file.

The format should be as follows:

```
SendMsg <uuid>
call-command: execute
execute-app-name: <one of the applications>
execute-app-arg: <application data>
loops: <number of times to invoke the command, default: 1>
```

As an example, the following `SendMsg` command would play a file named `test.wav` to the channel specified in `<uuid>`.

```
SendMsg <uuid>
call-command: execute
execute-app-name: playback
execute-app-arg: /tmp/test.wav
```

If you have data that exceeds 2048 characters which needs to be passed in as an argument via the `SendMsg` command, you can use a slightly different format when submitting your commands as follows:

```
SendMsg <uuid>
call-command: execute
execute-app-name: <one of the applications>
loops: <number of times to invoke the command, default: 1>
content-type: text/plain
content-length: <content length>
<application data>
```

Note the highlighted lines. You can specify the length of the text used to invoke your application and then send in the application data in full.

hangup

This command hangs up an active call.

Format:

```
SendMsg <uuid>
call-command: hangup
hangup-cause: <recognized hangup cause>
```

nomedia

You can control whether or not FreeSWITCH is in the media path real-time with the nomedia command. This command allows you to turn on or off media handling for a specific channel.

Usage:

```
SendMsg <uuid>
call-command: nomedia
nomedia-uuid: <noinfo>
```

log <level>

This command enables log output. You can specify a logging level that you wish to see. This allows you to receive all the log events just as if you were on the FreeSWITCH CLI.

Usage:

```
log <level>
```

nolog

This command disables log output previously enabled by the nolog command.

Usage:

```
nolog
```

noevents

This command disables all events that were previously enabled with event.

Usage:

```
noevents
```

Event-based applications

Several applications exist that take advantage of the Event Socket system. The most commonly used application is the fs_cli. We will also go over a demo PHP and Perl script to get you familiar with utilizing the event system.

FreeSWITCH Console application

Most people do not realize it, but if they have used the FreeSWITCH Console application (fs_cli), then they have already used the FreeSWITCH event socket subsystem. fs_cli is a C application that connects to the FreeSWITCH event socket provided by mod_event_socket, as previously discussed. It consumes all system events, colorizes them and provides an interface for sending commands back in the form of event messages. The entire FreeSWITCH console has been completely recreated by this application. (You can view the source code for fs_cli in libs/ esl/fs_cli.c under the FreeSWITCH source directory.)

PHP Socket connections

The FreePBX v3 project introduced a class that allows for connecting to the FreeSWITCH event socket system via PHP. You can use the class as a standalone class—it handles all the work of connecting to the event system via mod_event_ socket, receiving and parsing events, and presenting them to the user in a friendly, easy-to-use array.

The FreePBX v3 project is discussed further in *Chapter 10, Advanced Features and Further Reading*.

Perl Socket connections

There is a Perl FreeSWITCH program named **FSSocket** that utilizes the Perl Object Environment and mod_event_socket in FreeSWITCH to provide an easy-to-use interface for working with FreeSWITCH from Perl. The project is at http://search. cpan.org/~ptinsley/POE-Filter-FSSocket-0.07/lib/POE/Filter/FSSocket. pm. On running the program you will get a text-based ncurses screen prompting you to enter commands and listing the output of their commands.

These are just two simple examples of using the event socket for controlling FreeSWITCH externally. However, there is a powerful abstraction library that simplifies the process of using the event socket, namely, The FreeSWITCH Event Socket Library.

Event Socket Library

The FreeSWITCH **Event Socket Library** (**ESL**) is a set of standard APIs made available as loadable modules for various programming languages. Generally speaking, the APIs, when loaded into a programming language of your choice, provide native function calls for accessing FreeSWITCH event functionality — without the need to set up a TCP or network socket or otherwise concern yourself with how FreeSWITCH is reached.

Supported libraries

FreeSWITCH utilizes SWIG (`www.swig.org`) to create a standardized set of APIs. **SWIG** takes a defined list of variable and function calls and automatically creates libraries that link the core FreeSWITCH code to the programming language's native loadable module interfaces. The following languages are supported by default:

- Perl
- PHP
- LUA
- Python
- Ruby
- C
- TCL
- .NET

The following objects and methods apply to any language that can build ESL extensions. Once you have loaded the corresponding module for your particular programming language, you can utilize any of the standard ESL objects, functions, and variables. The generic function calls are listed as follows. The FreeSWITCH ESL uses SWIG to take care of most type conversions for you, so try using your language's native type casting or variable structures when using these commands.

ESLObject

`ESLObject` is the core ESL object. You can set the `loglevel` information you wish to receive for events that you are receiving from FreeSWITCH.

eslSetLogLevel($loglevel)

eslSetLogLevel($loglevel) sets the log level on the server. $loglevel is an integer between 0 and 7. The values for $loglevel mean:

- 0 is EMERG
- 1 is ALERT
- 2 is CRIT
- 3 is ERROR
- 4 is WARNING
- 5 is NOTICE
- 6 is INFO
- 7 is DEBUG

ESLevent object

When an event is received, you will get an ESLevent object. This object has various helper functions available to help parse and process the event that was received.

serialize([$format])

serialize([$format]) turns an event into colon-separated 'name: value' pairs similar to a SIP/e-mail packet.

setPriority([$number])

setPriority([$number]) sets the priority of an event to $number in case it is fired.

getHeader($header_name)

getHeader($header_name) gets the header with the key of $header_name from an event object.

getBody()

getBody() gets the body of an event object.

getType()

getType() gets the event type of an event object.

addBody($value)

addBody($value) adds $value to the body of an event object. This can be called multiple times for the same event object.

addHeader($header_name, $value)

addHeader($header_name, $value) adds a header where the key is $header_name and value is $value to an event object. This can be called multiple times for the same event object.

delHeader($header_name)

delHeader($header_name) deletes the header with key $header_name from an event object.

firstHeader()

firstHeader() sets the pointer to the first header in an event object, and returns its key name. This must be called before nextHeader is called.

nextHeader()

nextHeader() moves the pointer to the next header in an event object, and returns its key name. firstHeader must be called before this method to set the pointer. If you are already on the last header when this method is called, it will return "NULL".

ESLconnection object

The ESLconnection object maintains a connection to FreeSWITCH for event handling. This object maintains connectivity to FreeSWITCH and handles sending and receiving of messages.

new($host, $port, $password)

This command initializes a new instance of ESLconnection, and connects to the host $host on the port $port, and supplies $password to the FreeSWITCH server.

This is intended only for an event socket in "inbound" mode. Use this function when creating a connection to FreeSWITCH that is not initially bound to any particular call or channel.

new($fd)

This command initializes a new instance of ESLconnection, using the existing file number (file descriptor) contained in $fd.

You can use this with Event Socket outbound connections. It will fail on inbound connections, even if passed a valid inbound socket.

socketDescriptor()

This command returns the UNIX file descriptor for the connection object if a connection exists. This is the same file descriptor that was passed to new($fd), when used in outbound mode.

connected()

This command tests if the connection object is connected. Returns 1 if connected, 0 otherwise.

getInfo()

When FreeSWITCH connects to an "Event Socket Outbound" handler, it sends a CHANNEL_DATA event as the first event after the initial connection. getInfo() returns an ESLevent that contains this Channel Data.

getInfo() returns NULL when used on an "Event Socket Inbound" connection.

send($command)

This command sends a command to FreeSWITCH, and it does not wait for a reply.

You can call recvEvent or recvEventTimed in a loop to receive a reply. The reply event will have a header named "content-type" that has a value of "api/response" or "command/reply".

To automatically wait for the reply event, use sendRecv() instead of send().

sendRecv($command)

Internally sendRecv($command) calls send($command) and then recvEvent(), and returns an instance of ESLevent.

recvEvent() is called in a loop until it receives an event with a header named "content-type" that has a value of "api/response" or "command/reply", and then returns it as an instance of ESLevent.

Any events received by recvEvent() that are unrelated to this transaction are queued up, and will be returned on subsequent calls to recvEvent() in your program.

api($command[, $arguments])

Send an API command to the FreeSWITCH server. This method blocks further execution until the command has been executed.

api($command, $args) is identical to sendRecv("api $command $args").

bgapi($command[, $arguments])

Send a background API command to the FreeSWITCH server to be executed in its own thread and is non-blocking.

bgapi($command, $args) is identical to sendRecv("bgapi $command $args").

sendEvent($send_me)

Inject an event into the FreeSWITCH event system. This allows you to send an event into FreeSWITCH where event consumers can process and utilize the event.

recvEvent()

This returns the next event from FreeSWITCH. If no events are waiting, this call will block until an event arrives.

If any events were queued during a call to sendRecv(), then the first one will be returned, and removed from the queue. Otherwise, then next event will be read from the connection.

recvEventTimed($milliseconds)

This command is similar to recvEvent(), except that it will block for (at most) the time specified in $milliseconds.

A call to recvEventTimed(0) will return immediately. This is useful for polling of events.

filter($header, $value)

See the event socket filter command.

events($event_type,$value)

`$event_type` can have the value "plain" or "xml". Any other value specified for `$event_type` gets replaced with "plain".

execute($app[, $arg][, $uuid])

Execute a Dialplan application, and wait for a response from the server. On socket connections not anchored to a channel (most of the time inbound), all three arguments are required. `$uuid` specifies the channel on which to execute the application.

`execute()` returns an `ESLevent` object containing the response from the server. The `getHeader("Reply-Text")` method of this `ESLevent` object returns the server's response. The server's response will contain "+OK [Success Message]" on success or "-ERR [Error Message]" on failure.

executeAsync($app[, $arg][, $uuid])

This command is identical to it does not wait for a response from the server.

This works by causing the underlying call to `execute()` to append "async: true" header in the message sent to the channel.

setAsyncExecute($value)

Force `async` mode on for a socket connection. This command has no effect on outbound socket connections that are set to "async" in the Dialplan and inbound socket connections, since these connections are already set to `async` mode on.

`$value` should be 1 to force `async` mode, and 0 not to force it.

Specifically, calling `setAsyncExecute(1)` operates by causing future calls to `execute()` to include the "async: true" header in the message sent to the channel. Other event socket library routines are not affected by this call.

setEventLock($value)

Force `sync` mode on for a socket connection. This command has no effect on outbound socket connections that are not set to "async" in the Dialplan, since these connections are already set to `sync` mode.

`$value` should be 1 to force `sync` mode, and 0 not to force it.

Specifically, calling `setEventLock(1)` operates by causing future calls to `execute()` to include the "event-lock: true" header in the message sent to the channel. Other event socket library routines are not affected by this call.

disconnect()

Close the socket connection to the FreeSWITCH server.

Events in practice

Let's look at a few specific examples that demonstrate the use of events.

Event Socket Library example: running a command

The following PHP example shows how you can write a simple script to take one-line commands and, using the FreeSWITCH Event Socket Library, send those commands to FreeSWITCH, and wait for the response.

```php
// Include FreeSWITCH ESL Library. Note that ESL.php comes
// with the FreeSWITCH PHP ESL module.
require_once('ESL.php');

if ($argc <= 1) {
printf("ERROR: You Need To Pass A Command\nUsage:\n\t%s <command>",
  $argv[0]);
exit();
}

// Strip off the executable's name ($argv[0])
array_shift($argv);
$command = sprintf('%s', implode(' ', $argv));
printf("Command to run is: %s\n", $command);

// Connect to FreeSWITCH
$sock = new ESLconnection('localhost', '8021', 'ClueCon');

// Send the Command
$res = $sock->api($command);

// Print the response
printf("%s\n", $res->getBody());
```

Examples of sending events to FreeSWITCH

The following examples are useful in demonstrating what you can do with the event socket by sending (or "injecting") events right into the FreeSWITCH event system.

Setting phone lights

Many phones support turning line lights on and off via SIP presence messages. You can use the event socket to turn these lights on and off yourself.

Turn lights on

You can turn a phone's lights on by sending a presence event to FreeSWITCH, which will then send a SIP presence message to the phone. Connect to the FreeSWITCH event socket and send the following event:

```
sendevent PRESENCE_IN
proto: sip
from: 1000@example.com
login: 1000@example.com
event_type: presence
alt_event_type: dialog
Presence-Call-Direction: outbound
answer-state: confirmed
```

Anyone who has a line button for `1000@example.com` should see that line's light turn on. Note carefully the `answer-state`—confirmed key/value pair. This means there is an active call happening (or we are simulating one) and the light should be turned on.

Turn lights off

You can turn a phone's light off by sending a presence event to FreeSWITCH, just like turning the lights on. After connecting to the FreeSWITCH event socket send the following event:

```
sendevent PRESENCE_IN
proto: sip
from: 1000@example.com
login: 1000@example.com
event_type: presence
Presence-Call-Direction: outbound
alt_event_type: dialog
answer-state: terminated
```

Note carefully that the "terminated" `answer-state` means there is no call on this line (turn the light off).

Rebooting a phone

FreeSWITCH has the ability to send a request to SIP phones to ask them to reboot. This is useful if you have changed a configuration entry and wish to make the phone get the new configuration, which most phones will do automatically when booting during their provisioning phase.

You will need to know the Call-Id field for the registered phone you are interested in rebooting. You can get this from issuing `sofia profile <profile_name> status` command and finding the party in the list. You can then issue `sofia profile <profile_name> <call_id> reboot`. The phone should reboot.

You can connect to the FreeSWITCH event socket to perform both these actions. The commands would be prefaced by `api`, as follows:

```
# Search for the Call-Id of interest from within your program
api sofia status profile <profile_name>

# Reboot the phone
api sofia profile <profile_name> <call_id> reboot
```

Requesting phone reconfiguration

Some phones support the feature of being reconfigured. To have Snom phones reread their settings from the settings server you can use the following:

```
sendevent NOTIFY
profile: internal
event-string: check-sync;reboot=false
user: 1000
host: 192.168.10.4
content-type: application/simple-message-summary
```

Custom notify messages

You can send custom notify messages with arbitrary content via event firing. As an example, if you have sent the following:

```
sendevent NOTIFY
profile: internal
content-type: application/simple-message-summary
event-string: check-sync
user: 1005
host: 99.157.44.194
content-length: 2

OK
```

A packet similar to the following one would be generated:

```
NOTIFY sip:1005@99.157.44.203 SIP/2.0
Via: SIP/2.0/UDP 99.157.44.194;rport;branch=z9hG4bKpH2DtBDcDtg0N
Max-Forwards: 70
From: <sip:1005@99.157.44.194>;tag=Dy3c6Q1y15v5S
To: <sip:1005@99.157.44.194>
Call-ID: 129d1446-0063-122c-15aa-001a923f6a0f
CSeq: 104766492 NOTIFY
Contact: <sip:mod_sofia@99.157.44.194:5060>
User-Agent: FreeSWITCH-mod_sofia/1.0.trunk-9578:9586
Allow: INVITE, ACK, BYE, CANCEL, OPTIONS, PRACK, MESSAGE, SUBSCRIBE,
   NOTIFY, REFER, UPDATE, REGISTER, INFO, PUBLISH
Supported: 100rel, timer, precondition, path, replaces
Event: check-sync
Allow-Events: talk, presence, dialog, call-info, sla, include-
   session-description, presence.winfo, message-summary
Subscription-State: terminated;timeout
Content-Type: application/simple-message-summary
Content-Length: 2
```

```
OK
```

Note that aside from the SIP notify message itself being generated because of our request, the specific fields we included in the request were passed directly into the SIP message.

Summary

Once you understand how rich the event system in FreeSWITCH is and have tried it out yourself, you begin to realize that there are literally thousands of things you can do with the FreeSWITCH application. Unlike previous topics on making phone calls or configuring modules, this is one piece of FreeSWITCH that truly lets you and your users interact with FreeSWITCH in real time, in any way you can possibly imagine. The eventing engine is powerful and robust, and its applications are limitless.

10
Advanced Features and Further Reading

There are two general categories of applications that can utilize FreeSWITCH—ones that are built in C as modules that live inside FreeSWITCH, and ones which control or manage FreeSWITCH externally. Both topics will be covered briefly in this chapter.

FreeSWITCH contains a variety of application modules that provide functionality and features that direct calls and otherwise make switching decisions while calls are in progress. These modules range from Caller ID lookup modules to real-time billing modules to multi-party conferencing modules. Modules can be used with each other to enrich the general Dialplan application set, to supervise calls, or to provide other functionality.

In addition, an entire community of open source FreeSWITCH applications has grown to provide various software programs that can fully (or partially) manage FreeSWITCH.

In this chapter, we'll presume you already have some basic understanding of how FreeSWITCH operates. We'll review various applications or modules which enable applications within FreeSWITCH, scratching only the surface of what they do. We'll also briefly cover some third-party tools you can use to expand your utilization of FreeSWITCH further.

We will discuss the following topics:

- Multi-User Conferencing (`mod_conference`)
- Nibblebill (`mod_nibblebill`)
- XML/Curl (`mod_xml_curl`)
- Other endpoint types: Skype, GSM, and TDM
- Web GUIs and other projects

Multi-user conferencing

FreeSWITCH includes a powerful built-in multi-user conferencing module mod_conference, which allows the mixing of audio channels between callers in a multi-user audio conferencing system. This system also allows for full control of all audio mixing and caller interaction features, such as detection of touch-tones, management of send and receive audio paths per channel, volume controls, gain controls, and more. You can create as many conferences as you like, as long as there still are free system resources (that is, memory, CPU cycles, and so forth) left.

Configuration

mod_conference is configured in the conference section of the XML files. This is generally located in the autoload_configs/conference.conf.xml file. The configuration defines how conferences behave, through a series of profiles. These profiles can be applied to conferences when they are created via the Dialplan.

The conference configuration file is divided into several sections, each with its own set of parameters. These sections are detailed in this chapter.

Conference profiles

Conference profiles are templates of settings that can be applied to a particular conference. In combination with caller-controls (discussed in this section), conference profiles allow for the complete customization of the behavior of individual conferences. You can create template types and apply them across many conferences, create a profile for each conference you intend to utilize, or you can simply utilize the defaults.

Conference profiles are named profiles that contain lists of parameters within each named profile element. The general structure is as follows:

```
<profiles>
    <profile name="default">
      <param name="paramName" value="paramValue"/>
    </profile>
</profiles>
```

You can have any number of `<profile>` tags, and each `<profile>` tag can have any number of `<param>` tags. The following is a list of parameters that are available:

- `rate`: The `rate` parameter specifies the default (and highest) sampling rate that the conference bridge will utilize. All callers who call into this channel will have their audio transcoded into this sampling rate if they are not already at that rate. For the purposes of audio mixing, this defines your "weakest link" in relation to the system — if two callers have HD phones but call in to a conference where the rate is 8000, those callers will have their audio sampled down to the lower rate.

  Command syntax: `<param name="rate" value="8000"/>`

  Default: 8000

  Available options: 8000, 12000, 16000, 24000, 32000, 48000 (possibly others in the future)

- `caller-controls`: Specifies the `caller-controls` profile to use with this conference bridge (see the following syntax).

  Command syntax: `<param name="caller-controls" value="default">`

- `auto-record`: It specifies whether to automatically record conferences on this conference bridge or not. Recording will begin once two or more parties are on the line. This option, if set, must consist of a path that can be written to for the purposes of recording the conference.

  Command syntax: `<param name="auto-record" value="filename"/>`

  Default: off

  Sample filename: `/usr/local/freeswitch/sounds/conferences/`
  `${conference_name}.wav`

  The sample filename listed would record conferences into a file based on the conference bridge's name.

- `interval`: The number of milliseconds per frame is the value for `interval`. This setting is similar to how `ptime` works, but it may vary from the `ptime` in SIP SDP headers or your TDM driver's settings. Higher numbers require less CPU but can cause conversation quality issues, so experiment with your setup. The default is usually OK.

  Command syntax: `<param name="interval" value="20">`

  Default: 20

- energy-level: Energy level (or strength/volume of audio) required for audio to be sent to the other users. The energy level is a threshold that dictates the level at which a person is determined to be speaking versus the receiving of background noise. This feature helps remove background or ambient noise from being mixed into the conference. If this option is too high it can also result in clipping at the beginning, and at the end of audio. 0 disables the detection and will bridge all packets even if they are only background noise.

  Command syntax: `<param name="energy-level" value="20">`

  Default: 20

  Set 0 to disable completely.

- member-flags: Member flags allow for setting member-specific flags or parameters on individual conference members. These options include whether to be "wasteful" with packet mixing (that is send audio to individuals even when no speaking is happening in the conference), whether or not a specific member is the leader of a conference (and thus, the conference should terminate when they leave), and so on. Options should be separated by a pipe | character.

  Command syntax: `<param name="member-flags" value="waste|endconf">`

  Options:

  - deaf: Prevents the members from listening to other members in the conference by default (this can be changed after the conference has begun via events).
  - waste: Send audio to channels even when no speaking is occurring.
  - dist-dtmf: Distribute DTMF signals to each channel. When someone pushes a DTMF tone, it is normally absorbed and processed by FreeSWITCH. This option prevents that from happening and instead echoes the DTMF tone to all other members.
  - endconf: Specifies that the conference should end when this party exits.

- conference-flags: Conference flags set conference-wide flags that dictate how the conference behaves. The only currently available option is to force users to wait for the moderator before the conference begins. Moderators are determined via the Dialplan when bridged to the conference by passing an extra flag. While waiting, callers hear music on hold.

  Command syntax: `<param name="conference-flags" value="wait-mod">`

- `tts-engine`: The Text-To-Speech engine to utilize within this conference bridge.

  Command syntax: `<param name="tts-engine" value="cepstral">`

- `tts-voice`: Which Text-To-Speech engine's voice to utilize within this conference bridge.

  Command syntax: `<param name="tts-voice" value="david">`

- `pin`: PIN code (that is pass code or password) that must be entered before user is allowed to enter the conference.

  Command syntax: `<param name="pin" value="12345">`

- `max-members`: The maximum number of members allowed in the conference. If this number is reached and an additional member tries to join, the `max-members-sound` will be played and the caller will not be allowed to enter the conference bridge.

  Command syntax: `<param name="max-members" value="20">`

- `caller-id-name`: The Caller ID name to set when making an outbound call from within this conference bridge.

  Command syntax: `<param name="caller-id-name" value="John Doe">`

- `caller-id-number`: The Caller ID number to set when making an outbound call from within this conference bridge.

  Command syntax: `<param name="caller-id-number" value="4158867900">`

- `comfort-noise`: The volume level of background white noise to add to the conference. Sometimes callers think they have been dropped from a conference if the audio level remains too quiet. This comfort noise setting provides white noise on the line so the caller knows the line is still connected. Note that at higher audio sampling rates this noise can become bothersome, so you may wish to tweak this setting if you go above 8000 Hz sampling rates.

  Command syntax: `<param name="comfort-noise" value="1000">`

- `announce-count`: The system will speak the total number of callers in the conference when a new person joins, but only when the threshold specified in this parameter is reached. It requires a valid text-to-speech engine.

  Command syntax: `<param name="announce-count" value="5">`

- `suppress-events`: This is for use with the FreeSWITCH event system. This special configuration option denotes that certain types of events should NOT be fired to other parties who may be listening for conference events.

- sound-prefix: Set a default path from which to retrieve conference audio files.

  Command syntax: `<param name="sound-prefix"`
                              `value="/usr/local/freeswitch/sounds/">`

- Custom Sounds: The following parameters are available for setting custom sounds to play from within the conference bridge when certain activities occur. All sounds are played to individual caller channels, not to all parties in the conference, with the exception of enter-sound and exit-sound, which are played to all members.

  All sound files are specified with the format:

  `<param name="sound-name" value="file.wav">`

  - muted-sound : Played when a caller has been muted.
  - unmuted-sound : Played when a caller is no longer muted.
  - alone-sound : Played to caller when they are the only remaining party.
  - enter-sound : Played to caller when they join the conference.
  - exit-sound : Played to caller when they exit the conference.
  - kicked-sound : Played when a caller is kicked out from the conference.
  - locked-sound : Played to callers who try to join a locked conference.
  - is-locked-sound : Played to conference participants when a conference is locked.
  - is-unlocked-sound : Played to conference participants when a conference is unlocked.
  - pin-sound : Prompt used when asking for a conference pin.
  - bad-pin-sound : Played when an invalid pin number is entered.
  - perpetual-sound : A special setting — this plays a sound in a continuous loop, forever, when parties are in the conference.
  - moh-sound : A file or resource handle that plays a particular music-on-hold stream to the conference when there is only one member in the conference. When a second member joins, the audio will stop, unless mod-wait settings have been specified (as mentioned earlier).
  - max-members-sound : If someone tries to join a conference that already has the maximum amount of members, this file is played.

Caller controls

Caller controls help you specify what commands are available to callers via touch-tones from within an active conference. Commands can include modifying the volume of the conference, mute/un-mute or more advanced options like playing menus to individuals or moving people from one conference to another.

Caller controls are templates that get used by conferences when they are first started. For example, you can specify a list of controls that are available (such as 0 for mute, 1 for lower volume, 3 for higher volume) and then apply those controls to three different conferences. The name of a caller-controls group need not reflect the name of a conference bridge.

Caller controls are set up when the conference is first started. They are applied across the entire conference. You cannot have one party enter the conference with one set of controls and another party enter with another set of controls.

Warning: Do not name your `caller-controls` "default" or "none". Those words are reserved for the default key mappings or no key mappings, respectively.

```
<caller-controls>
  <group name="somekeys">
    <control action="vol talk dn"        digits="1"/>
    <control action="vol talk zero"      digits="2"/>
    <control action="vol talk up"        digits="3"/>
    <control action="transfer"           digits="5"
            data="100 XML default"/>
    <control action="execute_application" digits="0"
            data="playback conf_help.wav"/>
    <control action="execute_application" digits="#"
            data="execute_Dialplan conference-menu"/>
  </group>
</caller-controls>
```

The preceding example shows how to create a `caller-controls` profile named `somekeys` and assign keys 1 through 3 to lowering/normalizing/raising the volume, key 5 to transferring the call, and keys 0 and # to executing a Dialplan command.

Advertise

The `advertise` section of the conference configuration file allows you to generate presence events ("advertisements") to services and subscribed parties via the FreeSWITCH event system. The idea is to set up permanent room names that generate presence events just like a phone or other device would. An outside program can then monitor whether a conference room is in use or not.

Advertise settings contain a room name in each element within `advertise` tags, as shown in this example:

```
<advertise>
  <room name="888@$${subdomain}" status="FreeSWITCH"/>
</advertise>
```

Sending and receiving XMPP events

The conference module allows for XMPP servers such as gtalk to accept commands via Jabber/XMPP. These commands can include things like kicking users, transferring calls, and so on. The configurations are simple to use. Examples are as follows:

```
<chat-permissions>
  <profile name="default">
    <user name="bob@somewhere.com" commands="all"/>
    <user name="harry@somewhere.com" commands="|deaf|dial|energy|kick
|list|lock|mute|norecord|play|record|relate|say|saymember|stop|trans
fer|undeaf|unlock|unmute|volume_in|volume_out|"/>
  </profile>
</chat-permissions>
```

Connecting callers to the conference

Callers are connected to conferences via the conference application, which can be invoked from the XML Dialplan or from the event socket via API calls. The general syntax for connecting a caller to a conference is as follows:

```
<action application="conference" data="confname@profilename">
```

`confname` is the conference room's name, and `profilename` is the profile to use from the conference configuration file (as specified earlier in this chapter).

You can optionally pass specific parameters in to the conference by appending `+flags` at the end of a conference profile name, as shown here:

```
<action application="conference" data="confname@profilename+flags{
mute|deaf|waste|moderator}+[conference pin number]">
```

When someone attempts to join a conference that has no other members currently in it, the conference does not actually exist and therefore must be created. Upon creation, the settings from the active profile along with the specified conference PIN number are recorded in memory with the conference. Any future participants who join the conference must specify the same PIN number, if one existed when the conference was created.

The profile name you specify should match a named profile from your `conf/autoload_configs/conference.conf.xml` file.

Dynamically created conferences stay alive until the number of members drops below one.

Here are some examples of values to specify in the data section when bridging a call to a conference:

Action data	Description
`confname`	profile is "default", no flags or PIN
`confname+1234`	profile is "default", pin is 1234
`confname@profilename+1234`	no flags
`confname+1234+flags{mute,waste}`	profile is "default", multiple flags with PIN

Note that while some parameters are optional, their order is very important

Controlling active conferences

A number of CLI and API commands exist for controlling an active conference. The most commonly used commands involve kicking members, adjusting volumes, and originating calls (to add people to a conference). While these items are outside the scope of this tutorial, you should consult the FreeSWITCH wiki for more examples of how to use CLI commands to control a conference bridge.

Nibblebill

`mod_nibblebill` is a credit/debit module for FreeSWITCH. The module was initially written by Darren Schreiber to fill the gaps of a professional grade trunking system that lacked the ability to detect fraud real-time. Its purpose is to allow real-time debiting of credit or cash from a database while calls are in progress. Darren had the following goals:

- Debit credit/cash from accounts real-time
- Allow for billing at different rates during a single call
- Allow for warning callers when their balance is low (via audio, in-channel)
- Allow for disconnecting or re-routing calls when balance is depleted
- Allow billing functions listed above to operate with multiple concurrent calls

Use cases

mod_nibblebill can be used in a variety of use cases, some of which are listed below.

Billing (pre-pay)

You can allow people to put cash into an account and "nibble" away at it. In addition, when callers have almost depleted their account, a tone or other message can play (or another action can occur) warning the caller of this.

Upon full depletion of their account, the call can either be transferred to an extension that allows them to recharge their balance via touch-tones or otherwise, or the call can simply be disconnected.

Billing (post-pay)

If your database column allows it, you can make the warning and out-of-cash thresholds a negative number. Then, callers can "dip into" negative numbers in the database, and then you can bill them after their usage. In this way, you are also able to protect yourself from abuse, since callers will still be terminated if they go below some (negative) threshold you set (that is spent too much money in a month).

This is a more typical approach to billing for landlines and it allows for an account to be automatically cut off if excessive usage occurs without someone paying their bill.

Pay-per-call service billing

You could bill for providing a special service, either via fixed fee or via per-minute after a certain event (entering a credit card number and being approved, for example).

Maximum credit and/or fraud prevention

You can set up a credit field that gets depleted by your users, similar to pre-pay above, but just not tell them about it. When they deplete all their credit for a day/ week/month/and so on they can't make any more calls. You can use an external script to deposit more credit into their account at a pre-set interval. This would allow something like "100 minutes a day free" or other such promotions to work.

Design goals

- Concurrent design—allows for supervision of multiple in-progress channels that belong to the same account/account code
- Scalability—allow for different heartbeat intervals (or turning off supervision during calls altogether). This allows the administrator to tweak checks depending on system load
- Flexibility—allow warning levels and "out-of-funds" levels to be flexible on a global and per-user basis, and allow customization as to what happens when the caller is out of funds
- Customizable—all settings should be customizable, including when people are terminated or warned and what happens when they are terminated or warned

Installation and configuration

`mod_nibblebill` is part of the main FreeSWITCH source tree. It requires database/ODBC support to function properly. Linux/Unix users must compile `mod_nibblebill` as it is disabled by default:

Enabling `mod_nibblebill` is very similar to the process we used in Chapter 2 where we enabled `mod_flite`:

1. Open `modules.conf` in the FreeSWITCH source directory and locate this line:

   ```
   #applications/mod_nibblebill
   ```

   Remove the # and save the file.

2. Open `modules.conf.xml` in the `conf/autoload_configs` directory and locate this line:

   ```
   <!-- <load module="mod_nibblebill"/> -->
   ```

   Remove the `<!--` and `-->` tags and save the file.

3. Build and compile `mod_lua` from the FreeSWITCH source directory:

   make mod_nibblebill-install

4. Modify the database connection settings in `conf/autoload_configs/nibblebill.conf.xml`:

   ```
   <param name="db_username" value="bandwidth.com"/>

   <param name="db_password" value="password"/>

   <param name="db_dsn" value="bandwidth.com"/>
   ```

5. Save the file and exit.

Now `mod_nibblebill` will load automatically when FreeSWITCH starts. Note: you may also `load` or `unload mod_nibblebill` without restarting FreeSWITCH. This allows you to make changes to your Nibblebill configuration without bringing down your entire system.

Database tables

Per your configuration file (from `nibblebill.conf.xml` above), make sure you have an ODBC database driver and database that is accessible and contains the correct database, table, and column names.

A sample table is below

```
mysql> use tcapi;
mysql> select * from accounts;
+--------+--------------+----------+
| id     | name         | cash     |
+--------+--------------+----------+
|      1 | Darren       | 41.4161  |
|      2 | Joe          |       50 |
|      9 | tester9      |       50 |
|     10 | tester10     | 44.8213  |
| 837269 | My Company   |       50 |
+--------+--------------+----------+
5 rows in set (0.00 sec)
```

In the above example, a table named `accounts` exists in the database `tcapi`. That table contains `id` and `cash` columns for use by the billing script. `id` represents the account code, and cash represents the amount of money the user is allowed to spend. The corresponding settings in your `nibblebill.conf.xml` file for the above setup would be:

```
<param name="db_dsn" value="tcapi"/>
<param name="db_table" value="accounts"/>
<param name="db_column_cash" value="cash"/>
<param name="db_column_account" value="id"/>
```

Creating the database table for PostgreSQL

Use this SQL command to create a table in Postgres:

```
create table accounts (
  id bigserial not null,
  name varchar( 256 ),
  cash double precision not null
);
```

Creating the database table for MySQL

Use this SQL command to create a table in MySQL:

```
CREATE TABLE accounts
(
   id int NOT NULL PRIMARY KEY,
   name VARCHAR(255),
   cash double precision NOT NULL
);
```

Billing a call

There are several methods available to employ for billing calls.

Nibble method (default)

The default method of billing is based on the concept of a FreeSWITCH heartbeat. For every X seconds, we deduct Y amount from an account.

To bill a call, you must set a minimum of two variables on an in-progress channel. The variables are `nibble_rate` and `nibble_account`. As a neat feature, `mod_nibblebill` doesn't really care where you set up the billing variables from, as long as they exist before a hangup occurs. That means you can set them in the Dialplan, in the directory, in a Lua script—wherever.

In its simplest form, you can add this to a user's directory entry:

```
<variable name="nibble_rate" value="0.03"/>
<variable name="nibble_account" value="18238"/>
```

Now that user will be billed $0.03/minute for every call made or received. The billing will go against account 18238.

By default, a heartbeat is set at 60 seconds. This means that every 60 seconds, 0.03 is deducted from their account. Note that all mathematical calculations are done using FreeSWITCH's internal microseconds counters. This means a few things:

1. If a heartbeat does not fire exactly ontime you will get a fraction of a cent billed. You should make sure your underlying database can support that.

2. Counters count the time in-between ticks exactly. There is no "lost" billing.

3. Billing of minimums does not exist (yet).

You can modify the heartbeat interval globally with this parameter:

```
<param name="global_heartbeat" value="300">
```

That would make the heartbeat fire every 300 seconds, or every five minutes. Heartbeats can go as low as every second (though this is really not wise, as you're making a database call every second, per channel).

Alternative to nibble billings

It is possible to use this module without heartbeats enabled. That means you just bill a call at the end of the call. You set the same variables as listed above, but you also set one additional variable in your `mod_nibblebill.conf.xml` file:

```
<param name="global_heartbeat" value="off">
```

By doing this, billing will only occur at the end of a call (on hang up). The time calculation will be from when the call was answered until the end of the call. If a call is never answered, billing is skipped.

The formula used to bill calls when this parameter is set is:

[time call ended] - [time call answered] x [rate per minute] = total bill rate

NOTE: This method does not allow for any supervision of a call in progress, meaning fraud can occur and people can go over their allotted limits.

Examples

The following examples demonstrate how to implement various billing scenarios.

Different rates per user

It is possible to have different rates per minute, per user. This can work *in addition* to the Dialplan examples listed below, as long as you take care not to delete the variables. Here is an example.

Let's say you have two users—one is billed at $0.05/minute and one at $0.10/minute. Neither is billed when calling a toll-free 800 number. You would set up their directory entries like this:

```
<user id="dschreiber">
  <params>
    <param name="password" value="1234"/>
  </params>
  <variables>
    <variable name="nibble_rate" value="0.05"/>
    <variable name="nibble_account" value="8182"/>
    <variable name="default_areacode" value="415"/>
    <variable name="toll_allow" value="domestic,international,local"
```

```
/>
      <variable name="user_context" value="default"/>
   </variables>
 </user>
 <user id="expensive_guy">
   <params>
     <param name="password" value="1234"/>
   </params>
   <variables>
     <variable name="nibble_rate" value="0.10"/>
     <variable name="nibble_account" value="2932"/>
     <variable name="default_areacode" value="212"/>
     <variable name="toll_allow" value="domestic,international,local"
/>
      <variable name="user_context" value="default"/>
   </variables>
 </user>
```

Then in your Dialplan, override the bill rates for toll-free calls only:

```
<extension name="tollfree800">
   <condition field="destination_number" expression="^1?(800\d{7})$">
    <action application="set" data="nibble_rate=0"/>
    <action application="bridge" data="sofia/gateway/bandwidth.
com/$1"/>
   </condition>
 </extension>
```

All non-800 number calls will be billed at the rates set on the user's account, while toll-free calls will be billed 0 (equivalent to no billing).

Single rate for all users

On your user accounts:

```
<include>
  <user id="diegoviola">
    <params>
      <param name="password" value="1234"/>
    </params>
    <variables>
      <variable name="toll_allow" value="domestic,international,local
"/>
      <variable name="user_context" value="default"/>
      <variable name="nibble_account" value="1"/>
    </variables>
  </user>
</include>
```

and:

```
<include>
  <user id="dschreiber">
    <params>
      <param name="password" value="1234"/>
    </params>
    <variables>
      <variable name="toll_allow" value="domestic,international,local
"/>
      <variable name="user_context" value="default"/>
      <variable name="nibble_account" value="2"/>
    </variables>
  </user>
</include>
```

On the extension, you want to bill:

```
<extension name="outbound">
  <condition field="destination_number" expression="^91?(\d{10,})$">
    <action application="set" data="nibble_rate=0.05"/>
    <action application="set" data="$${nibble_account}"/>
    <action application="bridge" data="sofia/gateway/teliax/$1"/>
  </condition>
</extension>
```

Different rates per area code

This example bills all calls at $0.05/minute, except calls to area code 919 which are $0.07/minute and calls to 800 numbers, which are free. Calls are billed to whatever account code is set for the user in their directory profile.

Note: In this example, we set the rate from the Dialplan. Be careful! This overrides any variable set on the user/directory level!

```
<extension name="tollfree800">
  <condition field="destination_number" expression="^1?(800\d{7})$">
    <action application="set" data="nibble_account=${accountcode}"/>
    <action application="set" data="nibble_rate=0"/>
    <action application="bridge" data="sofia/gateway/bandwidth.
com/$1"/>
  </condition>
</extension>

<extension name="special919rate">
  <condition field="destination_number" expression="^1{0,1}(919\
d{7})$">
    <action application="set" data="nibble_account=${accountcode}"/>
    <action application="set" data="nibble_rate=0.07"/>
```

```
      <action application="bridge" data="sofia/gateway/bandwidth.
com/$1"/>
    </condition>
  </extension>

  <extension name="domestic">
    <condition field="destination_number" expression="^(1{0,1}\
d{10})$">
      <action application="set" data="nibble_account=${accountcode}"/>
      <action application="set" data="nibble_rate=0.05"/>
      <action application="bridge" data="sofia/gateway/bandwidth.
com/$1"/>
    </condition>
  </extension>
```

Different rates per service delivery

This idea encompasses the concept of changing the nibble_rate while the call is in progress.

Here is the idea: A caller could call in and for the first part of their call, they might be getting billed at $1.00/minute, maybe to talk to Tier 1 support. If they need Tier 2 support, the rate goes to $5.00/minute. The rate changes when the call is transferred, simply by changing the variable. You can even set the amount to 0 while the caller is on hold or in a FIFO queue.

```
<extension name="tier1">
  <condition field="destination_number" expression="^2000$">
    <!-- Save anything billed at a previous rate -->
    <action application="nibblebill" data="flush"/>
    <!-- Change the rate -->
    <action application="set" data="nibble_rate=1.00"/>
    <!-- Transfer to Tier1 rep -->
    <action application="transfer" data="1000 XML default"/>
  </condition>
</extension>

<extension name="tier2">
  <condition field="destination_number" expression="^2000$">
    <!-- Save anything billed at a previous rate -->
    <action application="nibblebill" data="flush"/>
    <!-- Change the rate -->
    <action application="set" data="nibble_rate=5.00"/>
    <!-- Transfer to Tier2 rep -->
    <action application="transfer" data="1001 XML default"/>
  </condition>
</extension>
```

Another possible use of this is to bill a caller while they're talking to support, but to stop billing after the call when you give them a survey. Same concept as above, but done this way:

```
<extension name="survey-after-call">
  <condition field="destination_number" expression="^2000$">

    <!-- Handle support request here at $1.00/minute via extension 1001
-->
    <action application="set" data="nibble_rate=1.00"/>
    <action application="set" data="hangup_after_bridge=false"/>
    <action application="bridge" data="sofia/internal/
1001@$${domain}"/>
    <action application="nibblebill" data="flush"/>

    <!-- Set rate to 0, then transfer caller to the survey IVR -->
    <action application="set" data="nibble_rate=0.00"/>
    <action application="bridge" data="sofia/internal/
1002@$${domain}"/>
  </condition>
</extension>
```

WARNING: There is a "catch" to this method. You should flush the current call's billings to the database before the call's rate changes. This is to write out any billed seconds since the last query to DB with the old rate.

Hang up the call when the balance is depleted

When the balance of an account drops below the setting you have specified in the configuration for `nobal_amt`, the call gets transferred to an extension of your choice. This allows you to play a message such as, "Your call has been terminated due to insufficient funds." Since we're really just transferring the call to an extension and suspending billing, you could get fancy and potentially make the user key in their credit card number to replete their funds.

In your `conf/autoload_configs/nibblebill.conf.xml` file add something like this:

```
<param name="nobal_amt" value="0"/>
<param name="nobal_action" value="hangup XML default"/>
```

In this example, note the `nobal_action` of "hangup XML default". This tells `mod_nibblebill` to transfer the call to the extension named "hangup" in the default context of your XML Dialplan when the balance reaches the `nobal_amt` threshold. You can then add this to your Dialplan:

```
<extension name="hangup">
  <condition field="destination_number" expression="^(hangup)$">
    <action application="playback" data="no_more_funds.wav"/>
    <action application="hangup"/>
  </condition>
</extension>
```

In this example, when a caller's balance reaches zero their call will be transferred to the hangup extension. That extension will play a message stating that they are out of funds (assuming you record a sound filename no_more_funds.wav) and the call will disconnect.

Note carefully that the B leg currently also gets transferred to the same extension.

Application/CLI/API commands

The following commands can be used from the Dialplan, CLI or API. The syntax is basically the same for each, with the somewhat obvious difference being that applications are in the format:

```
<action application="nibblebill" data="action [params]">
```

Whereas CLI and API commands are just:

```
nibblebill <channel-uuid> <action> [params]
```

Check

Inserting check in your application or using it on the CLI with a UUID returns the balance that has been billed so far. This does not include any increments that are not written to the database yet.

```
<action application="nibblebill" data="check"/>
```

Flush

Insert this in your Dialplan:

```
<action application="nibblebill" data="flush"/>
```

The preceding code will immediately write to the database any pending billings. Billing will continue, but everything that needed to be billed up to this point in time will be calculated and recorded.

This has no effect when billing is paused.

Pause

Insert this in your Dialplan:

```
<action application="nibblebill" data="pause"/>
```

This will set a flag to pause billing. If the call is terminated while billing is paused, no billing from the time the call was paused onward will be calculated, but billing prior to the pause will still get recorded. You can also manually resume billing later on during the call with the `resume` command (discussed in the next section).

Note that if you call the pause command when a call is already paused, the call is ignored.

Resume

Insert this in your Dialplan:

```
<action application="nibblebill" data="resume"/>
```

This will resume billing during a call that was previously paused. The time in-between pause and resume is not billed. Note that you can pause and resume a call multiple times and the amount of time in between each pause period will be tracked.

Reset

Insert this in your Dialplan:

```
<action application="nibblebill" data="reset"/>
```

This will reset the billing timer to the current time. Note that all you are doing here is resetting all the internal counters that track the call's progress to the current time, so any time that would have been billed prior to now (but has not yet been committed to disk) will be "lost" and considered "free."

> Any amounts already deducted in the database for a particular account are considered committed—a done deal. This command has no impact on commits already made to disk.

Adding and deducting funds

Insert this in your Dialplan:

```
<action application="nibblebill" data="adjust 5.00"/>
```

It adds or deducts a certain amount of funds from an account (in this case, we are adding $5.00). Note that this occurs immediately and currently circumvents any protections that exist for when the database is down. It is your responsibility to deal with having a functioning database when you use this command.

Use negative numbers to deduct from an account.

Enabling session heartbeat

Enabling the session heartbeat is done during a call as follows:

```
<action application="nibblebill" data="heartbeat 60"/>
```

This sets the heartbeat for the current call (only) to 60 seconds. You can set this differently per-call.

Bill based on B leg only

If you want to bill only B Leg `enable_heartbeat_events` variable must be enabled on the B Leg channel. You can enable these `hearbeats` by setting the heartbeat events in the `bridge` command. As we discussed earlier in the book, variables in brackets on the `bridge` command are passed to the B Leg.

Here is an example:

```
<action application="bridge" data="{enable_heartbeat_events=5,nibble_
rate=1,nibble_account=0838833133}sofia/external/$1@tel.co.th"/>
```

XML/Curl

`mod_xml_curl` can be used to dynamically control the behavior of FreeSWITCH. `mod_xml_curl` hooks into FreeSWITCH at times when configuration files or sections of configuration files are requested. Instead of retrieving the data for those requested configuration options from the in-memory XML structure, `mod_xml_curl` will look to see if the configuration category matches a known `mod_xml_curl` category and will then attempt to retrieve the configuration data, real-time, from an external source. By using `mod_xml_curl` you can provide configurations to multiple instances of FreeSWITCH without having to duplicate the configuration, and the configurations can be served up by any software program that can generate XML. The software does not even need to be on the same server that FreeSWITCH is on. This solution is very helpful when building out robust, multi-server platforms.

`mod_xml_curl` can be used to get any information that would normally be in `freeswitch.xml`. XML configuration section names are utilized to determine what server URLs should be accessed depending on what type of information is being requested. Some sample section names that you can link to external URLs include:

- `configuration`: Configuration items, that is for mod_sofia or mod_dingaling
- `directory`: User directory (dial-by-name, and so on)
- `ivr`: For IVR menu options and items
- `Dialplan`: Dialplan items (for call routing)
- `phrases`: Phrases for the say API

Once you load the `mod_xml_curl` module, all future attempts to access XML will be sent first to `mod_xml_curl`, which can then query a web server if the section being requested has a configuration "binding". The web server can optionally return nothing and FreeSWITCH will fail back to the normal method of looking in-memory for an XML match. This also means that if your Web server isn't reachable you can place fail back scenarios into your in-memory XML configuration.

Installation

To use `mod_xml_curl` you must first ensure it is enabled. If you compiled FreeSWITCH from source, you'll want to ensure that the `mod_xml_curl` module is also compiled and installed. Do just as we did with `mod_flite` back in Chapter 2:

1. Open `modules.conf` in the FreeSWITCH source directory and locate this line:

   `#xml_int/mod_xml_curl`

   Remove the # and save the file.

2. Open `modules.conf.xml` in the `conf/autoload_configs` directory and locate this line:

   `<!-- <load module="mod_xml_curl"/> -->`

   Remove the `<!--` and `-->` tags and save the file.

3. Build and compile `mod_xml_curl` from the FreeSWITCH source directory:

   `make mod_xml_curl-install`

`mod_xml_curl` is now configured to load automatically when FreeSWITCH starts. You may restart FreeSWITCH or type `load mod_xml_curl` at the `fs_cli`.

> Modules in `autoload_configs/modules.conf.xml` are loaded in order. If you intend to use `mod_xml_curl` to provide configuration information to other modules that load, make sure `mod_xml_curl` is at the top of the `modules.conf.xml` file.

Configuration

The file `autoload_configs/xml_curl.conf.xml` is used in the default FreeSWITCH setup. It contains a series of bindings that specify what configuration sections are located on which host. Individual bindings are specified as such:

```
<param name="gateway-url" value="http://localhost:8080"
bindings="Dialplan"/>
```

In the preceding example, you are stating that there is a URL of `http://localhost:8080` which should be called each time something in the Dialplan is requested. FreeSWITCH will "bind" (or tie) all future Dialplan requests to this URL first. (Bindings are discussed in the next section.) When a Dialplan entry is actually needed, FreeSWITCH will call the URL specified with a series of HTTP POST data that gives details about which Dialplan entry is desired. Your web server can then execute a program or script that returns only information for that Dialplan entry.

Note that bindings can be made to a single URL for multiple types of configuration sections. In the `bindings="Dialplan"` parameter, just add additional section names, each separated by a pipe. Here is an example of using the same URL and binding configuration option for both Dialplan and directory entries:

```
<param name="gateway-url" value="http://localhost:8080" bindings="Dial
plan|directory"/>
```

Note the addition of directory right after Dialplan, separated by a pipe.

Including all other required tags, the full configuration would look something like this:

```
<configuration name="xml_curl.conf" description="cURL XML Gateway">
  <bindings>
    <binding name="Dialplan fetcher">
      <param name="gateway-url" value="http://localhost:8080"
             bindings="Dialplan"/>
    </binding>
  </bindings>
</configuration>
```

It is possible that your primary web server is unavailable. In this scenario, you may specify an alternate web server to try to reach. Note carefully, however, that in using the option there is a timeout that will need to occur first before a backup server is attempted, which might delay call processing and have undesirable consequences. It is generally a better strategy to use a professional load-balancing device in front of your web servers if you are going to cluster web servers together to serve up XML information.

Here is more advanced configuration that includes a backup server. The binding statements are processed in sequential order in a failover manner.

```
<configuration name="xml_curl.conf" description="cURL XML Gateway">
  <bindings>
    <binding name="Dialplan_A">
      <param name="gateway-url" value="http://localhost:8080"
bindings="Dialplan"/>
    </binding>
    <binding name="Dialplan_B">
      <param name="gateway-url" value="http://backuphost:8080"
bindings="Dialplan"/>
    </binding>
  </bindings>
</configuration>
```

If you are using `lighttpd`, `nginx`, `thin` and probably a few others as your web server, you might receive some errors regarding "Expect: 100" or have performance problems. You can turn this off by adding this string to your binding:

```
<param name="disable-100-continue" value="true"/>
```

Bindings

Bindings are relationships between configuration sections (such as directory, Dialplan, IVR, and so on) and settings for URL retrieval. You may have different types of bindings that hit different servers depending on your setup; for example, you may get your directory entries (that is, allowed users and devices) from one server but your Dialplan entries come from another server. Each one of these relationships is called a "binding."

Bindings do not just have to be plain HTTP URLs. You can include authentication credentials and a few options as well. HTTP-Basic is available for authentication and will be used by default, although it is generally less secure as passwords are transmitted in plain text. If you are only accessing a local web server on the same machine, this solution is the fastest. HTTP-Digest is also supported.

You specify authentication schemes by using the auth-scheme parameter, as in this example:

```
    <binding name="Dialplan">
      <param name="gateway-url" value="http://localhost:8080"
bindings="Dialplan"/>
      <param name="gateway-credentials" value="user:password"/>
      <param name="auth-scheme" value="basic"/>
    </binding>
```

The emboldened entries specify the username/password to use and the authentication scheme to use.

HTTP requests

When mod_xml_curl seeks information, it will make a standard HTTP request to the URL specified. With each request, a set of POST data will be sent that your script can utilize to figure out what information is needed by FreeSWITCH. The POST will contain a querystring with the following values:

- key_value: This field contains the configuration section name/filename that is being requested. Examples include "acl.conf" or "sofia.conf" and so forth.
- key_name: This reflects a parameter name or setting that is being queried.
- section = configuration: This reflects the specific configuration section within the file that is being requested.
- tag_name = configuration: This parameter is always sent as an indicator that configuration data is being requested.

HTTP response

Your web server must respond with data that is formatted as a complete XML document containing the section header and XML information FreeSWITCH needs. Note carefully that even though FreeSWITCH is only requesting a subsection of configuration data, you must properly format a full XML response document.

The response format is:

```
<document type="freeswitch/xml">
  <section name="configuration">
    <configuration name="SECTIONNAME.conf">
       <!-- YOUR XML CONFIG RESPONSE HERE -->
    </configuration>
  </section>
</document>
```

In the preceding example you would replace SECTIONNAME.conf with a section name like sofia.conf and then place your settings, parameters, or other XML return tags within the configuration section, just as if they were in the flat files.

> **NOTE:** It is possible to return more data than is necessary. FreeSWITCH will still parse the new XML data and look only for the specific information it needs. So if you are returning Dialplan information from your script, you can return multiple extensions, and FreeSWITCH will still process the condition statements to ensure that only the intended destinations that match are executed.

Optimization

In general, your XML responses via mod_xml_curl should be as small as possible. On small systems, this is less important, but on larger systems, returning extraneous amounts of data can actually be slower then just using the built-in flat XML files that get loaded into memory. This is because each request entails making an HTTP call, downloading XML data, parsing it and then using the XML data, versus just searching in-memory and using data. Responding with as little as necessary is advisable to avoid CPU spikes related to processing large XML documents.

Order of requests

Depending on when you load_mod_curl in the conf/autoload_configs/modules. conf.xml file, you can grab configuration data for other modules during their startup phase from external files. Such scenarios are useful when modules, such as mod_sofia, might get information like their IP address and profile data from a database that resides on your web server.

Request/response examples

As a general reference, below you will find some examples of requests and responses when utilizing mod_xml_curl. Listed first is the POST data that should be received by your server when mod_xml_curl is bound to a specific module and makes a request. Following that is a sample response your web server could return that would result in the configuration of FreeSWITCH.

mod_sofia

When mod_sofia loads, it requests information about the directory and gateways on the system. You do not have to return information about any of your users at this time. This request will also occur is someone restarts or rescans in mod_sofia. The following is an example request for the default internal profile:

```
[hostname] => myswitch
[section] => directory
[tag_name] =>
[key_name] =>
[key_value] =>
[Event-Name] => REQUEST_PARAMS
[Core-UUID] => abca98daa-5023-15b1-1b10-dbabca89dba
[FreeSWITCH-Hostname] => myswitch
[FreeSWITCH-IPv4] => 192.168.0.50
[FreeSWITCH-IPv6] => ::1
[Event-Date-Local] => 2010-04-16 00:21:29
[Event-Date-GMT] => Tue, 16 Apr 2010 00:21:29 GMT
[Event-Date-Timestamp] => 1256629972839876
[Event-Calling-File] => sofia.c
[Event-Calling-Function] => config_sofia
[Event-Calling-Line-Number] => 3056
[purpose] => gateways
[profile] => internal
```

A sample response to this request might be as follows. This response would tell mod_sofia about two existing domains in the system, clientA.myswitch.com and clientB.myswitch.com (useful if you are hosting two clients on the same machine).

```
<document type="freeswitch/xml">
  <section name="directory">
    <domain name="clientA.myswitch.com">
      <params>
        <param name="dial-string" value="{presence_id=${dialed_
user}@${dialed_domain}}${sofia_contact(${dialed_user}@${dialed_
domain})}"/>
      </params>
    </domain>
    <domain name="clientB.myswitch.com">
      <params>
        <param name="dial-string" value="{presence_id=${dialed_
user}@${dialed_domain}}${sofia_contact(${dialed_user}@${dialed_
domain})}"/>
      </params>
      <user id="default" />
    </domain>
  </section>
</document>
```

ACL

When access control lists are needed, they also can be queried real-time. A query would be made that provides information on the domain hitting the system and for what purposes it is asking (that is directory retrieval). In the below scenario, on host `myswitch`, someone from `192.168.0.2` is requesting directory information in relation to the allowed network-list.

```
[hostname]  => myswitch
[section]   => directory
[tag_name]  => domain
[key_name]  => name
[key_value] => 192.168.0.2
[domain]    => 192.168.0.2
[purpose]   => network-list
```

Authorization

When a user attempts to register to a FreeSWITCH instance, `mod_xml_curl` can query your web server to see if they are a valid user, and if they are, to pass a list of parameters to FreeSWITCH that tells information about that user. An example registration is shown below. In this example, the user `1000@clientA.myswitch.com` is trying to register using authentication.

```
[hostname]  => myswitch
[section]   => directory
[tag_name]  => domain
[key_name]  => name
[key_value] => clientA.myswitch.com
[Event-Name] => REQUEST_PARAMS
[Core-UUID] => c5c8cbf4-60c3-45a2-b110-933da620cfd2
[FreeSWITCH-Hostname] => 25515_1_36308_177178
[FreeSWITCH-IPv4] => 192.168.0.50
[FreeSWITCH-IPv6] => ::1
[Event-Date-Local] => 2009-10-27 00:47:10
[Event-Date-GMT] => Tue, 27 Oct 2009 07:47:10 GMT
[Event-Date-Timestamp] => 1256629630733916
[Event-Calling-File] => sofia_reg.c
[Event-Calling-Function] => sofia_reg_parse_auth
[Event-Calling-Line-Number] => 1671
[action] => sip_auth
[sip_profile] => internal
[sip_user_agent] => PolycomSoundPointIP-SPIP_320-UA/3.1.0.0084
[sip_auth_username] => 1000
[sip_auth_realm] => clientA.myswitch.com
[sip_auth_nonce] => 533c5264-12cb-4f8b-bcdb-5ecabe5e540f
[sip_auth_uri] => sip:clientA.myswitch.com:5060
[sip_contact_user] => 1000
```

```
[sip_contact_host] => 192.168.1.100
[sip_to_user] => 1000
[sip_to_host] => clientA.myswitch.com
[sip_from_user] => 1000
[sip_from_host] => clientA.myswitch.com
[sip_request_host] => clientA.myswitch.com
[sip_request_port] => 5060
[sip_auth_qop] => auth
[sip_auth_cnonce] => hSVnPb32nA/OtkY
[sip_auth_nc] => 00000001
[sip_auth_response] => 6e4e611d7593d52e02451b70900071d8
[sip_auth_method] => REGISTER
[key] => id
[user] => 1000
[domain] => clientA.myswitch.com
[ip] => 192.168.1.100
```

At first glance the information in the POST you receive from FreeSWITCH can be a bit overwhelming. If we review only what is critical to generating a response for mod_xml_curl, we can pay attention to these fields:

```
[hostname] => myswitch
[section] => directory
[tag_name] => domain
[key_name] => name
[key_value] => clientA.myswitch.com
[key] => id
[user] => 1000
[domain] => clientA.myswitch.com
```

This is a little more manageable. This shortened piece of information says that we need the information available about user 1000 on clientA.myswitch.com. We then use a script on our web server to find data about this user and return a response, like this:

```
<?xml version="1.0" encoding="UTF-8" standalone="no"?>
<document type="freeswitch/xml">
  <section name="directory">
    <domain name="clientA.myswitch.com">
      <groups>
        <group name="default">
          <users>
            <user id="1000">
              <params>
                <param name="password" value="some_password"/>
              </params>
            </user>
          </users>
        </group>
```

```
      </groups>
    </domain>
  </section>
</document>
```

This example allows an auth/challenge to happen with user `1000` on domain `clientA.myswitch.com` with the password `some_password`. If you do not wish to communicate passwords in plain text over your network, you can use the `a1-hash` parameter. Simply replace the `password param` in the above example with this tag:

```
<param name="a1-hash" value="50046ba744759aa83e045ba0b996e7a9"/>
```

In the above example, the md5 hash is generated by running `md5` on the password `1234`. Any program that can generate a proper md5 hash will work for creating this.

Voicemail request

`mod_voicemail` occasionally needs to look up a user's id. You respond to requests for voicemail box information in the same way you respond to `mod_sofia` authentication requests. As an example, FreeSWITCH will post this request to you looking up a voicemail box named `Support`.

```
[hostname] => testmachine
[section] => directory
[tag_name] => domain
[key_name] => name
[key_value] => clientA.myswitch.com
[Event-Name] => GENERAL
[Core-UUID] => c5c8cbf4-60c3-45a2-b110-933da620cfd2
[FreeSWITCH-Hostname] => myswitch
[FreeSWITCH-IPv4] => 192.168.1.10
[FreeSWITCH-IPv6] => ::1
[Event-Date-Local] => 2009-10-27 00:47:40
[Event-Date-GMT] => Tue, 27 Oct 2009 07:47:40 GMT
[Event-Date-Timestamp] => 1256629660158410
[Event-Calling-File] => mod_voicemail.c
[Event-Calling-Function] => resolve_id
[Event-Calling-Line-Number] => 1278
[action] => message-count
[key] => id
[user] => Support
[domain] => clientA.myswitch.com
```

You would respond to the voicemail box request with XML code that looks like this:

```
<?xml version="1.0" encoding="UTF-8" standalone="no"?>
<document type="freeswitch/xml">
 <section name="directory">
  <domain name="clientA.myswitch.com">
   <groups>
```

```
      <group name="default">
        <users>
          <user id="Support">
            <params>
              <param name="vm-password" value="1234"/>
            </params>
          </user>
        </users>
      </group>
    </groups>
  </domain>
</section>
</document>
```

This would result in a mailbox named Support being accessible with the password 1234.

Dialplan bindings

One of the most commonly used mod_xml_curl bindings is the Dialplan binding. This binding allows for the routing decisions made by FreeSWITCH to be offloaded to an external web server's script. Note that the mod_xml_curl Dialplan binding gathers XML information to be used as the Dialplan during the ROUTING phase—call flow still proceeds into the EXECUTE phase where the commands specified are actually run.

Request

FreeSWITCH will POST a request to your Web server with information about the incoming call when a routing decision must be made. The query string will contain the same basic POST data as talked about earlier along with some additional fields. These fields are described as follows:

- context: The numbering context to retrieve (normally "default").
- destination_number: Number that was dialed/called.
- caller_id_name: Name of the calling user.
- caller_id_number: Number of the calling user.
- network_addr: IP address of the calling user.
- ani: Phone number that the user called from (if known).
- rdnis: Redirected number information. Set by providers if this call is actually the result of a forwarded call to a different number. This field will contain the number that was originally dialed.

- source: Source module who created the call (such as mod_sofia, mod_portaudio, and so on).

- chan_name: Channel name.

- uuid: This call's unique identifier.

- endpoint_disposition: The state the call was in when mod_xml_curl asked for information. It is useful if a call is actually the result of a transfer or has already been answered for some other reason.

Reply

When you receive a request for Dialplan information, you would process the POST data and decide how to respond. Here is a sample response:

```xml
<?xml version="1.0" encoding="UTF-8" standalone="no"?>
<document type="freeswitch/xml">
  <section name="Dialplan">
    <context name="default">
      <extension name="dialed_number">
        <condition field="destination_number" expression="^123$">
          <action application="bridge" data="sofia/user/123"/>
        </condition>
      </extension>
    </context>
  </section>
</document>
```

This sample response would create an extension named dialed_number which matched the number that was dialed (123 in this example) and bridge the call to the SIP user registered to 123.

Other bindings

It is possible to bind to other modules within the FreeSWITCH system as well. Any modules that search for configuration data using the standard FreeSWITCH configuration API functions will call the same event/hook system that allows mod_xml_curl to operate. Such modules include IVRs, mod_directory, mod_sofia, and others.

General "Not found" reply

You can tell FreeSWITCH to stop processing (that is no match/no route to destination) if you like. Simply return a not found message, like this:

```
<?xml version="1.0" encoding="UTF-8" standalone="no"?>
<document type="freeswitch/xml">
  <section name="result">
    <result status="not found" />
  </section>
</document>
```

Note carefully that if you fail return the not found result, FreeSWITCH will keep looking for a match in the Dialplan and will fail back to the flat-file XML system.

Important: The default configuration in FreeSWITCH includes extensions and Dialplan entries that could allow someone to register and make calls on your system without your knowledge! If you are exclusively using mod_xml_curl as your Dialplan and the directory parsing engine, make sure you remove the stock configuration files in conf/Dialplan and conf/directory, accordingly.

Debugging

You can use the following FreeSWITCH command to help with debugging your configuration. It will return a filename with the resulting XML for each xml_curl query.

xml_curl debug_on

Failing back

When a module needs a piece of configuration data, it will ask FreeSWITCH for that data using a common API. FreeSWITCH then searches for that data in the following order:

1. Any dynamic sources that were registered, in the order they were registered. Typically, if you use mod_xml_curl, then it will be the only dynamic source you need to worry about.

2. The in-memory configuration data built from your local XML files of the conf directory.

FreeSWITCH will stop looking as soon as it finds the requested data. In this way, it is possible to either provide new configuration data that is not present in your static files or to override your static data with dynamic data.

Alternative endpoints

While most users of FreeSWITCH will use SIP (and thus `mod_sofia`), there are other ways for FreeSWITCH to communicate with the world. Here are brief descriptions of three methods that you may wish to investigate further.

Skype and GSM endpoints

Not everyone has the budget to buy hardware or services to connect to the Skype and **GSM (Global System** for **Mobile Communications)** networks, especially when first learning a new technology. FreeSWITCH has an alternative to offer to those willing to do a little work: a pair of endpoints (that is, channel drivers) that allow inbound and outbound voice calls and messaging (chatting, SMSs) in the cheapest possible way.

Both `mod_skypopen` and `mod_gsmopen` support full integration with all the FreeSWITCH features, have CLI commands for diagnostic and control, full events interaction, and can be used in the same way as the Sofia SIP workhorse endpoint module.

Both the `mod_skypopen` and `mod_gsmopen` modules have the same general structure: they control an external entity (an "interface") via its own signaling protocol, and redirect the audio stream from/to FreeSWITCH via the interface to/from the destination network.

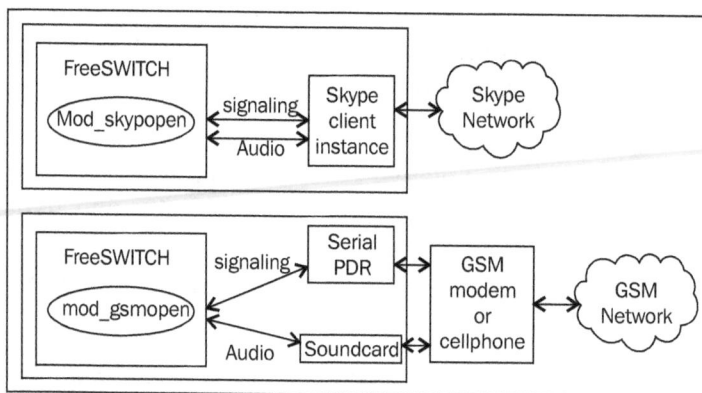

For `mod_skypopen` the "interface" is an instance of the regular Skype client software that interacts natively with the Skype network, redirecting the audio flow to FreeSWITCH. The Skype client instance is controlled by `mod_skypopen` through the Skype API native commands (signaling).

For `mod_gsmopen` the "interface" is a GSM modem (or perhaps a second-hand cell phone) that interacts natively with the GSM network. The GSM interface is controlled by `mod_gsmopen` via serial port commands, often regular AT commands (signaling), while the audio flows through a soundcard.

Both `skypopen` and `gsmopen` fully support voice calls and chatting, using the regular FreeSWITCH APIs, Dialplans, and events. So, if your application works with SIP or Jabber, both for voice and/or messaging, it will work unmodified on GSM and Skype networks as well, including inbound/outbound chatting and SMS messages.

Skype with mod_skypopen

You will need to compile and load the `mod_skypopen` module, and start at least one instance of the regular native Skype client on the same machine FreeSWITCH is running on.

No external hardware, no reverse engineering, and nothing nefarious is happening. `mod_skypopen` is simply a legal usage of the Skype API. While `mod_skypopen` uses the Skype API in full accordance with the Skype license agreement, it is not endorsed, certified, or otherwise approved in any way by Skype.

Linux and Windows are fully supported and you can have dozens of concurrent Skypopen calls on a machine that has enough RAM and CPU power to run dozens of Skype client instances. On Mac, only one instance is possible as of this writing.

On Linux and Windows, you can have multiple instances answering inbound Skype calls/chat for the same Skype username (that is dozens of concurrent inbound calls for "mycompany_tech_support").

Multiple outbound calls/chat can be originated from the same Skype username on Linux (that is dozens of concurrent calls placed by "mycompany_sales" Skype username), while on Windows each outbound call has to be placed by a different Skype username ("mycompany_sales01", "mycompany_sales02", and so on).

Both on Linux and Windows Skypopen and the Skype client instances can run "headless", without the need (and the overhead) of a desktop installation. (for example, on a regular "server" installation, on Linux using Xvfb).

Skypopen allows for placing and receiving outbound/inbound calls to/from other Skype usernames (the classic regular "Skype-to-Skype" calls), for placing "SkypeOut" calls to PSTN or cell phone numbers around the world (you must buy from Skype credit for the Skype username used by the "interface" Skype client instance), for receiving "SkypeIn" calls originally destined for a PSTN number somewhere in the world (you must buy the service from Skype), and for chatting (inbound/outbound) with other Skype usernames. Skype SMS service is not yet supported as of this writing.

Further information is available on the Skypopen wiki page at `http://wiki.freeswitch.org/wiki/Skypopen`.

GSM with mod_gsmopen

You will need to compile and load the `mod_gsmopen` module, and the following:

- one or more GSM modem or second-hand cellphone (the "interface")
- one or more serial port (most often just a USB port)
- one or more soundcard (most often a USB cheap "dongle")
- cables for the serial and audio connection between the "interface" and serial port/soundcard

Each "interface" is the combination made by all of the listed items.

Most cell phones out there can be directly connected to serial port (USB) via their own data cable, while for audio you will need to make an audio cable from the hands-free jack to the in/out jacks of the soundcard.

There are very nice cheap embedded compound devices on the market (fully supported by GSMOpen) that comprise the GSM modem, the soundcard, and an internal USB hub (a complete "interface"). With those devices you'll have one only standard USB cable running from the FreeSWITCH machine to the "black box" complete interface.

For multiple lines installation, just use USB hubs (more details, supported cell phones/devices, and so on on wiki), and you can have concurrent calls and SMSs to/from the numbers of each SIM (one "interface", one SIM, one number).

For usage as SMS gateway only (no voice calls needed) you only want the serial part of the "interface" (no soundcard, no audio cable). You can connect as many second-hand cell phones you wish with USB hubs (multi-serial support is very good in Linux), and the CPU load at full SMS throughput is negligible.

Each "interface" has its own SIM card, with its own cell number, and the best contract you can have from your GSM carrier. Note that most carriers offer free intra-carriers calls, "SME plans", "family plans", free minutes, or special offers on special hours.

You can mix and match interfaces with different carriers and plans, and have outbound calls and SMSs made from the less costly "interface" via Dialplan and least cost routing.

At the time of writing, GSMOpen runs only on Linux, however Windows support will be available soon.

For an up-to-date list of supported hardware ("black box" complete devices, cell phones, cables, and so on) and detailed instructions on the various use cases, refer to the GSMOpen wiki page at `http://wiki.freeswitch.org/wiki/Gsmopen`.

TDM with OpenZAP and FreeTDM

FreeSWITCH is fully compatible with many types of telephony interface cards. Various types of interface cards are manufactured by Sangoma, Digium, OpenVox, Rhino Technologies, RedFone, and others. The FreeSWITCH developers created a BSD-licensed abstraction library named OpenZAP. This abstraction layer allows FreeSWITCH to communicate with both Sangoma and Digium-based cards and their requisite drivers. FreeTDM, sponsored by Sangoma Technologies Corporation, is a new abstraction layer that will eventually replace OpenZAP completely. We recommend that those interested in using telephony cards with FreeSWITCH start by visiting the OpenZAP wiki page at `http://wiki.freeswitch.org/wiki/OpenZAP`.

Configuration tools and related projects

The FreeSWITCH community has grown tremendously over the past few years with many different people using the software for a variety of purposes. These purposes range from running small home PBXs to large telephone companies. Along the way a variety of people have created different bits of code that allow you to save time or allow FreeSWITCH to operate in unique ways. Contributions range from complete open-source GUIs and frameworks to small single-purposes libraries. We briefly discuss some of these items below.

Web GUIs

There are a number of Web Graphical User Interfaces (GUIs) available for FreeSWITCH today. Some are graphical tools that generate XML configuration files while others take the approach of abstracting the switch configuration completely and providing simplified but flexible user interfaces to end-users. We cover some of the more popular ones below.

Note that choosing the right PBX is really a personal decision based on your preferences. Some people prefer one language over another. Some people are strictly about features. Some people focus on scalability. Since most distributions come with easy to install ISOs, you should try out all the interfaces you can find before making a decision on which one you like best.

WikiPBX

WikiPBX is a Python-based FreeSWITCH GUI and was one of the original GUIs for FreeSWITCH. It utilizes many of the same architectural patterns as FreePBX thanks to its utilization of Django and its abstraction of databases. From the WikiPBX homepage, the core features of WikiPBX are listed as:

- Multiple 'accounts' per server instance—each account is effectively a completely independent PBX. (multi-tenant).
- Layered configuration—XML files goes on top of what is stored in database. Allows you to use a database, but stays out of your way if you choose to use flat files.
- Configure extensions, SIP endpoints, and gateways via web interface.
- View/hangup/transfer live calls.
- View call history (CDR records) over the web interface.
- Web interface for managing (add/edit/update) IVRs written in Python, JavaScript, or Java.
- Easily record "sound clips" for use in Dialplan or IVRs.
- Inject audio or text-to-speech into live calls.

While WikiPBX paused development somewhat in 2009, development has resumed and is progressing rapidly with periodic releases and updates to the websites published roadmap.

WikiPBX is located at `http://www.wikipbx.org`.

FreePBX v3

FreePBX has been a thriving community for some time in relation to the Asterisk PBX ecosystem. In December of 2009, the FreePBX brand name was acquired by a corporate entity who sponsored a rewrite of the project. The FreePBX team decided to bring on a full-time engineer to rewrite the entire FreePBX stack in a way that would allow it to scale better while also allowing it to take advantage of multiple soft-switch engines. The first engine they addressed was FreeSWITCH. The product was later expanded to work with Asterisk as well.

FreePBX v3 was initially started by Darren Schreiber as the TCAPI (`tcapi.org`) project. Other core contributors include Michael Phillips and Karl Anderson. As a ground-up rewrite with the support and backing of a professional UI designer and input from the community, the project released its first 1.0 version in May, 2010. It is written fully in PHP.

The project encompasses multiple concepts:

- A layered ORM database model that works with Postgres, MySQL, and other engines
- Strong adherence to the MVC architectural pattern, which separates out components of the application so they can easily grow in the future
- A modular application and plugin system that allows for individual features to be installed and removed, and to impact other pages, easily
- Simplicity
- The ability to work across multiple engines, such as FreeSWITCH, Asterisk, YATE, and others

One of the most interesting features of the configuration engine is its ability to generate the FreeSWITCH XML files dynamically or in real-time without affecting existing systems. This means that even if the GUI does not do exactly what you need it to, you can always go "under the hood" and add the pieces you require to the configuration files.

The layering of various code pieces adds a significant amount of complexity for PHP coders, though much of it is well documented on the FreePBX website. There is also internationalization support, multi-tenant support, and various other features not found in v2 or other products currently available.

The community around v3 is very active with multiple core developers contributing code to the current implementation.

You can learn more about FreePBX at `http://www.freepbx.org/v3/`.

FusionPBX

FusionPBX is an open source graphical interface written in PHP. The project started as the FreeSWITCH package on the pfSense firewall, then later it was renamed to "FusionPBX" and released with multi-platform support including Linux, BSD, Windows, Mac OS X, and others. It supports multiple databases including PostgreSQL, MySQL, and SQlite.

Features include unlimited extensions, IVR menu, voicemail-to-e-mail, hunt groups, fax server, interactive conference controls, active calls and extensions, queues, call forward, click-to-call, DISA, provisioning, multi-tenant, and more.

FusionPBX is highly customizable. For example a user assigned to the "superadmin" group can log in to the web interface and perform many administrative functions including customizing the menu, content, themes, user groups, multi-tenant configuration, and feature permissions.

Additional information such as documentation and screenshots are available on the website (http://www.fusionpbx.com).

2600hz

The 2600hz project was created by the core team who started FreePBX v3. The project was a natural next step in development for open source telephony platforms. It is designed to be a distributed cloud and premise hybrid that allows for separation of various telecommunications pieces into a series of APIs. The GUI, call-handling APIs, database storage engine, and messaging engines have all been abstracted into independent modules, allowing you to choose which pieces to utilize for your own application.

Taking their experiences (both positive and negative) from the FreePBX v3 project, the team embarked on a mission to allow for heavy scalability in any architectural platform while fixing some of the user interface issues missing from the v3 project. Specific goals were to replace an inflexible database layer and to deliver a solid, highly scalable eventing mechanism. PHP simply was not well-suited for handling the massive number of events that the FreeSWITCH architecture can generate and alternatives like Java were too bloated for their liking.

Leveraging newer open source projects and libraries in combination with their PHP and C coding skills, the 2600hz project attempts to solve the scalability issues that exist in all the current open source GUI projects. While the project is still under heavy development, its main focus is in distributed cloud computing technologies that leverage FreeSWITCH's excellent event system and call-handling abilities.

If you are interested in the hosted or distributed communications market you should check out the early releases of the 2600hz project.

You can learn more about the 2600hz project at http://www.2600hz.com.

Supporting libraries

In addition to the ESL abstraction library supplied with FreeSWITCH, there are third-party libraries that expand upon (or eschew entirely) ESL while adding specific functionality to certain programming languages.

Liverpie (Ruby)

Liverpie (language independent IVR proxy) is a free piece of software, written in Ruby, that talks to FreeSWITCH on one side, and to any web application on the other, regardless of language, platform, and so on. It translates FreeSWITCH `mod_event_socket` dialogue into HTTP markup (embedding various parameters in HTTP headers), so you can write your own HTTP-speaking finite state machine and hook it to FreeSWITCH via Liverpie. Note also that Liverpie expects the response in YAML so you can save yourself the pain of providing XML if you are comfortable with Liverpie doing the translation.

You can learn more about Liverpie at `http://www.liverpie.com`.

FreeSWITCHeR (Ruby)

FreeSWITCHeR is an EventMachine-based Ruby library for interacting with FreeSWITCH. FreeSWITCHeR interacts through `mod_event_socket`. It can create both inbound and outbound event listeners and can power an entire call from a Ruby library. Significant amounts of documentation and sample code to get you started are available.

You can learn more about FreeSWITCHeR at `http://code.rubyists.com/projects/fs`.

Librevox (Ruby)

Librevox eventually came to life during a major rewrite of FreeSWITCHeR. Harry Vangberg, who participated in the original FreeSWITCHeR code, decided to rewrite FreeSWITCHeR and this is the result. From the website: "Librevox and Freeswitcher look much alike on the outside, but Librevox tries to take a simpler approach on the inside." As with FreeSWITCHeR, there is a good amount of documentation and sample code to get you started.

You can learn more about Librevox at `http://github.com/ichverstehe/librevox`.

EventSocket (Python/Twisted)

EventSocket is a Twisted protocol for the FreeSWITCH event socket. This protocol provides support for both inbound and outbound methods of the event socket in a single-file class. It may be used for a wide variety of purposes. It aims to be simple and extensible, and to export all the functionality of the FreeSWITCH to Twisted-based applications. Moreover, it is totally event-driven and allows easy implementation of complex applications aiming at controlling the FreeSWITCH through the event socket.

This code is part of the core of the Nuswit Telephony API (http://nuswit.com), a full-featured web-based dialer currently operating in Brazil and Colombia.

Source code, examples and documentation are available at http://github.com/fiorix/eventsocket.

FSSocket (Perl)

The FSSocket perl library, based on the Perl Object Environment (POE) framework, allows for easy integration with the FreeSWITCH event socket system from Perl. It parses FreeSWITCH events into hashes. You can ask for as many event types as you like or all for everything.

Source code, examples, and documentation are available at: http://search.cpan.org/~ptinsley/POE-Filter-FSSocket-0.07/.

Summary

FreeSWITCH provides a powerful toolset for creating rich applications. The modules bundled with FreeSWITCH today are an early example of what you can do with the powerful internal APIs that are available. In addition, a thriving community of FreeSWITCH enthusiasts is taking the software development available to the next level. Expect many hosted, cloud and premise-based solutions to thrive in the coming years for various purposes in the VoIP and communications space, based on the FreeSWITCH core.

A
The FreeSWITCH
Online Community

One of the good things about many open source software projects is that people from around the world connect on a regular basis to form a community of interested, and in many cases passionate, users. FreeSWITCH is certainly one of these.

In this appendix we will introduce several aspects of the online community. They are as follows:

- FreeSWITCH mailing lists
- Real-time interaction via IRC
- Main FreeSWITCH website and wiki
- The annual ClueCon telephony conference in Chicago

This appendix will help you to become a part of this vibrant, worldwide community.

The FreeSWITCH mailing lists

The FreeSWITCH project maintains several mailing lists at `http://lists.freeswitch.org`. The primary list for most users is appropriately named `freeswitch-users`. Like many projects, the lists are powered by the GNU mailing list manager, `MailMan`.

To join one of the lists, simply browse to x and click on the name of the list as shown in the following screenshot:

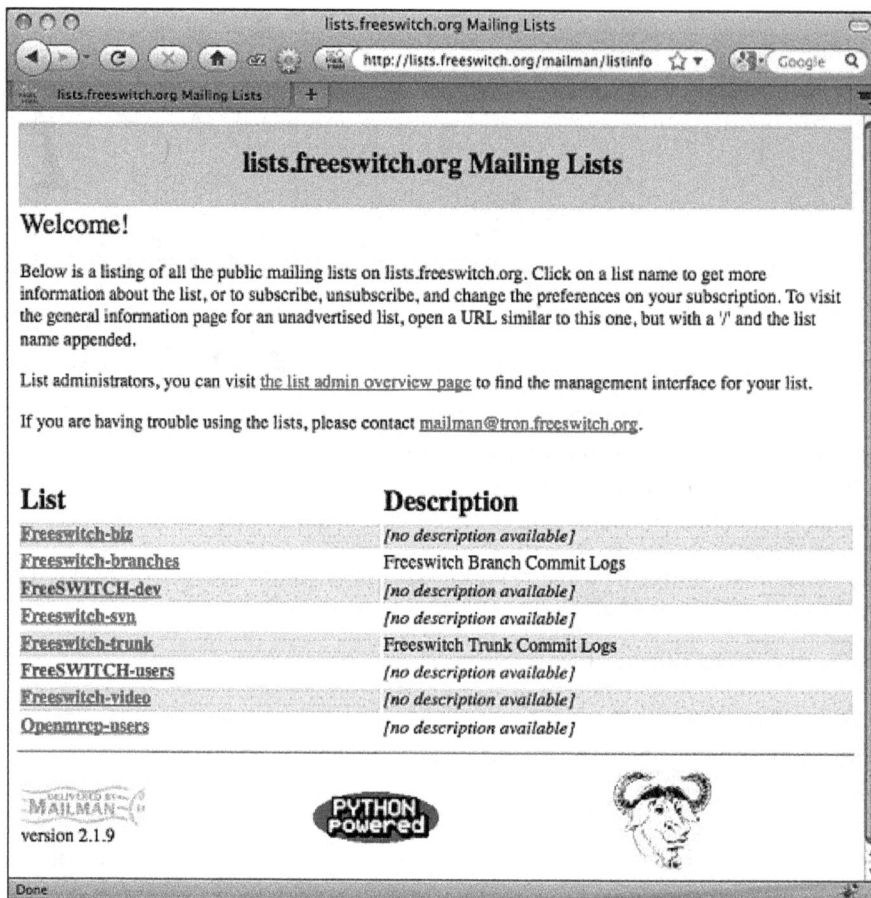

New users should join only the FreeSWITCH-users list, until they are comfortable with the project. The other lists are very technical in nature, except for the FreeSWITCH-biz list, which is used for discussing commercial endeavors with FreeSWITCH.

You will need to input a username and password when subscribing to a list. Keep this information handy so that you can make adjustments to your e-mail subscriptions. One important setting that you can change is whether or not to receive "digest" e-mails. A digest is an amalgamation of several e-mails into a single transmission. The digest method is handy for those who may be casual readers of the e-mail traffic flowing through the mailing lists. However, if you wish to interact with others then you should not use the digest because it will be difficult to participate in a particular discussion thread.

Some points to keep in mind when using the mailing list are as follows:

- Use an e-mail client that handles threads so that you can more easily follow specific discussions.

- Do not "hijack" threads! A hijack occurs when someone replies to an existing thread and changes the subject line of the e-mail. Always start with a new message to the list if you need to discuss a new subject.

- Try not to become overwhelmed when you first join. There are lots of messages coming through each day. You can only absorb so much, so pace yourself and give yourself time to get acclimated.

- Use the site archives to search for discussions on a particular subject. An example is to use Google. Search Google for `site:lists.freeswitch.org "early media"` to see all list threads that discuss the topic of "early media".

The mailing lists are a great resource for interacting with people all over the world. However, sometimes you need to have a dialog. In cases like this you will appreciate chatting with others in real-time.

Talking in real-time via IRC

IRC or Internet Relay Chat or is a venerable means for chatting with other users. The FreeSWITCH team has several chat rooms on `irc.freenode.net`. They are as follows:

- `#freeswitch`
- `#freeswitch-dev`
- `#freeswitch-social`
- `#openzap`

Using IRC is simple once you know what to do. You will need an IRC client for your computer. There are many to choose from, including the following:

- Chatzilla: A Firefox addon
- IRSSI: A text-based IRC client
- Colloquy: An IRC client for Mac OSX
- mIRC: An IRC client for Windows

You can also join the `#freeswitch` channel using the Java applet on the main FreeSWITCH website (see the following).

To use IRC you will need to choose a nickname, known as a "nick" for short. Choose something unique, and if possible register your nick with Freenode. Visit `http://freenode.net/faq.shtml#userregistration` to learn more about setting up your nick and getting it registered.

A few nicks that you will probably see online are as follows:

- anthm: Anthony Minessale
- bkw_: Brian K West
- mikej: Michael Jerris
- mercutioviz: Michael S Collins
- pyite: Darren Schreiber
- Math: Mathieu Rene
- intralanman: Raymond Chandler

These are all active members of the FreeSWITCH community. There are many others who stay online throughout the day (and night, depending on your time zone). Following are a few things to keep in mind when using IRC:

- It is a public place with persons from varying backgrounds and standards of decency.
- Be polite, even when others are not.
- Do not "flood" the channel with long pastes of information. If you have more than two or three lines of information to share, then use the pastebin found at `http://pastebin.freeswitch.org`.
- When joining the room there is no need to ask if you may pose a question. Simply ask your question. For example, "I'm a new user trying to set up a gateway. Why does FreeSWITCH say that username and password are REQUIRED parameters when my provider uses IP authentication?"
- Be patient! Usually someone will answer within a few minutes, but keep in mind that usually there are more people in the channel during North American business hours.
- People from all backgrounds are welcome. The main #freeswitch channel is in English, but there are many who speak other languages, including Spanish, French, Italian, German, Portuguese, and Chinese.
- Always respect user c888!

Feel free to join the FreeSWITCH IRC channel and see what topics are being discussed.

The FreeSWITCH main website and wiki

There are two primary websites for the FreeSWITCH project:

- `www.freeswitch.org`: The main project page
- `wiki.freeswitch.org`: The public wiki page

The main FreeSWITCH page— www.freeswitch.org

The FreeSWITCH main web page is the starting point for all things related to the project. From the main page you can do many things as follows:

- Read up on FreeSWITCH and VoIP news
- Download or browse the source code
- Report bugs or feature requests
- View documentation
- Join the `#freeswitch` IRC channel with the Freenode Java applet

New content is added to the main page every few days, so check back frequently.

The FreeSWITCH Wiki page— wiki.freeswitch.org

The FreeSWITCH wiki is the primary source for FreeSWITCH documentation. A wiki is a website that allows users to add, edit, or delete content and link to other content. A classic example of a wiki page is Wikipedia. The FreeSWITCH wiki page uses MediaWiki (`http://www.mediawiki.org`), the same wiki engine used by Wikipedia.

The FreeSWITCH wiki is a community resource. While Michael S. Collins is the primary wiki administrator, all FreeSWITCH users are welcome to add or update content on the site. Like most wiki sites there is a lot of content. Sometimes searching for information can be challenging. We recommend that you use Google site search (`site:wiki.freeswitch.org <search topic>`) if you are having trouble locating a particular subject. After using the wiki for a while you will begin to get a feel for where certain pieces of information are located.

Prospective wiki contributors should keep a few things in mind, they are as follows:

- Do a search before adding content—it may be that the information you want to add is already on the wiki and simply needs to be updated or better indexed.

- Make sure that any content you add is properly linked to.

- Make sure that any content you add is part of a site category.

- Feel free to make mistakes! Others will be happy to help you make corrections.

Documentation of open source software is almost always a challenge, so if you are in a position to assist please contact Michael at `msc@freeswitch.org`. There is always a need for skills such as proofreading, verifying facts, testing configurations and examples, and translating text into other languages.

The annual ClueCon open source developer conference

Each year in Chicago, we have a three-day conference where open source telephony professionals and enthusiasts gather to discuss many topics. The conference is held in the first week of August and is a great way to interact with a wide range of personalities in the telephony world. Visit `http://www.cluecon.com` to see details about the upcoming conference and to get links to presentations and videos from previous conferences.

Although ClueCon is "by developers, for developers", it has been growing each year and many non-developers have been attending. Most presentations are still relatively technical in nature; however, there are many talks that focus on non-technical aspects of telephony, such as demonstrations of new products. The conference is designed for users, developers, and vendors to connect with one another. Users appreciate being able meet developers and vendors in person, and vendors appreciate the focus being on interacting with developers and vendors rather than on spending many hours in a sales booth.

ClueCon invites people from all open source telephony projects to come and give presentations. Over the years there have been presentations on Asterisk, FreeSWITCH, and OpenSIPS, as well as from vendors such as Sangoma and Dialogic, who have been supportive of open source telephony projects.

We encourage all FreeSWITCH users to become acquainted with one another by means of these resources.

B

The History Of FreeSWITCH

In order to properly explain the origin of FreeSWITCH we have to go back to the time before we even had the idea to write it. The VoIP revolution really began to take shape at the turn of the century with the creation of both the Asterisk PBX and OpenH323. Both of these pioneering software packages enabled many developers to have access to VoIP resources without paying for a costly commercial solution. This led to many new innovations in both projects, and the rapid spread of the evidence that true usability of IP telephony did indeed exist.

I first got involved in the industry in 2002, when my company at the time was selling outsourced technical support and we needed a way to manage the calls and send the traffic to an off-site location. We were using a commercial solution but it was costly to deploy and had very over-priced per-seat charges on top of that. I had done a lot of work with open source applications such as Apache and MySQL in my past duties as a web hosting platform architect so I decided to do some research on the existence of any open source telephony applications. Enter Asterisk.

When I first downloaded Asterisk, I was amazed. I got some analog telephone cards to use with it and here I was at my house, with a dial tone on a phone that was plugged into the back of my Linux PC. Wow! That's crazy... It wasn't long before I started immersing myself in the code, trying to figure out how it worked. I learned quickly that it was possible to extend this software to do other things based on loadable dynamic modules just like Apache. I started digging around and worked up a few test modules. This was better than ever. Now I was not only making my phone talk to this PC, I was making it execute my own code when I dialed a certain number.

I played around with a few ideas and then the thought dawned on me. Hey! I **really** like Perl and this telephone stuff is pretty cool too. What if I try to combine them? I looked into the documentation on embedding Perl into a C application and before I knew it I had `app_perl.so`, a loadable module for Asterisk that would allow me to execute Perl code of my choice when a call was routed to my module. It wasn't perfect and I started to learn quickly about the challenge of embedding Perl in a multi-threaded application, but it was at least an awesome proof of concept and quite the accomplishment for a few days of tinkering.

As time progressed, I was drawn deeper into the Asterisk online community. After playing with the code for a few weeks, I began working on some call-center solutions using Asterisk as the telephony engine and some homegrown web applications as a frontend. Along the way, I encountered some bugs in Asterisk, so I submitted them to the issue tracker for inclusion to the development branch. The more this process repeated, the deeper my involvement in the project grew, and I began creating improvements to the software as well as just sporadic fixes to bugs. By 2004, I was actually fixing bugs that other people reported as well as my own. It was the least I felt I could do for having a free solution to all of my problems. If my problems would actually be solved, still remained to be seen.

When I was testing my application, I would make many calls to the system and watch for the web page to update, control the queues and watch the stats build up. However, one thing I was not paying attention to was the number of simultaneous calls and the call volume itself. I was really only making a call or two at a time, and I was not really fully testing my application. When I put it into production for the first time, it was also the first time I ever saw what happened when multi-threaded software had an irresolvable conflict in the locking contention, better known as a dead lock. I was quite familiar with the segmentation fault, as I had encountered many of those along the way when I was working on my own modules, but I was surprised to also see a rise in the number of inexplicable random ones happening only some of the time.

A segmentation fault is a violation that an application commits where it makes inappropriate access to memory by destroying the same memory more than once or accessing memory addresses that are out of bounds or do not exist. You will run into them a lot in C programming, since you have lower-level access to the operating system and there is nothing to protect you from making errors besides your own discipline. I don't give up easily, which you could consider a curse or a blessing, so when I started to encounter some problems, I was prepared to get to the bottom of it. I spent countless hours studying the output from the GNU debugger and trying to simulate the traffic that caused my problems. After a little trial and error, we find success! I managed to duplicate the crash in my test lab using a load generator. I even managed to figure out where the problem was and fixed it! That was a great feeling that lasted right up until later that afternoon, when I learned there was another new problem with similar symptoms somewhere else in the code.

I managed to slowly back out the features in my application that increased the likelihood of a deadlock or segmentation fault, but I could not completely eliminate all of the problems. I eventually discovered that the `app_queue` module was causing most of my grief which was not the best news considering that was the module I was using the most in my call-center application. Some of the changes I wanted to make were too intrusive for inclusion in the main code distribution so I ended up using my own copy of the code so I could continue to update the rest of Asterisk. This kept things stable, but only stable enough to seek another solution.

By this time I had written a fairly large amount of features into Asterisk and was really starting to have some big ideas for new functionality. I created a new concept called "function variables" allowing modules to expose an interface that could be expanded from the dial plan (if you read the rest of this book that idea may sound familiar). I still was wrestling with the queue problems, so I got together with another Asterisk community member and started brainstorming on a new ACD queue module for Asterisk called `mod_icd`.

ICD stood for Intelligent Call Distribution, a play on the acronym ACD meaning Automatic Call Distribution. We had identified all of the shortcomings of the `app_queue` module with regards to functionality and we had a common interest in making a more stable module that would not cause countless crashes and deadlocks. We had a working prototype and a lot of work to do. We used state machines and higher-level memory management abstractions with data pools and several other inspiring concepts that we felt were lacking in the standard Asterisk. The problem was, I think we over-engineered the module too much, almost as if we were trying to edge out the entire Asterisk core, which was of course not completely possible being only a loadable module within that core.

We never quite finished `mod_icd`. It was late 2004 and my opportunities with call-center solutions lay smashed on the rocks, washed away by the unforgiving seas of segmentation faults and deadlocks. We started focusing more on other telephony services that did not involve queuing. I developed a new offering of toll-free termination and fax-to-e-mail services. Using several new features I added to the mainline Asterisk and some of my less-popular modules that were not approved, I built a cluster of seven Asterisk boxes and connected them to a large telecom circuit. This deployment of Asterisk was not problem-free but, on the bright side, if some of the machines crashed there was more to take its place while we restarted them.

At this point I had accumulated several new ideas, some tested, some not, some that were going to require some major changes to Asterisk. My team, Brian West, Michael Jerris and I were donating a lot of time to the Asterisk project. We helped maintain the issue tracker. We fixed bugs and helped out every week by hosting a developer's conference call. We even hosted a mirror of the code on our site. We were very involved yet some of our new ideas were causing some political turmoil in the Asterisk community, as there was an unnecessary competition among the various developers. Every contributor to Asterisk must sign a form stating that all the code you write, that may be included in the Asterisk code base, will automatically have a royaltyfree license for Digium, the owner of Asterisk, to do what it pleases with your code. This was so they could sell the unrestricted licensing to would-be buyers for a high price. Not exactly the spirit of open source but that's another story. I think this alienation caused some strife between the volunteer developers like myself and the developers who were hired outright by Digium to work on Asterisk.

Even with the tension, we were dedicated to the project and really wanted to see it succeed. We were having those regular weekly conference calls and they were really starting to help get the developers motivated. We decided that we should have a live in-person meeting so we could all share our knowledge of telephony and hang out for a few days. We had no idea what we were doing, but we decided to do it anyway and call it ClueCon. Having a clue meant you knew what you were doing, so ClueCon was a conference to help everyone to "get a clue". I do acknowledge, I just said we did not know what were doing either, so there was a bit of irony that people with no clue would start a clue con. However, that turned out to be more of a blessing than a problem and the clue we were referring to was in regards to telephony not to running conferences.

Therefore, with several months until the first ClueCon, in the spring of 2005, we had one of our usual weekly conference calls and began talking particularly in detail about several shortcomings of Asterisk. This is not uncommon, because our primary goal was to identify the problems and convert them into solutions. There was, at the time, a fairly large unruly crowd who was tired of the endless problems they were experiencing with Asterisk. Many of them joined this weekly call, hoping to persuade us to look at one of their issues. The more I thought about it, the bigger the task seemed to unravel some of the big architectural problems that were plaguing us. Many concepts were monolithic in nature and would not scale. Many features had several users dependant on them and changing them with a goal of improvement could lead to regressions in functionality. It just seemed like some of the problems could only be solved with a sledgehammer, yanking out some older code and doing some serious rewrites to some of the deeper recesses of the core code. This did not seem very viable since it would render Asterisk unusable for months if not a year or more. That's when I had the idea, let's make a 2.0!

It was not the worst idea; I knew it would be challenging but, hey, I thought we could start a new code base alongside the old one, so we could tear out the parts of the code that caused the most problems and replace them while still maintaining the original code for the users who depended on something that worked. I was pretty excited about the idea and equally shocked when the project leader reacted to my suggestion of the idea, and he appeared was equally shocked that I would even suggest such a thing so, in short, we did not make an Asterisk 2.0. Here I was, with a ton of ideas and a clear mind on exactly what I did and did not like about Asterisk with nowhere to write them down.

I gazed at that empty text-editor buffer open in an empty directory for an hour. I knew what I wanted to do, but it was hard to bring it to words. I never could find the words until I added in several oddly arranged punctuation around them. Those were not your everyday words, they were symbol names and variable declarations. I was writing C code. In a few days, I drafted up a basic application in C, tying together some of my favorite tools from my past experience in programming. I had the Apache Portable Runtime or APR library, the Perl language, and a few other packages. I built a core and a loadable module structure, a few helper functions to use memory pools and I had a simple command-line prompt that would allow you to type help if you wanted to see a sarcastic comment about there being no help for you, and exit to shut the application down. I made a sample module that would let you telnet to a specific TCP port and have it echo back everything you typed and a very basic state machine. I called it Choir. I thought of my idea as a series of parts working together to make one unified voice like a choir. After that initial coding session, I put it down for a while. ClueCon was coming and I did not want to rush things as I still thought that there was much to consider.

August of 2005 was the first annual ClueCon conference. We had several open source VoIP project leaders including Craig Southeren, one of the authors of OpenH323 and Mark Spencer, creator of Asterisk and the same person who did not like my Asterisk 2.0 idea. However, it was awesome to get these guys in the same room. We filled the day with presentations, with discussions going back and forth, and we really got everyone thinking. It was a huge success and I left the conference energized and ready to work on my Choir code again. However, I didn't. Instead I talked it through on our conference call for months while trying to keep my struggling Asterisk based platform afloat. It was fall now and the turmoil in the Asterisk community finally erupted into a rebellion. A large percentage of the community forked Asterisk into a new application called OpenPBX.

I totally understood why they did it, and I supported them the best I could. I donated all of the code I had written for Asterisk, for them to do what they pleased. I helped when I had a chance, but could never fully get involved with the effort because I still had the same problem — I saw a need to really tear everything down to the basic level and the founders of the new project were mostly interested in fixing specific pressing issues that were not being addressed in a timely manner by the Asterisk core team. We still had the conference calls, but mostly nobody would show up from the Asterisk project because they were not happy with the idea of cavorting with the rebels. I apologized one day because I could not try to solve any problem in OpenPBX that would not boil down to totally gutting everything and writing a new core. That's when someone asked me, "How long do you think it would take to get your new code to make a call?" Like Mr. Owl from the tootsie pop commercials, I had no idea so I decided to find out. A-one, a-two, a-three weeks (give or take).

The first module that actually produced sound was called mod_woomera; it was an endpoint module using the Woomera protocol written by Craig Southeren, the same person I had just met at ClueCon. I made a similar module for Asterisk and it was a simple protocol and required no codecs or anything fancy. The idea was that it would take the complexity out of H323 and allow applications to use it via this simple protocol that could be easily integrated into VoIP applications, so it seemed like a great place to start. As I started to work, I realized that I needed more elements in my basic core and slowly started to bring the code together to a point where I could make a call to the Woomera-powered H323 listener process and get activity in my Pandora code. Yes, I renamed it to Pandora because nobody liked the name Choir. I joyously listened to the Alan Parsons Project hit *Sirius* stream into my speakers from my application for the first time. This was even more exciting than the first time I made Asterisk work because I actually wrote this code myself from scratch and it was doing something.

Now I was getting somewhere; I figured out how to make two channels bridge, then how to support some other protocols and do a few basic things beyond a sarcastic help message and an exit routine. The idea came and went to dub this code OpenPBX 2 and finally when I had enough with naming arguments, I decided once and for all what I wanted to call the application: FreeSWITCH. I finally had a name I knew I was going to stick with and some working code, and a lot of ambition. I put my head down and just began coding. There was work to be done everywhere. It was too overwhelming to think about it really. I just kept plowing through the code and by the time I reached January of 2006, I had enough to share with the public. We opened up our code repository to developers asking them to register for a developer account to gain access to the code as a way to make sure only those who were serious would bother to complete the registration process. We had some people checking it out and providing feedback and we really started to feel like we had a real project.

We had a module to bridge calls, one to play sounds, a few codecs, some examples of Dialplan modules, and a few other things. Oh and did I mention it worked on Windows too?

Our original site is still preserved, though none of the links are active: http://www.freeswitch.org/old_index.html.

Somewhere along the way from all that planning, we actually produced code that could run on Windows as well as Linux and Mac OSX. My original team mates, Michael and Brian were there from the beginning and Mike, having a lot of experience in Windows, made sure we could compile and run the code in MSVC. It was a struggle at first, but after having to correct tons of compiler errors on many occasions, I began to learn how to code in a way that would be friendly on most platforms on the first try. Time started to fly and before I knew it, it was ClueCon time again. That year I gave my first presentation on FreeSWITCH demonstrating the core design and fundamentals that are outlined in the opening chapter of this book. We saw far exciting modules, such as an endpoint module that can communicate with Google Talk. My presentation featured a live demonstration of several thousand calls being set up and torn down by our mod_exosip SIP module. It was a nice demo, but we still weren't happy.

Exosip was a SIP library that was really nothing more than a helper library to Osip, an open source SIP library that provided most of the functionality. The Exosip made it a bit easier to get an endpoint moving and we decided to use it but we encountered several mishaps with it and I started to feel that same sinking feeling I had when I was trying to get Asterisk working, so we started looking for a replacement. It didn't help that there was potential licensing conflicts because Exosip claimed to be GPL despite the fact that its parent library was LGPL (which, in my opinion, is a much more reasonable license). As we chose MPL for our project, it was forbidden by the GPL to allow GPL'd code to be included in an MPL app. License debates are fun and a good way to get people excited but that was not the time for one.

We searched the land of open source far and wide, for both a new SIP stack and an RTP stack to use in FreeSWITCH since there was quite the high demand for SIP functionality. We auditioned several libraries for both roles and we ended trying at least five different stacks for both protocols. I never found an RTP stack that satisfied me, so I wrote my own. I was not foolish enough to try the same thing with SIP. Having a front row seat to the mess caused by Asterisk trying to write a SIP stack from scratch and the failure with Exosip in my rear-view window, I continued to search for a SIP stack until I found Sofia-SIP, a SIP stack written by Nokia. We built a functional mod sofia to test things out and we were highly impressed. We continued to polish the module until we reached the point where we could drop `mod_exosip` and use mod_sofia as our primary SIP endpoint module. This was only

the beginning really, as I still find myself adding code to mod_sofia on a regular basis to this day. SIP is a complicated and frightening protocol that brings many unpleasant thoughts to mind even saying its name , but now is not the time for that conversation.

We gave another presentation on FreeSWITCH at ClueCon 2007, this time with a new SIP module and a lot more code. Now we also had OpenZAP, a TDM library to connect FreeSWITCH to telephone hardware. I experienced the joy of making the very same cards I got working on Asterisk so long ago, to work with FreeSWITCH as well. We had announced that soon we would be releasing the 1.0 edition of FreeSWITCH. Anyone who read our original homepage that I posted earlier might notice we announced that an official release was "coming soon" way back then. This was announced in January of 2006 and we were trying desperately to make things the way we wanted them ever since. We really wanted to focus on making a stable core before all else and we were making real progress, but we still were not ready to release 1.0.

By spring of 2008 we had stable SIP, we had the event socket to remotely control FreeSWITCH, we had a module to interface with our API commands over http, we had XML curl and a nice big list of features. We finally decided it was the right time for a release, so we bit the bullet and released FreeSWITCH 1.0 Phoenix. I chose Phoenix as the release name because I felt that all of our hard work was born from the ashes of our previous failures and though it had been used by a lot of others, including NASA who was launching the Phoenix to Mars at the same exact time, I think it was the appropriate title.

ClueCon 2008 featured the announcement that 1.0 had been finally released earlier that year in late May. Several presentations also related to FreeSWITCH as well as the other open source projects such as Asterisk who had produced a 1.6 release that year. We spent the next entire year focusing on wideband audio support and other advanced features such as on-the-fly re-sampling of unlike audio streams. We added many new SIP features like presence indications and other fancy things beyond simple call setup and a follow-up 1.0.1 release.

In 2009, we released 1.0.2 to 1.0.4 versions and presented FreeSWITCH again at the fifth annual ClueCon. Some of our early innovations matched up with reality by that time, as we were able to demonstrate Polycom phones using high-definition audio on their new Siren codec as well as support for the Skype protocol as an endpoint module. The FreeSWITCH presentation was an overview of the things you probably didn't realize you could do unless you learn to think fourth-dimensionally, as Doc Emmitt Brown from *Back To The Future* and I both like to put it. We have some similarities to Asterisk in behavior, but we also have an entirely new paradigm that opens the door to some incredible things you can do with just a PC and a telephone.

As the new decade begins we are still working hard on making stable code and building new features into FreeSWITCH. We will soon be releasing 1.0.5, and we have a long list of new ideas to work on as well as a wonderful online community who supports us and contributes code, feedback, and much more on a regular basis. ClueCon MMX (2010) is scheduled to take place in the first week of August; we hope to see you all there and I hope you have managed to learn a little bit more about FreeSWITCH and why I decided to start typing those first few characters in that empty text-editor.

Index

E

L

language independent IVR proxy. See
  Liverpie
language module 20
lcr action 172
LIBNCURSES 25
libraries, FreeSWITCH
  about 270
  EventSocket 271
  FreeSWITCHeR 271
  FSSocket (Perl) 272
  Librevox 271
  Liverpie 271
Librevox
  about 271
  URL 271
LIBTOOL 25
Linux 25
  FreeSWITCH, compiling 28
Linux/Unix executable files
  versus Windows executable files 47
listen-ip parameter 204
listen-port parameter 205
Liverpie
  about 271
  URL 271
loadable dialplan modules
  about 157
  advantages 157
Local_Extension Dialplan entry
  modifying 68
locked-sound option 236
log <level> command 218
log action 171
loglevel information 220
looping 131
Lua
  about 123
  enabling, steps 124
  script 125, 126
  scripting, tips 152, 153
  scripts, running from Dialplan 124, 125
  syntax 125
Lua patterns
  syntax, URL 151
  versus regular expressions 151

Lua script
  about 125, 126
  running, from Dialplan 124, 125
  tips 152, 153
LuaSQL
  database, connecting 141-146
luasql.postgres module 144

M

Mac OS X
  FreeSWITCH, compiling 28
  requisites 25
macros
  voicemail_enter_pass macro 117
  voicemail_goodbye macro 117
  voicemail_message_count macro 119
mailing lists, FreeSWITCH
  about 273
  FreeSWITCH-biz list 274
  freeswitch-users 273
  FreeSWITCH-users list 274
  freeswitch-users list 274
  tips 275
  URL 273
Makefile 30
make install utility
  running 30, 31
make utility
  about 30
  running 30, 31
match tag 16
max-failures attribute 110
max-members-sound option 236
max-members parameter 235
max-timeouts attribute 110
mday variable 169
member-flags parameter 234
member-flags parameter, options
  deaf 234
  dist-dtmf 234
  endconf 234
  waste 234
menu-back action 113
menu-exec-api action 112, 113
menu-exec-app action 111, 112
menu-play-sound action 113

U

Unix
  about 25
  FreeSWITCH, compiling 28
unmuted-sound option 236
unset action 172
use cases, mod_nibblebill module
  billing (post-pay) 240
  billing (pre-pay) 240
  fraud, preventing 240
  maximum credit 240
  pay-per-call service billing 240
user
  adding, to FreeSWITCH user directory
    67-69
  XML file, creating for 68
user@domain 64
user_context variable 67
user agents. *See* **SIP profile**
user element 66
uuid variable 169

V

variables, FreeSWITCH
  caller profile fields 184, 185
  channel variables 185
  global variables 187
  passing, call headers used 192
  testing, regular expressions used 184
  utilizing 184
variables, FreeSWITCH user directory
  accountcode 67
  callgroup 67
  effective_caller_id_name 67
  effective_caller_id_number 67
  outbound_caller_id_name 67
  outbound_caller_id_number 67
  toll_allow 67
  user_context 67
variables element 66
verbose_events action 172
version command 37, 49
vi text editor 26
voice applications, FreeSWITCH
  about 16

building 126-129
  conditions 131-139
  example 14, 16
  IVR, interacting with caller 129, 130
  looping 131-139
voicemail
  testing 70, 71
voicemail_enter_pass macro 117
voicemail_goodbye macro 117
voicemail_message_count macro 119

W

waste option 234
wday variable 169
web call
  making, curl used 146-151
Web Graphical User Interfaces. *See* **Web
  GUIs**
Web GUIs 267
Web GUIs, FreeSWITCH
  2600hz project 270
  FreePBX 268, 269
  FusionPBX 269
  WikiPBX 268
week variable 169
WGET 25
while loop 134, 140
WikiPBX
  about 268
  features 268
  URL 268
Windows
  FreeSwitch, compiling 33
  requisites 25
Windows executable files
  versus Linux/Unix executable files 47
WinRAR
  URL 25
WinZip
  URL 25

X

X-Lite 49
X-Lite soft phone
  about 51, 52

configuration error 53

X-PRE-PROCESS tag 187

XML

alternatives 198

XML Dialplan, scenarios

about 192

called number, matching 194, 195

called number, matching with IP address 194

DIDs, routing to extensions 197

digits, capturing 194, 195

IP address verification, number dialling 192, 193

local extension, trying 197

prefix, adding 195

registered devices, bridging to 195

user authentication, verifying 196

XML Dialplan module

about 11, 159, 164

commands 174-178

condition variables 169, 170

contexts 43

functions 187, 188

inline execution 170

pitfalls 172, 173

using 44

XML registry

about 19

configuration section 19

dialplan section 19

directory section 19

phrases section 19

XMPP events

receiving 238

sending 238

Y

YAML 199

yday variable 169

year variable 169

[PACKT] open source
PUBLISHING
community experience distilled

Thank you for buying
FreeSWITCH 1.0.6

About Packt Publishing

Packt, pronounced 'packed', published its first book *"Mastering phpMyAdmin for Effective MySQL Management"* in April 2004 and subsequently continued to specialize in publishing highly focused books on specific technologies and solutions.

Our books and publications share the experiences of your fellow IT professionals in adapting and customizing today's systems, applications, and frameworks. Our solution based books give you the knowledge and power to customize the software and technologies you're using to get the job done. Packt books are more specific and less general than the IT books you have seen in the past. Our unique business model allows us to bring you more focused information, giving you more of what you need to know, and less of what you don't.

Packt is a modern, yet unique publishing company, which focuses on producing quality, cutting-edge books for communities of developers, administrators, and newbies alike. For more information, please visit our website: www.packtpub.com.

About Packt Open Source

In 2010, Packt launched two new brands, Packt Open Source and Packt Enterprise, in order to continue its focus on specialization. This book is part of the Packt Open Source brand, home to books published on software built around Open Source licences, and offering information to anybody from advanced developers to budding web designers. The Open Source brand also runs Packt's Open Source Royalty Scheme, by which Packt gives a royalty to each Open Source project about whose software a book is sold.

Writing for Packt

We welcome all inquiries from people who are interested in authoring. Book proposals should be sent to author@packtpub.com. If your book idea is still at an early stage and you would like to discuss it first before writing a formal book proposal, contact us; one of our commissioning editors will get in touch with you.

We're not just looking for published authors; if you have strong technical skills but no writing experience, our experienced editors can help you develop a writing career, or simply get some additional reward for your expertise.

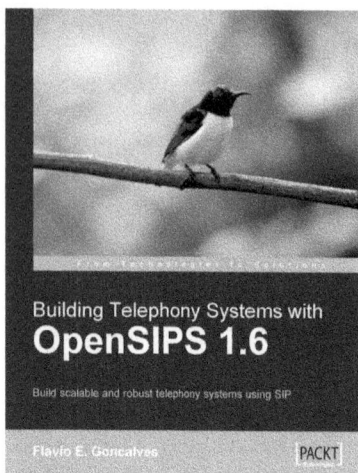

Building Telephony Systems with OpenSIPS 1.6

ISBN: 978-1-8495107-45-1   Paperback: 284 pages

Build scalable and robust telephony systems using SIP

1. Build a VoIP Provider based on the SIP Protocol

2. Cater to scores of subscribers efficiently with a robust telephony system based in pure SIP

3. Gain a competitive edge using the most scalable VoIP technology

4. Learn how to avoid pitfalls using precise billing

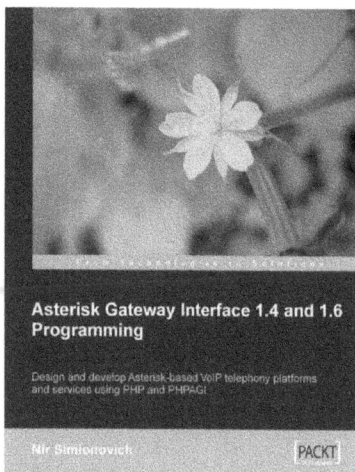

Asterisk Gateway Interface 1.4 and 1.6 Programming

ISBN: 978-1-847194-46-6   Paperback: 220 pages

Design and develop Asterisk-based VoIP telephony platforms and services using PHP and PHPAGI

1. Develop voice-enabled applications utilizing the collective power of Asterisk, PHP, and the PHPAGI class library

2. Learn basic elements of a FastAGI server utilizing PHP and PHPAGI

3. Develop new Voice 2.0 mash ups using the Asterisk Manager

4. Add Asterisk application development skills to your development arsenal, enriching your market offering and experience

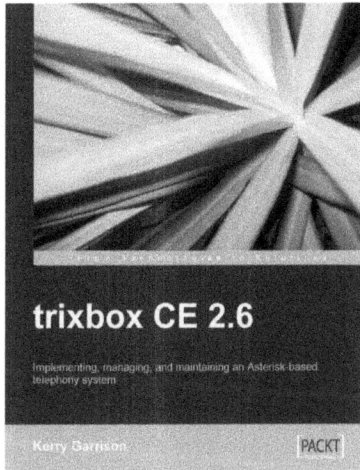

trixbox CE 2.6

ISBN: 978-1-847192-99-8   Paperback: 344 pages

Implementing, managing, and maintaining an Asterisk-based telephony system

1. Install and configure a complete VoIP and telephonic system of your own; even if this is your first time using trixbox

2. In-depth troubleshooting and maintenance

3. Packed with real-world examples and case studies along with useful screenshots and diagrams

4. Best practices and expert tips straight from the Community Director of trixbox, Kerry Garrison

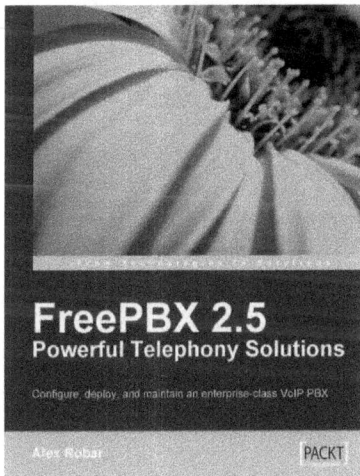

FreePBX 2.5 Powerful Telephony Solutions

ISBN: 978-1-847194-72-5   Paperback: 292 pages

Configure, deploy, and maintain an enterprise-class VoIP PBX

1. Fully configure an Asterisk PBX without editing the individual text-based configuration files

2. Add enterprise-class features such as voicemail, least-cost routing, and digital receptionists to your system

3. Secure your PBX against intrusion by managing MySQL passwords, FreePBX administrative accounts, account permissions, and unauthenticated calls

Please check **www.PacktPub.com** for information on our titles

www.ingramcontent.com/pod-product-compliance
Lightning Source LLC
Chambersburg PA
CBHW080929220326
41598CB00034B/5732